THE CHARACTER OF AMERICAN HISTORY

By the same author

★

AN AMERICAN CRISIS: CONGRESS AND
RECONSTRUCTION, 1865-7

THE CHARACTER OF AMERICAN HISTORY

BY

W. R. BROCK

Fellow of Selwyn College, Cambridge
University Lecturer in American History

SECOND EDITION

MACMILLAN
London · Melbourne · Toronto

ST MARTIN'S PRESS
New York
1965

First Edition 1960
Second Edition 1965

MACMILLAN AND COMPANY LIMITED
Little Essex Street London WC2
also Bombay Calcutta Madras Melbourne

THE MACMILLAN COMPANY OF CANADA LIMITED
70 Bond Street Toronto 2

ST MARTIN'S PRESS INC
175 Fifth Avenue New York NY 10010

Library of Congress Catalogue Card Number 66–12687

PRINTED IN GREAT BRITAIN

TO HELEN

PREFACE TO THE FIRST EDITION

THIS BOOK is intended primarily for those with little previous knowledge of the history of the United States; but it is hoped that those already acquainted with the history of that country will find its pages not altogether unprofitable. There is much omitted: there is little about the history of the West, military history makes but one brief appearance, intellectual history often receives cursory treatment, and geographical factors receive short measure. For these omissions I make no apology. The main concern of the book is with politics in their broadest sense, with the art of living together in society, and I have chosen the incidents and arguments which seem to me to throw most light upon American political evolution. For me the great success of the United States lies in their political achievement, while the greatest challenge to modern Americans is the proper use of their political power.

I have not attempted to equip the book with an apparatus of bibliographical references, and the footnotes are intended to illustrate, occasionally to amuse, and to introduce the reader in a fragmentary way to the rich literature of American history. This book is not an academic exercise, but I hope that those who read it will nevertheless be able to find in it some of the merits of professional history.

W. R. BROCK

Cambridge
June 1959

PREFACE TO THE SECOND EDITION

I HAVE made a number of minor corrections, rearranged and expanded material in the last two chapters, and brought the narrative of events up to the death of President Kennedy. I have also revised the Guide to Further Reading.

W. R. BROCK

Cambridge
September 1964

ACKNOWLEDGEMENTS

A BOOK such as this necessarily owes much to the ideas of other men. I have tried to indicate my indebtedness in the footnotes or in the Guide to Further Reading, but it is impossible to record in detail the help which I have received from conversations with American historians. I am however glad to have an opportunity of acknowledging my debt to members of the History Departments in the three American Universities with which I have been fortunate to be associated — Yale, Berkeley and Johns Hopkins. Nor can a Cambridge historian fail to pay tribute to the succession of distinguished Americans who have come to his University as Pitt Professors of American History and Institutions. I also owe much to the teaching and friendship of the American staff on the three Fulbright Conferences which I was able to attend, and to my colleagues in the British Association for American Studies. I share with many other British scholars a sense of gratitude and obligation to the Commonwealth Fund of New York, and in particular to Mr E. K. Wickman and to Mr Lansing Hammond of the Fund's Division of Education. Lastly I must thank the University of Cambridge and my own College for a generosity which made possible two highly instructive visits to the United States.

CONTENTS

LIST OF MAPS

[1]

The Features of American History

From Europe have come the dynamic forces which make the history of the United States. Westward migration, beginning in prehistory in the heartlands of Asia, has filled the American continent and reached its great climax in the early years of this century. The immediate impetus for migration came from the great increase of European population in modern times. The philosophy of America derives from that European rationalistic and scientific revolution which has transformed the modes of thought in every aspect of human life. The economy of America is that produced by the European revolution in technology, industry and communications. The political system of America derives in part from English constitutionalism and in part from the European revolt against the *ancien régime* which has overthrown traditional authority, dissolved social hierarchies, and substituted utility for religion as the ultimate standard in human relations. In America, as in Europe, the city has triumphed over the countryside and produced an urbanized civilization with consequences still uncertain; in America, as in Europe, the power of central government has grown and mass democracy threatens to submerge both individualism and local autonomy. If this last revolution is still incomplete in America, it may only be because conformity is so generally accepted as a social virtue that direction is unnecessary.

Is American civilization purely derivative? Are imitation, reception and assimilation its only themes? Most Americans would maintain that they have added to their inheritance something which is distinctively their own. Many foreigners would agree

I

that Americanism cannot be mistaken for anything else, and an Englishman will often feel that a common language, a common heritage, and some similarities in political institutions emphasize rather than obscure the present divergencies. It would be harder for either the American or the foreigner to describe what Americanism is; no more than an Englishman is able to explain what it is to be English, can an American describe the experience of being American.[1] Americanism is not a fashion but something complex, imponderable, and deep rooted.

The United States form neither the largest nor the most populous country in the world; Russia, Canada, China and Brazil cover more territory; Russia, China and India contain more people.[2] But no other large country has been so rapidly settled and no other populous country has provided its people with so high a standard of living. The rapid expansion of the nation has been achieved without disunion and without recourse to despotic government. The increase of national wealth has been achieved with the smallest possible concession to that collectivism which has followed elsewhere in the train of economic advance. Compared with the compact states of Europe, the United States have divided authority between central government and state governments with extensive and exclusive powers; in contrast with the sovereign majorities of unitary states they have such a profusion of checks and balances that it is sometimes difficult to understand how any public purpose is ever fulfilled. In economic affairs the balance sheet is different; while business in the Old World is either under state control or lacking confidence in itself, American business has enormous self-confidence, great political influence, rides a loose rein, and seems to possess the power to remake the world which it has already changed. To a European the evident satisfaction of Americans with their political and economic institutions is a perpetual surprise; violent differences of opinion

[1] The most recent and most comprehensive example of the American attempt to substitute the concept of a 'way of life' for the traditional loyalties of older societies is Max Lerner, *America as a Civilisation*, New York and London, 1958.

[2] The comparison of geographical extent refers to the contiguous continental territory of the United States; with the inclusion of Alaska and Hawaii the United States are larger than China and Brazil and slightly smaller than Canada.

are frequent but they seldom touch the fundamentals of a system which seems so open to criticism. Yet this uniformity has been imposed upon peoples more varied than those of any other nation.

The ancestors of nearly all modern Americans crossed the Atlantic; emerging from European society they underwent an experience which made their sons and grandsons more and more like each other and less and less like their cousins at home. By a process, which is not less peculiar because it is familiar, the first generation immigrant remained alien, the second belonged to two worlds, and the third became wholly American. The millions of Irishmen in America have never sought an American Irish Free State; racial minorities have often felt grievances but they have always claimed that the remedy lies in their rights as American citizens; the drab and complex government of the United States has proved more attractive as a focus for loyalty than all the splendid monarchies and national traditions of Europe. In an era in which racial nationalism has been an explosive and disruptive force in history, America has succeeded in imposing upon many races a nationalism which ignores race.[1] This remarkable growth has its roots in the hopes and achievements of the Atlantic migrants.

Why did men migrate? It is no easy decision to leave an ancestral home even when life in it seems intolerable, and although there is a will, the way has still to be found. Any large migration will carry along the shiftless, the vicious, the mentally retarded and the physically weak, but somewhere there must be purpose and determination. A significant feature of the Atlantic migration was that the decision was seldom made at a higher level than the family; men might catch the infection from strong-willed

---

[1] In 1924 it was estimated that the Nations of Europe which had contributed most to the population of the United States were (in order of the size of their contributions): Great Britain and Northern Ireland, Germany, Eire, Poland, Italy, Sweden, the Netherlands, France, Czechoslovakia, Russia, Norway, Switzerland, Austria, Belgium and Denmark. The contribution of countries other than those of northern Europe increased very greatly in the last years of the nineteenth and the first of the twentieth century. In 1930 the national origins and numbers (in millions) of the foreign born were: Italy 1·8, Germany 1·6, Russia 1·5, Poland 1·3, other central European countries 1·3, Canada 1·3, Great Britain 1·2, Scandinavia 1·1, Ireland ·9, Mexico ·6 (*Historical Statistics of the United States*, Series B, 279–303).

associates but the decision to move remained an individual one, and no one obeyed the commands of a superior. The transportation of convicts in the eighteenth century form a minor, and the African slave trade a major, exception to this rule. Since migration usually involved so large an element of personal decision the selection of migrants is less fortuitous than one might imagine. Migration seldom appealed to the well-to-do, the destitute could not find the means to move (unless, as with the great Irish migration, earlier emigrants sent home the money), and America had the greatest attractions for those who wished to possess land of their own. Migration might sometimes be impelled by political or religious persecution, but a more likely cause was chronic irritation with the burdens and restraints of a society dominated by hereditary privilege and encumbered with feudal survivals. Occasionally, as with the Irish famine of 1845, there was direct correlation between migration and economic distress, but the 'pull' of good times in America was usually stronger than the 'push' of hard times at home. Compared with the blindness of earlier migrations the Atlantic migrant was well informed about the prospects before him. Fraud and delusion were not uncommon from the land companies, shipping companies and railways, but there is no reason to suppose that the migrant was more gullible, when his whole future and past savings were at stake, than his descendant of today.

The Atlantic migrants thus had certain common characteristics which helped to override their diversity of racial origin. They came in the main from those labouring, peasant and lower-middle-class elements which were also to provide Europe with industrial leaders in the nineteenth century and political leaders in the twentieth. They were often men with grievances, but deep-seated resentment was more common than flaming passion. Though many townsmen came along, men from the country or with rural origins predominated. They had made a deliberate choice based on fairly good information; but however much men knew, the decision to move was still an act of courage inspired as much by faith as by material calculation.

If acceptance of the New World was an act of faith, rejection of the Old was a rational decision. The migrant did not know what was coming to him, he did know what he was leaving behind. There must have been regrets for the old home, but it is the nature of man to make the best of what he has and to depreciate that which he has voluntarily abandoned. The picture of the Old World as an abode of sorrow deepened in its colours as the years went by. The exactions of the landlord and the tax-collector, hunger, disease, and the ceaseless struggle for life with little purpose, might well appear more dreadful in the tales of a grandfather than they had been in reality. This rejection of the Old World is one of the first and perhaps the most important of the acquired American characteristics.

The immigrant's world view would have been shattered had America failed to provide him with something not wholly unlike his dreams. There was an abundance of land, there were opportunities in industry and business, the social barriers seemed hardly to exist for the industrious man, and almost every year came the experience of participation in the government of nation, state or municipality. Failures were many, but always enough successes to bring the American legend to life; and for many European peasants, hard times on a farm of their own was still success beyond their wildest dreams. Psychologically it was important that the immigrant found himself in a society where conventions of equality reigned. Great differences existed between rich and poor, and these tended to increase with economic progress, but America was not a deferential society.[1] The poor man was not expected to know his place but to rise from it; no privileged individual enjoyed the legal right to determine the destinies of his humble fellow men; economic inequality was one of the facts of life but subordination was not treated as a moral virtue. These conventions of equality prevailed even over the social differentiation of a capitalist society; in Europe the new class of industrial leaders modelled themselves upon the older aristocracy and

---

[1] The generalization applies to the Northern, Mid-Western and Western States, to which the great majority of nineteenth-century immigrants were directed; it would have to be qualified for the more stratified society of the South.

B

expected to receive the same deference, while the industrial proletariat adopted from peasants and middle-class radicals the
language with which hereditary aristocracies had been attacked.
The idea of class conflict — essentially the product of a stratified
society — was unlikely to take root in a rapidly expanding
economy with a high degree of social mobility.

*   *   *   *

In eighteenth-century America very few white men were
economically dependent upon other white men. This interesting
and important fact is a key to much which follows. It is natural
for colonial societies to become stratified — there is an inevitable
distinction between old and new settlers — but in large colonial
countries it is also difficult to find the labour force for the support
of the aristocracy. Land is plentiful and the honest settler seeks
land for himself, the rebellious servant can disappear into the
wilderness, and a labour force disintegrates as soon as it is formed.
A remedy for the upper class is to impose discipline by making
access to the land difficult and expensive, by obtaining severe laws
against runaways and by establishing servile traditions based
upon the idea of natural inequality. From this degradation the
poor white man was delivered by the African slave, New England
terrain and Quaker idealism.

The African Negro was admirably fitted for the white planters'
labour force: he was strong, docile, content with a low standard
of life, amenable to agricultural training, and marked out by his
colour for recapture should he become a fugitive. The poor white
farmer realized instinctively his debt to the African and repaid
him by accepting the relationship of master and slave as the only
one possible between black and white. White equality under the
law, despite great economic inequalities, became the cornerstone
of Southern political thought. Two different societies — that of
the plantation and that of the small farmer — were enabled to
exist side by side; the planter gentry were able to develop a
patrician liberalism which was the glory of eighteenth-century
Virginia, while the yeomen were respectful without being sub-

servient, and established leadership was reconciled with popular representation.

In New England the terrain never favoured the great estate, men of talent turned to the sea or to the professions, and the upper class became one of merchants, ministers and lawyers. Such an upper class requires a small labour force in relation to its wealth, and the poorer colonists became freeholders, seamen, craftsmen and small traders. During much of the seventeenth century power remained largely in the hands of a distinguished oligarchy, part capitalist and part theocratic; but the tendency of Puritan settlements to develop religious schisms and the ambitions of pushful entrepreneurs both fostered the establishment of new settlements. The idea of the congregation — the core of Puritan church organization — guided men towards compact rather than dispersed settlements, and memories of English village life influenced the development of the New English township. But it was a village without a squire, with an established church organized not by remote bishops but by elders and ministers on the spot, and in which the majority of adult males were freeholders. There was a predetermined social organization but no established pattern of leadership. The promoters of the settlement and the ministers might form a natural group of leaders, but there was no convention by which they could retain leadership; the manifold tasks of a new settlement called for wide dispersion of responsibility, and the possibility of a further schism, bringing about a break-down of the settlement, was always present. The logic of the situation pointed therefore to self-government, and in the 'town meeting', which became the typical instrument of local government, all freeholders had a voice. Here then was another society, different from Europe and fostering among its people a vigorous participation in their own government.

New York and Pennsylvania might well have reproduced the society of the *ancien régime*. At an early stage the Hudson valley of New York had been parcelled out among great landowners, but this system was confined to a comparatively small area, did not spread, and was outflanked by New England migration into the upper part of the state. In Pennsylvania during the eighteenth century thousands of European migrants (mostly Germans) sold themselves as indentured servants into virtual slavery for a term of years. Quakers usually refused to hold Negro slaves, but neither would a Quaker hold a man beyond the just period and so create a permanent white labour force. More significant was the unicameral government with a wide franchise which had been William Penn's last gift to his colony; this ensured that Pennsylvania would attract free white settlers, that small freeholders would hold a majority in the assembly, and that it would be impossible to pass restrictive land laws. Increasingly the wealthy Pennsylvanians turned to the opportunities of what became a great commercial centre at Philadelphia, while retaining their estates as social adjuncts rather than as commercial propositions. Meanwhile the Germans, Scotch-Irish (Ulstermen) and others formed a rural society which was as diffuse as that of Virginia and as free from upper-class dominance as that of New England.

Thus even before the Revolution American society was very unlike that of Europe. Economic dependence, the cement of society in an aristocratic régime, was rare and traditions of equality and of popular participation in government were already strong. The ascendancy of the upper classes was based upon wealth not upon hereditary right, and though some of the habits of the deferential society were carried over into the New World it was hard to maintain them against the facts of physical and social mobility.

The peculiar characteristics of colonial society were carried over and intensified during the great period of expansion which followed. In a famous sentence written in 1893 F. J. Turner, the most influential of all American historians, declared that 'American democracy was born of no theorist's dream; it was not carried in the *Susan Constant* to Virginia nor in the *Mayflower* to Plymouth. It came out of the American forest, and it gained new strength each time it touched a new frontier.' Though Turner's theories have been much criticized of late years, there remains an essential germ of truth in the thesis that democratic behaviour owed much to the process of settlement in the wilderness.[1] The men immediately attracted to the West were the small farmers of the South, Pennsylvanian farmers, New Englanders forced from their original homes by a terrain which could support only a limited number of farmers, and vigorous immigrants coming direct from Europe. Life on the frontier placed little value upon hereditary distinction, much upon enterprise, mutual help to overcome the difficulties of forest settlement and Indian resistance, and the ability to cope with local problems. Even in the most primitive settlement there were jobs to be done; lacking a ready-made governing class authority was forced upon humble settlers, and lacking any other rule of leadership democratic election was the natural mode of procedure.

*   *   *   *

The facts of social life were reflected in political institutions. There has been controversy among historians about the extent of the suffrage in colonial America — ranging from an assertion that there were unenfranchised 'masses' to a belief that most adult white men had the vote — but there must be agreement that, compared with England, the franchise was both wide and rational. Most colonies imposed property qualifications for the vote, but a great many colonists owned property and a straightforward disenfranchisement of the propertyless was different in principle from the archaic and haphazard qualifications which determined the right to vote in England and Scotland. A colonial assembly represented 'the people' in a manner quite different from Parliament; there were no rotten or pocket boroughs, no territorial magnates nominating representatives and no need to resort to theories of virtual representation to explain why large towns were unrepresented while two members sat for decayed villages. Save that the governors were appointed or approved by the King,

---

[1] But less truth in his assumption of a necessary connection between frontier democracy and political virtue. 'Il y a bien souvent de la différence entre la volonté de tous et la volonté générale; celle-ci ne regarde qu'a l'intérêt commun; l'autre regarde à l'intérêt privé et n'est qu'une somme de volontés particulières' (Rousseau, *Du Contrat Social*, Livre II, Ch. III).

there was no hereditary principle in colonial government. An upper house did not exist in Pennsylvania and Georgia, was elected by the lower house in Massachusetts, and appointed by the Crown elsewhere; nowhere did a man have a prescriptive or hereditary right to sit in these upper houses or councils.[1]

There were to be constitutional struggles during and after the Revolution, but the ultimate responsibility of the government to the people was never questioned. America found it easy to dispense with an external principle of authority and to substitute the sovereignty of the people for the mystical sanctions of government, which European nations continued to seek even after a century of revolution.[2] By 1830 most white male Americans had the vote (a condition which was not achieved in England until 1884), no qualification prevented any citizen from rising to the highest positions, and upper houses were ceasing to be the special guardians of property and were becoming, rather, gatherings of particularly successful politicians entrusted with power for a longer period than those of the lower house.

The aspirations of European radicals had become practical politics. Here was a land in which there were no kings and no aristocrats, in which the peasant could become a proprietor, the outcast a respectable citizen, and the labouring man could make his fortune. Conscience was free and save in New England men were little troubled by established churches; the man who spoke his mind was applauded for his candour rather than condemned for his presumption. To upper-class Englishmen it seemed shabby, plebian and dominated by dangerous passions; to its citizens it seemed the best hope of mankind; and to an acute observer, such

---

[1] The Pennsylvania constitution of 1776 vested the supreme legislative power in an assembly which was elected by all resident and tax-paying freemen. Executive power was vested in a president and council; the former was elected jointly by assembly and council from members of the council; the council itself was elected (one member for each county) for three years. 'By this mode of election and continual rotation,' the constitution explained, '. . . the danger of forming an inconvenient aristocracy will be effectually prevented.' Many Americans deprecated the extreme democracy of Pennsylvania, but it was only on American soil that so emphatic a detestation of aristocracy could have received legal expression.

[2] New York, far from a radical state, declared in its 1777 constitution 'that no authority shall, on any pretence whatever, be exercised over the people or members of this state, but such as shall be derived from them'.

as the Frenchman, de Tocqueville, it seemed the shape of things to come.[1]

The American nation went through its formative stage when middle-class radicalism was progressive thought. A period in which technological revolution operating in an undeveloped continent kept open the door to opportunity, made middle-class ideals acceptable to the whole people, and raised no fundamental criticisms of the American political and social system. The great Civil War was not a quarrel about *how* men should be governed, and the constitution of the rebel Confederate states merely duplicated with slight modifications the Constitution of the United States.

Today the constitution has become a symbol of enormous power, capitalism has a prestige which it lacks even in other capitalist states, and a communist ruler may well envy the ideological solidarity of the American people. The lack of controversy over the fundamentals of society has meant that America since 1800 has been fertile in minor political experiments, conservative and unoriginal in political theory, and tolerant of a good deal of bad behaviour on the part of politicians so long as they inflict no radical proposals upon the country. Recently there have been signs that the confidence of earlier years has given place to fear of criticism and change — at the height of national power, American beliefs seem to have gone over to the defensive — but this change is perhaps more apparent than real, for the faith of the ordinary American citizen remains unshaken. If it should ever cease to be so a momentous change will have occurred in the character of the nation; for faith in the justice of his institutions was the principal thing which America gave to the immigrant, and in this belief rather than in material achievement are found the real bonds of union.

The survival of faith is not unconnected with economic

[1] 'Alors je reportais ma pensée vers notre hémisphère, et il me sembla que j'y distinguais quelque chose d'analogue au spectacle que m'offrait le Nouveau-Monde. Je vis l'égalité des conditions qui, sans y avoir atteint comme aux États-Unis ses limites extrêmes, s'en rapprochait chaque jour davantage; et cette même démocratie, qui régnait sur les sociétés américaines, me parut en Europe s'avancer rapidement vers le pouvoir' (Alexis de Tocqueville, *De la Démocratie en Amérique*, ed. André Gain, p. 2).

success. In undeveloped countries which have come under the influence of Western civilization, education and political practice have often run ahead of material well-being; men have the knowledge to frame their grievances before they have the rewards which render them content. In America the sequence has usually been reversed. The crudity of the rich American has been a standing joke in genteel European society, but it may be better for the health of a nation to have crude men with power than to have men of talent who are denied economic opportunity. There have been periods in American history when the gates of abundance seemed closed to the mass of the people and these periods — particularly from 1893 to 1896 and from 1929 to 1935 — are those in which there has been some attack upon the fundamentals of American beliefs and a real threat of revolution.

The evident force of political beliefs and of material achievement makes it easy to forget that the United States also took their modern shape during a period of great religious revival. For many early settlers the act of migration was an act of religious revolt, and the fervour of English non-conformity continued, and still continues, as a powerful influence upon American life. At a time when early enthusiasm was waning new evangelical tides invigorated the eastern Churches and flowed out in missionary zeal over the frontier. Where the older forms of Protestantism seemed to have come to a halt, Methodism, with its enthusiasm and its broad human appeal, took over. In the nineteenth century American Churches were fed by new currents of evangelical protest, multiplied and refined their own sectarian divisions, and took an important part in the great missionary ventures of the nineteenth century. At the same period Americans achieved a complete separation of Church and State, and the Calvinist stress upon the congregation became the central fact of American religious organization. As enthusiasm subsided the congregation tended to become a social group (usually composed of people with similar incomes), bound together by a form of worship and by a body of ethical beliefs. Usually these ethical codes blended with and lent support to the social values of American life, and the per-

sistent, pervasive and often unnoticed influence of religion underwrote the fundamentals of American life. In time even the Roman
Catholics would adapt themselves to this basic conformity which
lies concealed beneath the multiple variations of American religion.

*   *   *   *

While basic principles have been seldom called in question
there have been violent quarrels over means, implications, and
immediate objectives. America has experienced the classic conflicts which have divided modern society — town against country,
industry against agriculture, mass against *élite* — and has added
to them some of her own making. The Federalist and Republican
rivalry in the late eighteenth century, the battles of Jacksonian
democracy, the great Civil War, the successive waves of agrarian
radicalism in the late nineteenth century, middle-class progressivism in the early twentieth century, and bitter political struggles of
the New Deal era, are all witness to the difficulties of an expansive
society living through a period of shattering change. Each of
these conflicts deserves a study in itself but at this stage it will
suffice to trace some of their main factors.

The democratic character of the primitive Western settlements
has already been remarked, but the West rapidly developed
sectional characteristics. From Virginia and the other Southern
colonies a constant westward movement filled the present states
of Kentucky and Tennessee, pressed northward across the Ohio,
and moved south-west into the uplands of what are now the
states of Alabama and Mississippi. In the interior valleys of the
Appalachians this migration met and fused with another, mainly
composed of Scotch-Irish, moving south-west from Pennsylvania. By the end of the eighteenth century the planters themselves,
feeling the law of diminishing returns on overworked tobacco
lands, were also seeking new land in the West. The pattern of
settlement was first that of isolated clearings in the forest, each
the site of a family farm, but to clear the woods, shift the heavy
logs, build the first cabin, and gather the first harvest, help was

necessary, and there developed habits of neighbourly aid which were both kindly and essential. These rural meetings became an established part of Western life, and the open air feast or barbecue became the occasion for religion, politics, and local planning. There is eloquent tribute to the simple delights of these rustic occasions, yet as social institutions they were no substitute for the more developed forms which the Southerners failed to evolve. Even the increasing importance of the Southwest as a cotton producing area failed to stimulate the rise of towns or of commerce among the greater part of the people. Three reasons for this failure seem to stand out: the existence of a recognized ruling class, slavery, and the lack of complex needs among farmers engaged on subsistence agriculture. In its early stages the Southern society was lively but uncoordinated; social organization came with the success of some of the first settlers as planters and in the arrival of new migrants, with capital, from the Eastern plantations. Social differentiation then became marked, a recognized upper class developed, and whether the gentry came of old planting stock or were self-made men, they adopted the genteel culture of Virginia as their model. For the support of such an upper class a labour force was once more necessary; again the white settlers wanted land of their own, and again the solution was found in the slave system. Thus slavery migrated westward and the Negro must be numbered among the builders of the West. Plantations could be established only in districts which were suited for them by soil and climate; the planters had either to reach out to good lands beyond the range of settlement or buy out earlier small settlers. In either case the region tended to become divided into planting areas, where gentry lived the genteel life on large estates cultivated by slaves, and hilly or less fertile areas, where many small farmers lived at a low standard mainly upon subsistence agriculture. Between the regions there could be bitter jealousies, but neither wanted much from government and both could believe whole-heartedly that the best government was that which governed least. One finds the apparent paradox in the Southern states that while political conflicts are frequent political change is

rare. Though great differences of class existed the language of
political equality held the field and it was comparatively simple
for the rural demagogue to adapt himself to the requirements of
the planter class. Thus on the south-western frontier democracy
advanced rapidly through the first stage of its development —
that of the equalitarian frontier society — but failed to advance
once a balance had been worked out between the regions dominated by large planters and those occupied by small farmers.[1]

There can be no doubt that Southern life was pleasant, even
for those white men who seemed to gain little from it. The traditions of neighbourliness and mutual help continued even as they
became less necessary, but a poor white Southerner could also
pass his days without seeing a church or a school and his sole
contact with the world of commerce was the pedlar with his pack
who was probably a New Englander at that.[2] Agrarian democracy
might be real but it paid a heavy price for its purity. Nor was it
always so pure. The weakness of law and the cult of personal
honour led among the upper classes to an absurd prevalence of
duelling and among the plain people to quarrels in which the
contestants fought to the death with knives or with their bare
hands until one had gouged out the eye of the other. Genuine
kindliness could be accompanied by amazing callousness, while
the whole structure of society rested upon the Negroes whom
convention condemned to perpetual inferiority.

[1] The argument in this and the following paragraphs owes much to two articles by S.
Elkins and E. McKitrick ('A Meaning for Turner's Frontier,' *Political Science Quarterly*,
Vol. 69 (1954), 321ff. and 565ff.).

[2] 'The inhabitants had barred their doors and double-locked their money-tills in vain.
With scarcely a halt the peddler made his way into their houses, and silver lept into his
pockets. When his pack was unrolled, calicoes, glittering knives, razors, scissors, clocks,
cotton caps, shoes, and notions made a holiday at a fair. His razors were bright as the
morning star, cut quick as thought, and had been made by the light of a diamond in a cave
in Andalusia. He showed hickory cups and bowls and plates, and mentioned the haste
with which people in a neighbouring village had broken their crockery and thrown it into
the street since crockery was known to spread the plague. He told stories of the plague. In
the end he invaded every house. Every one bought. The Negroes came up from their
cabins to watch his driving pantomime and hear his slow, high talk. Staying the night at a
tavern, he traded the landlord out of bed and breakfast and left with most of the money in
the settlement.' So Constance Rourke describes the impact of a Yankee pedlar upon
Southern communities (*American Humor*, Anchor Books, p. 16). Southern society was
defenceless against such arts, and eventually repaid the Yankee with suspicion and
distrust; but one may surmise that the men got a better shave with the new razors than
heretofore.

In the northern migration the same stage of frontier democracy was encountered, but at first it seemed as though the great estate might become the Northern pattern. Great tracts north of the Ohio passed into the hands of land companies and individual speculators; but the land companies could not provide a ready-made race of squires to take charge of the primitive settlements. Responsibility necessarily devolved upon the settlers themselves. Curiously enough it was the efforts of the great landed interests to obtain a framework of order within which they could operate, which sealed their own fate. The Ordinance of 1787 set up government in the Northwest, provided a blue-print for transition to statehood through a stage in which locally elected legislatures controlled local affairs, and prohibited slavery north of the Ohio. Effective local power was therefore destined to fall into the hands of the small settlers and the region was sealed off from the slave labour on which an upper class might be erected. A natural hostility developed between the small settlers and the great proprietors which ended in the complete ruin of the latter. Nothing in American history is perhaps more notable than the collapse of these great vested interests under the relentless pressure of small settlers who demanded easy and cheap access to land, the right of squatters to pre-empt land which they had cultivated, and heavy taxes on unimproved land. Caught between public hostility, encroaching squatters, and penal taxation—and without the labour force to establish commercial farming—the great landowner disappeared from north-western history.

The absence of a ruling class threw greater responsibilities upon the humble settlers; it also opened to them greater opportunities. New Englanders who predominated in the northern migration had a natural fondness for small town life, and all the traditions of race urged that the little white church and the little red school house should follow in the wake of settlement. But the establishment of towns was neither by chance nor by government planning. In a few cases, as at Marietta on the Ohio, a land company had deliberately set up a New England township; but the great proliferation of towns which followed in the early nineteenth century was the result of individualistic speculation and promotion. The ambitions of the successful turned not to the establishment of a plantation but to founding a town. On a good town site, land values would rise and so also would the prosperity of the whole community. Success depended upon many things besides the initial suitability of the site: upon roads, trade, securing the county capital, and upon attracting more people of a useful type. The energy and communal activity of agrarian democracy flowed over into the small towns where every man's fortune might depend upon the decisions which they could obtain from authority. But as democratic procedures moved to their urban setting they changed their character, for the townsmen did not want to defend a simple rural existence but to get things done. The ideal element in politics might recede into the background but their practical utility greatly increased. These Westerners had very little respect for authority, but they knew instinctively the uses of power, and rewarded those who manipulated power to their best advantage. Nor amid the scramble for material gains were other amenities neglected; even at their lowest reckoning these had a cash value in raising the character of the town. It is no accident that along the trail of New England migration there were, by the time of the Civil War, the majority of the nation's commercial towns, the tracks of the main east to west railways and a majority of the institutions of higher education.

Here then were two societies which had little in common, each of which had developed distinctive patterns of behaviour, and in which an apparent agreement about the forms of political life concealed great divergence in the practice of politics. If the Northwest was still predominantly agricultural it was commercial agriculture, and the interests of banking, commerce and manufactures were increasingly important and vocal. If the South consisted in fact of two societies, it was represented at the national level entirely by planter gentry whose main concern was to preserve the price of cotton and their own local autonomy.[1] Moreover

---

[1] In 1819 Taylor of New York said in the House of Representatives, 'When have we seen a Representative on this floor, from that section of our Union, who was not a slave-

both Northern and Southern cultures were expansive. The Southerners might appear gracious and unhurried beside the busy grasping Northerners, but they were equally avaricious for new land on which to raise cotton, and in this land hunger they were backed by the small backcountry farmers who wanted to relieve the pressure on their poor fields. Many other disagreements flowed into the great conflict between North and South, but here were its essential characteristics, fruitful of misunderstanding, of bloody war, and of traditions which even the twentieth century has not reconciled.

The great rift between North and South dominates the history of the United States, but the clash between East and West has often been equally important. In colonial days and for some time thereafter a natural frontier existed at the limit of navigable water; east of it men were in close touch with the commerce of the Atlantic, west of it they depended upon short, bad and infrequent roads for the transport of goods. Without internal communications the West might have remained a primitive economy, or its more forward elements might have created a distinct society based upon the Mississippi and separated from the eastern seaboard by a wide area of sparsely populated territory. Some men were even tempted to think of a Western commonwealth at first under Spain and eventually independent. However feeble such a state might have been the Westerners would have been masters of their own destiny. Roads, canals, railways and the American acquisition of Louisiana decided otherwise, and the Western territories passed with marvellous rapidity from a primitive to an advanced economy. For this advance the price was the loss of independence.

Any agricultural economy is likely to come under the economic domination of those who supply capital, machines and markets, and the consequences of this dependence are likely to be deepened by the normal fluctuations of economic life. Heavy demand in war or from new markets causes expansion, the delayed effect of

holder? Who but slaveholders are elected to their state Legislatures? Who but they are appointed to fill their executive and judicial offices? I appeal to gentlemen, whether the selection of a labouring man, would not be considered an extraordinary event?' (*Congressional Record*, Feb. 15, 1819, 15th Congress, 2nd Sess. 1177).

expansion is over-production, and prolonged depression ensues. To this kind of fluctuation an economy operating upon the fringe of virgin land is particularly susceptible, for the temptation to bring too much into cultivation is almost irresistible and rural bankers, who supply the credit for expansion, are likely to be infected by the easy optimism of a growing society. The depression which follows is likely to be very severe and accompanied by the failure of many banks; the outsiders who have ultimate control demand the payment of debts and refuse to relax their usual standards of business practice because of what they regard as the improvidence of others. This was the recurrent experience of the Western farmer. Ridden by economic laws which he did not understand and could not control he sought remedies and scapegoats: relief for debtors, increased issues of currency to enable the farmer to borrow his way through the depression, and attacks upon monied men are the usual demands of agrarian radicalism from the eighteenth to the twentieth centuries.

What the debtor farmer was really trying to preserve was his independence; one could always subsist on a farm (save when flood or drought was added to the farmer's troubles) but debt threatened the farm itself. This explains both the passions and the limitations of agrarian radicalism. The emotions generated by attacks on the economic hierarchy are intense, but the farmer radical wanted to be an independent property owner and could not afford to reject the normal supports of a property-owning society. Even while he attacked the system on points of detail he came back to the sanctity of contract and the right of a man to do what he will with his own. Thus the most violent attacks upon the American capitalist system never questioned its fundamental assumptions, remained wholly unsympathetic to European socialism, and failed to achieve any permanent alliance with industrial labour. Not infrequently, however, the farmer could make common cause with small businessmen.

The strength of agrarian radicalism lay in its appeal to favourite symbols in American life. The innocence of the rural cultivator contrasted with the corruption of civilized life was a familiar conceit of eighteenth-century literature and was permanently enshrined in American thought by Thomas Jefferson, who wrote, 'Those who labor in the earth are the chosen people of God, if ever He had a chosen people, whose breasts He has made His peculiar deposit for substantial and genuine virtue. It is the focus in which He keeps the sacred fire, which otherwise might escape from the face of the earth. Corruption of morals in the mass of cultivators is a phenomenon of which no age nor nation has furnished an example.' The independent cultivator protecting his rights with his vote was the American prototype of the democratic man; in Europe it was the townsman bidding with his vote for social benefits. Even today it is conventional, not least among those who are careful never to set foot upon a farm, to pay tribute to the rural virtues. It is then not altogether surprising that the complaints of the farmer have led finally to government action which could hardly be contemplated for any other economic interest. Today, God's chosen people have become the foster children of the national government, draw substantial sums from the American taxpayer to ensure that they receive more for their produce than its market value, and are protected by complex laws against the changes and chances of economic life. The long chapter of agrarian radicalism may thus be said to have closed and can only be re-opened by some drastic change in national policy.

The conflict between town and country is wider than that between East and West, or between debtor and creditor. For over half a century more people have lived in large towns in the United States than in any other nation, and by 1920 more people lived in towns than in rural areas. A substantial number of those living in the country work in the towns or are directly under urban influence, and modern communications and mass media make the circle of this influence ever wider. For a long time there has been migration from the countryside to the towns and some important groups of immigrants — notably the Irish and the Italians — seldom got further than the big cities. A special example of recent movement into the cities has been the northward migration of Southern Negroes which has been directed almost entirely to the larger towns of the North.

In spite of the persistence of the agrarian cult American civilization has always been partly, and is now largely, a town-made product. Corporate business and organized labour are both based upon the cities and these two share with the national government the direction of economic life. One major party leans heavily upon urban businessmen, the other upon the mass vote of the bigger towns. Throughout the modern history of the Western world there has been a struggle between rural and urban civilization; in America it has been marked, first because by far the greater number of large towns were in the Northern states, and then because the cities contained so many whose allegiance to American values was doubtful. In a nation which is still dominated by Anglo-Saxon and Protestant traditions (and to a large extent by Anglo-Saxon and Protestant men) the great cities are predominantly Irish, Italian, Slav and Roman Catholic. In the nineteenth century they became the centres of corrupt politics, political machines, and socialism. Americans who were not directly concerned turned their eyes away from the city, its problems and its implications. No one has yet done for the influence of the city what F. J. Turner did for the influence of the frontier, but 'the shame of cities' is a conventional phrase which has passed into every textbook. Yet the Revolution owed more to Boston, Philadelphia, New York and Charleston than it did to the countryside, even when the contribution of Virginia is placed in the balance; there was radical democracy in the towns before it ever appealed to the farmer, and the city vote has been an important element in every 'progressive' movement save Populism. On the other hand American cities have perhaps demonstrated the vices of popular government with striking regularity.

The United States has no national metropolis. Washington is an administrative capital but not an economic or cultural capital; New York is an economic capital but it is not the political capital and its strong claims to be a cultural capital are disputed by other

c

regions. No one city can ever play the part which London and Paris play, but each of the great towns has its economic and cultural empire. In a countryside which is still sparsely populated compared with England, the pre-eminence of the city is more marked; so are the attempts of the countryside to restrain its influence. A curious triangular relationship has developed between farmer, urban businessman and urban labour. The farmer and the businessman are usually allied by race, fundamental beliefs, and a patriotic suspicion of what is 'red', European, and Catholic; but they are often opposed on immediate political issues, and the rural underdog may find something in common with the urban underdog. On a national scale this is seen in the vast, perplexing and enduring alliance of rural South with the Northern city masses which traditionally, though perhaps erroneously, dates from a 'botanizing expedition' made by Jefferson and Madison into New York state during the autumn of 1792. This alliance is the backbone of the Democratic Party, which Republicans perpetually try to break by appeals to the conservative South against Northern liberalism, and to city liberals against Southern reaction.

A third feature of the social map is the small town; by origin a rural market town it has usually remained one in character. It may have acquired some small factories but it is unlikely to have a large labouring population, and the dominant figures will be merchants, real estate agents, lawyers, and the owner of the local newspapers. This normally benevolent but narrow-minded oligarchy runs the local charities, the hospital, and the Republican party organization (or, in the South, the Democratic organization). Its members are the chief supporters of the Churches and probably influence the schools. In many ways the small town is the mean of American life; it is the legatee of all the American traditions, it typifies the strength and the weakness of the American system, it is the heart which must be won before any new idea or policy can take root. Even though the small business-man, like the farmer, is losing his independence and becoming the agent of the great corporate businesses, his social and political influence remains very great. Based on the small town — of which a good many are more than a thousand miles from the sea — fundamentally decent, but too often ignorant and opinionated, he has been forced to play a world role which he has not chosen and for which he is ill-equipped.

A special feature of the clash between urban and rural society has been the rise of big business and the reactions which it has occasioned. By 1860 most Americans had come to accept a doctrinaire version of *laissez-faire* and the virtues of free enterprise and free competition were held to be self-evident. At the very moment when these beliefs triumphed they were being challenged by the elimination of competition, by agreements between rivals, by the consolidation of business, and by the rise of monopoly capitalism. The theory of evolution, popularized as a scientific doctrine by Charles Darwin and as a philosophic principle by Herbert Spencer, sanctified the survival of the fittest and presented Americans with an intellectual problem which was to dog them for years to come: if the value of competition was to ensure that the fittest survived, how could it be maintained *after* the fittest had survived? Or, to put the problem in more practical terms, how could monopoly be restrained without sapping the roots of the competitive system? Attention was concentrated upon the problem because of the outrageous behaviour of a few magnates who were prepared to use force, fraud, and political corruption to attain their objects. The new *élite* was both powerful and unwilling to recognize the responsibilities of power. In 1870 a distinguished and sensitive American wrote that, 'The belief is common in America that the day is at hand when corporations . . . swaying power such as has never in the world's history been trusted in the hands of mere private citizens . . . and after having created a system of quiet but irresistible corruption . . . will ultimately succeed in directing government itself.'[1] The possibility may never have become an actuality, but the suspicion that it might do so remains; never was the fear so real as in the late nineteenth century. The conduct of the great railway corporations caused special

[1] Henry Adams, *The Gold Conspiracy*, in the *Westminster Review*, Oct. 1870.

alarm for no business is more likely to establish a monopoly, in none is the argument for consolidation more clear, and nowhere are its consequences more deplorable when guided by unscrupulous men. Almost as alarming was the oil-refining industry in which John D. Rockefeller established a reputation for ruthlessness which was more efficient than fair; his Standard Oil Company, which came to control 90 per cent of the refining business, seemed to illustrate the worst features of monopoly.

The challenge was met after a fashion. The Interstate Commerce Act of 1887 set up an independent commission to supervise railway operation, and the Sherman Anti-Trust Act of 1890 made it illegal to combine in restraint of trade. Neither act was immediately effective in the face of judicial suspicion, executive apathy, and the highly paid lawyers employed by the corporations. But a principle had been established that big business was susceptible to public regulation, and in the twentieth century the independent commissions have multiplied and the Anti-Trust Laws have become a complex code embodying the rules of the game. Big business has not been killed — that would perhaps have been a disaster for America — but total monopoly has been outlawed, real competition between the giants has been enforced, and the methods used against smaller rivals must be 'fair'. The spokesmen of big business claim that it has acquired a conscience and a convention of public service. Those less friendly may claim that its evils have been obscured rather than eradicated. It is perhaps more pertinent that the great corporations have become so vast, so impersonal and so bureaucratic that the insolence and trickery of the early monopolists have become impossible. If American big business today has its vices they are those of a system not those of individuals. And if criticism has sometimes been bitter, there has also been pride in the massive achievement.

*   *   *   *

The typical American wants to believe that men are reasonable, naturally good, and fundamentally idealistic. These decent convictions have clashed, throughout his history, with things as they are. The American is constantly faced with the paradox that the people must be entrusted with power, but that when they have power they cease to act decently. Fortunately for the nation the makers of its government were acutely aware that men could be corrupted, that passion could overthrow reason, and that men could not be governed merely by relying upon their good intentions. Alexander Hamilton was the supreme exponent of this philosophy, but so, in a more subtle way, was James Madison, the father of the Constitution, and even the idealistic Jefferson believed that liberty was a fragile thing easily lost by bad men and bad conditions.[1] The thought of these men was guided by the idea that government ought to be one of laws not men, that laws were likely to be better than the men who executed them and that, while government ought to derive from the people, an inviolable constitution should restrain those whom the people had chosen.

The government of the Union is a wholly artificial creation. It did not evolve, as did that of all European countries, from the semi-mystical majesty of kings, but it was made at a single moment in time, in the summer of 1787. The way had been prepared by a loose association between states known as the Confederation, but it was the work of the Federal Convention which made the government of the United States as it exists today. The Constitution embodies principles which are anathema to many political theorists; it is a matter of debate whether these heresies have done

[1] 'A large and well-organized republic can scarcely lose its liberty from any other cause than that of anarchy, to which a contempt of the laws is the high road' (*Works of Alexander Hamilton*, ed. Lodge, VI, 26). 'The instruments by which government must act are either the Authority of the laws or Force. If the first be destroyed, the last must be substituted; and where this becomes the ordinary instrument of government, there is an end to liberty' (*ibid.*, 27). 'In a representative republic, where the executive magistracy is carefully limited . . . and where the legislative power is exercised by an assembly, which is inspired by a supposed influence over the people, with an intrepid confidence in its own strength . . . it is against the enterprising ambition of this department, that the people ought to indulge all their jealousy and exhaust all their precautions' (Madison, *Federalist Letter*, LXVIII). Jefferson referred to the narrow margin by which the proposal to transfer power to a dictator in Virginia was defeated in 1781, 'Searching for the foundations of this proposition, I can find none which may pretend a color of right or reason, but the defect that . . . there being no barrier between the legislative, executive, and judiciary departments, the legislature may seize the whole; that having seized it, and possessing a right to fix their own quorum, they may reduce that quorum to one, whom they may call a chairman, speaker, dictator, or by any other name they please (*Notes on the State of Virginia*, Query XIII).

more to prolong its life or to make its operations obscure, complex and ineffective. The law of the United States is the supreme law of the land, yet it does not touch certain important human interests, and the states continue to perform important functions which are elsewhere regarded as national responsibilities. Nor, in general, does the reputation of the states for enlightened performance of their duties stand very high. At the centre, the powers of government — executive, legislative and judiciary — are separate and function independently. Congress is not sovereign as the British Parliament is sovereign; the President is not responsible to Congress as the British Prime Minister is responsible to Parliament; the judges do not execute without question the laws of Congress — as the British courts execute the law of Parliament — but only those laws which they deem to be constitutional. In theory the people are sovereign and they exercise this sovereignty by electing a President, Senators, Congressmen, state Governors, state senators, state assemblymen, a multitude of officials, and in some states the state judges; but each and every one of these elected authorities may be at loggerheads with all the others, and so far from the will of a sovereign majority prevailing through their elected representatives, numerous majorities produce different representatives whose mutual conflicts may well prevent anything from happening at all. American government moves slowly, jerkily, and often blindly; it is equally susceptible to waves of popular emotion and to the influence of minorities and pressure groups.

Since the Constitution is written in the plain and dignified prose of the eighteenth century and not in modern lawyers' language, it allows a wide measure of opinion into its interpretation, and the elderly men who compose the Supreme Court can act as a legislature rather than as a court. The prohibition of slavery in territories north of 36° 30′ under the Missouri Compromise was law for thirty-seven years before the Court declared it invalid; racial segregation in schools had been the unchallenged practice for over half a century in the Southern states before the Court declared it to be unconstitutional; early New Deal measures were invalidated on arguments which were philosophical rather than legal, against a President and Congressional majority which had won a landslide electoral victory. The anti-trust laws, intended to limit monopoly capitalism, have been twisted, contracted, extended and glossed by the Supreme Court; in one era emptied of all meaning, in another made to carry more meaning than their authors ever intended; applied to those to whom they were never meant to apply, interpreted loosely, interpreted strictly, until these acts—perhaps the most important on the statute book — mean what they do mean because the Supreme Court wills it so. Political theorists can thus extend themselves in their quest for defects in the American system of government which has, however, maintained in union peoples whom race and geography seemed to have divided, twice mobilized the national resources for total war, and commands the undivided loyalty of its citizens for whom it is the supreme symbol of national wisdom.

If the national government was an artificial creation, the political parties have evolved without design. With their eyes fixed upon the dangers of local faction, the makers of the Constitution did not anticipate national parties; but in creating power at the centre they ensured that men would seek the means to secure it. The only way to do this was by electing a Congress and a President, and for this the votes of no one class, section or region were adequate; there had to be an alliance of factions and at an early stage in national history the party became a loose alliance to elect a President. The various interests united in a party had to find some common cause, but it has usually been easier to find this in dislike of some policy or group of men than in a programme of action. It follows also that any declaration of party aims will be amorphous, will indicate an attitude rather than a conviction, will compromise important questions on which its elements cannot agree, and try to ignore what cannot be compromised. The most important political movements are liable to take place within the parties rather than in conflict between them, and the lack of clear distinction between the party programmes often arises because both are responding to the same currents of opinion in slightly different ways. The parties frequently seem to be moving on parallel courses carried along by the same currents which neither attempts to control.

From the nature of parties (and indirectly from the nature of the Constitution) certain results ensue. Men committed to definite policies are unlikely to rise to the top, for they are certain to antagonize some element essential to the alliance. The politician is likely to regard himself as a broker of power and opinion rather than as a leader. The machinery of politics is brought more to the fore than in England because the party is primarily a piece of political organization and not the instrument of ideological attack or defence. The parties have evolved internal checks and balances which serve to stifle rather than to discipline trouble-makers; in Great Britain the whole ponderous machinery of party is brought into action against a rebel, in America he is usually left untouched because he can accomplish very little. The individual politician has more freedom from national party bosses and more dependence upon his constituents (but may also owe a good deal to the local party boss).

The American tradition of a government of laws has its sordid obverse in a tradition of lawlessness. The two are not unconnected for a trust in the law has often obscured the need to make adequate arrangements for its enforcement. Indeed there is a crucial weakness at the heart of the American system which leaves the major responsibility for the prevention of crime with state governments which are often weak and sometimes corrupt. Lawlessness has appeared in three main forms: rough justice executed by respectable citizens when law enforcement has failed, evasion of unpopular laws by local authorities and backed by local public opinion, and plain criminality. What is peculiar about American history is not so much the scope and organization of the third as the involvement of decent citizens in the first two. The usurpation of royal authority and the coercion of Loyalists played an important part in the Revolution; so too did the vigilante committee (under that or another name) play in the history of the frontier. The history of the South since the Civil War has been largely the maintenance of white supremacy in contravention of the fourteenth and fifteenth amendments which give the Negro full civil and voting rights. On the other hand respectable opinion has often been strangely slow to act against corrupt politicians even when closely allied with organized vice and crime. Several reasons have been assigned for this lack of public spirit. Business often depended upon local politicians for necessary favours and much preferred a corrupt machine, with which it was possible to come to terms, than a reform administration which might be incalculable; respectable opinion, realizing that the mass vote must be organized, tacitly agreed that the 'boss' — for all his misuse of public money and blackmail of business — might offer the cheapest way of doing so; businessmen and lawyers have often been far too busy keeping abreast of the competitive struggle to waste time on politics. It may be, however, that corruption is a price which has been paid for agreement upon fundamentals; it is when men are bitten by radical bugs, when groups work for total change, when ideas get into politics that 'good men must associate'. However, the behaviour of the corrupt has been, from time to time, so outrageous that the 'reform' movement led by good citizens is a recurrent feature of American history, and in extreme instances becomes action of the vigilante type in which decent men take the law into their own hands.

*　　*　　*　　*

The political system has, in spite of its many oddities, fulfilled most of the tasks which have been set for it. Where there is a broad measure of agreement, where there is the will to compromise, and where the problems to be solved are not overwhelming, the American system can do its work well. If it encourages parochialism it is also responsive to public opinion; if the politician tends to be amoral or even immoral, it also produces a great number of common-sense men with an instinct for combining what is right with what is possible. It may however be asked whether the sensitive, sprawling, slow moving political system of the United States, so well-fitted in so many ways for reconciling the differences of a diverse people, is not too cumbersome for the conduct of foreign affairs? Alexander Hamilton once wrote, 'Whoever considers the nature of our government with discernment will see, that though obstacles and delays will frequently stand in the way of the adoption of good measures, yet, when once adopted, they are likely to be stable and permanent. It will be far more difficult to undo than to do.' A century and a half has greatly increased the 'obstacles and delays' so that American foreign policy often resembles a great liner set on its course without the means to avoid collision in the congested sea of modern international politics.

In the beginning Americans felt that they had created a new type of society, freed from the evils of the Old World, 'conceived in Liberty, and dedicated to the proposition that all men are created equal'. Innumerable orations and patriotic poems have hammered home the point that Americans are not as other men are. This conviction was able to grow and become a part of the character of American history partly because forces often beyond American control kept the nation in isolation from the rest of the world during the formative period of its growth. This isolation was more apparent than real: on the one hand the nation was made by forces emanating from Europe, and on the other it was the British navy which kept other European nations from transatlantic adventures. Nevertheless from 1815 to 1917 Americans were able to think primarily of their own domestic concerns. It would be tempting to remark 'happy is the country which has no foreign policy' had not the Civil War demonstrated that men can think too much about their own affairs.

In the twentieth century the United States have been forced to make a drastic readjustment of their traditional views. America is no longer required to reject Europe but to save it. Hostages to fortune have been given in every part of the world and demand protection. The domestic affairs of the American people are becoming international property, and the outcome of a debate in the Senate may affect directly the lives of men in far corners of the world. The Americans are forced to play this role in a world in which approximately half the population has been taught to identify wrong with Americanism, and in which even allies regard their influence with barely concealed jealousy. It remains to be seen whether the intellectual and emotional resources of American civilization are sufficient for the times.

[2]

The Era of the Revolution

The war of the Revolution was not fought because Great Britain wished to secure a paltry revenue or because the colonists wished to escape minor exactions. It was fought because men in England could not see how the vital interests of the country could be sustained unless Parliament was supreme over the whole Empire and because men in the colonies believed that this supremacy must endanger their essential rights. On both sides of the Atlantic there were dissentient minorities, and on both sides the majority tried to resist the conclusions to which logic and extremism were leading them. In England men such as Burke believed that British supremacy could be reconciled with colonial autonomy if Britain would rely upon colonial goodwill rather than upon coercive legislation. In America many conservatives felt the need for some external authority wielding residuary power to act as a guarantee of social order. On both sides of the Atlantic the debate passed through several stages — and no great conflict has ever been so thoroughly explored in anticipation by written and spoken discussion — but in the long run this debate served to isolate and emphasize the points upon which agreement was impossible rather than to explore the common ground.

By 1774 the point was reached at which the British government felt that it must back the authority of Parliament by force, while the colonists felt that submission to it would be an abrogation of the rights and dignity of men. Both sides had come to live in a world of fiction as much as in a world of fact: on the British side the acceptance of colonial autonomy was thought to be the first step in the wholesale destruction of British power, on the American side tyranny and military despotism were held to be the hidden though undeniable aims of British policy. The words of the Declaratory Act of 1766, passed by a government friendly to the colonies and intended as no more than an abstract statement of what was legally irrefutable — that Parliament had power to legislate for the colonies in all cases whatsoever — was twisted into a real intention to legislate colonial liberties out of existence. After this lapse of time it is possible to see how exaggerated, foolish and often malicious these fears were, but it is also possible to recognize that they arose because no man could believe both in the supremacy of Parliament and in the right of colonies to do as they pleased with their own.

The nature of the interests which Great Britain sought to protect were consequent upon her world position. Her success in war over the superior population, resources and military power of France was rightly attributed to her naval strength and her wealth derived from trade. The preservation of the navy and the safeguarding of commercial profits were therefore the cardinal aims of British policy and they had been knit together in a complex but coherent system of imperial regulation. Colonies had been acquired and developed to serve these ends; British shipping was given an almost complete monopoly of their trade; their most valuable products could be exported only to England; and, save for a few articles for which a special case could be made, foreigners were excluded from their markets. The necessity for such regulations was widely recognized in the colonies and under them the colonies had grown to prosperity; in exchange for certain restrictions and for a small but incalculable loss of profit the colonies gained protection, secured a market, and were able to contribute no less than a third to the merchant navy of Great Britain.[1] These

[1] John Dickinson was typical of the conservative revolutionaries who retained a strong sense of benefits of Empire. In the *Essay on the Constitutional Power of Great Britain* of 1774 he wrote, 'To a man, who has considered . . . it will not appear too bold to aver, that, if an archangel had planned the connexion between Great Britain and her colonies, he could not have fixed it on a more lasting and beneficial foundation, unless he could have changed human nature. A mighty naval power at the head of the whole — that power, a parent state with all the endearing sentiments attending to the relationship — that could never disoblige, but with design — the dependent states more apt to have feuds among themselves — she the umpire and controuler — those states producing every article

Laws of Trade and Navigation were in fact the very last instruments of British authority to be repudiated by the colonists and
on the eve of independence some were still anxious to retain them
as a matter of expediency while claiming colonial self-government
as a right. But if the effectiveness of the Laws of Trade and
Navigation was to depend upon colonial recognition of their
utility it was probable that British interests would be sacrificed
whenever a dispute arose.[1] The power and resources of Great
Britain would be eaten away piecemeal, until she joined Venice,
Poland, and Sweden in the company of powers who had grasped
greatness without the will to retain it. 'The dye is now cast,'
wrote George III at a crucial stage in the revolutionary war,
'whether this shall be a great Empire or the least dignified of the
European States.'[2]

While the preservation of the laws of trade and navigation
were the essential core of the British case, there were other reasons
which made it difficult to contemplate a contraction of imperial
authority. In any system of protection interests grow which must
perish if it is ended, while new interests coming into the field
demand the same consideration as the old. Thus British merchants
handling the growing exports of British manufactures asked for
protection against colonial competitors and a series of not very
effective laws restrained manufactures in the colonies. British
merchants had large sums laid out in the colonies, mainly as long
credits given to buyers and planters; these investments might be

necessary to her greatness — their interest, that she should continue free and flourishing
— their ability to throw a considerable weight in the scale, should her government get
unduly poised — she and all those states Protestant — are some of the circumstances,
that delineated by the masterly hand of a Beccaria, would exhibit a plan, vindicating the
ways of heaven and demonstrating, that humanity and policy are nearly related.'

[1] This point of view was put forcibly and well by Lord Lyttelton during the Stamp Act
debates. On Feb. 10, 1766, he is reported as having said, 'It is said that they will not submit
to the Stamp Act as it lays an internal tax; if this be admitted, the same reasoning extends
to all acts of Parliament. The Americans will find themselves crampt by the Act of
Navigation and oppose that too.... The only question ... is whether the American
colonies are a part of the dominions of Great Britain? If not, the parliament has no
jurisdiction, if they are ... they must be proper objects of our legislature: and by declaring
them exempt from one statute or law, you declare them no longer subjects of Great
Britain, and make them small independent communities not entitled to your protection.'

[2] The King to Lord North. Nov. 3, 1781 (*Correspondence of George III*, ed. Fortescue,
V, 297).

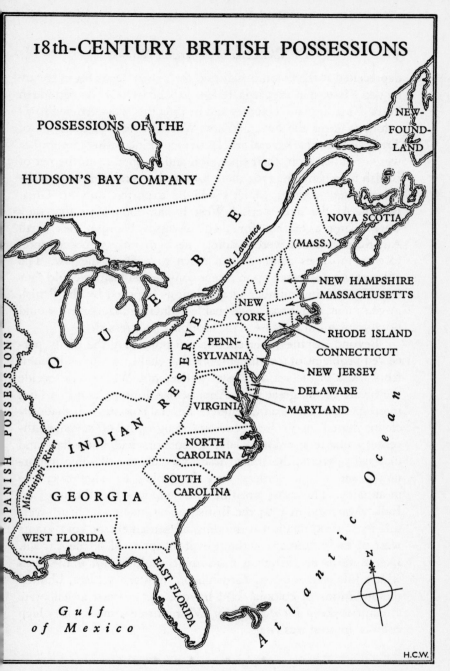

18th-CENTURY BRITISH POSSESSIONS

POSSESSIONS OF THE

HUDSON'S BAY COMPANY

NEW-FOUND-LAND

Q U E B E C

St. Lawrence

NOVA SCOTIA

(MASS.)

NEW HAMPSHIRE
MASSACHUSETTS

NEW YORK

RHODE ISLAND

PENN-SYLVANIA

CONNECTICUT

NEW JERSEY

DELAWARE

VIRGINIA

MARYLAND

I N D I A N   R E S E R V E

NORTH CAROLINA

SOUTH CAROLINA

GEORGIA

S P A N I S H   P O S S E S S I O N S

Mississippi River

WEST FLORIDA

EAST FLORIDA

Gulf of Mexico

A t l a n t i c   O c e a n

N

H.C.W.

The boundaries shown are those of 1774; the western boundaries of New
York, Pennsylvania, Maryland, Virginia and North Carolina had been limited
by the Proclamation of 1763 although these colonies had claims to western lands;
the boundary of Quebec had been advanced south of the Great Lakes by the
Quebec Act of 1774.

depreciated if the colonies satisfied their own needs for currency by paper issues; in 1751 legal tender paper currency was forbidden in the New England colonies and in 1764 this was extended to all colonies. After the Seven Years' War a review of the Acts of Trade showed that several articles of new or increasing importance were excluded from their operation and escaped from the net of British merchants; in 1764 there followed several additions to the 'enumerated' articles which could be exported only to Great Britain. At the same period West Indian complaints that they were losing a market for their molasses because the North American colonies were evading the high duty imposed upon foreign molasses resulted in a drive to enforce the law. The colonist who reflected upon recent commercial history could thus see an increasing number of regulations imposed by the British government, and it was a reasonable deduction that control would not diminish but increase as the economy progressed.

Beyond disputes over commercial policy lay the dimly perceived problems of a continent, offering challenges quite different from those of the sea or coastal settlements. Who would decide the future of the great trans-Appalachian Empire, and in whose interests should it be administered? Several colonies had shadowy claims based upon the generous geography of seventeenth-century charters; colonial land speculators had immediate and material interests; the Indian trade was already of some importance; and a few settlers were beginning to edge over the mountains. The most pressing problem was the threat of an Indian war, and in 1763 the British government sought to avert this by a Proclamation forbidding all settlement or land grants west of the mountains without express approval of the Crown. Defensible as an emergency measure, its prolongation in the years which followed inflicted hardship on Western settlers, blunted the ambitions of colonial land buyers, and seemed a deliberate attempt to keep for decision at Westminster a matter in which colonial interest was vital.

*   *   *   *

The precariousness of power in the pre-industrial age makes British anxieties comprehensible, but it is more difficult to understand what the colonists sought to gain by relaxing or dissolving the bonds of empire. Around 1763 the overall benefits of the imperial connection seemed evident in the growth and prosperity of the colonies: what strong motives could induce hard-headed lawyers, merchants and landowners to question the paternal care of the mother country, to risk the dangers of war, and to incur the dire penalties of treason? A modern historian is apt to seek the inner causes for such seemingly irrational behaviour in class conflicts which drive men blindly on to disrupt and destroy; from the search for such conflicts has arisen a school of interpretation which sees the American Revolution as primarily an internal revolution aimed at the displacement of a colonial 'aristocracy'. But the men who led the colonies into the Revolution belonged to the same economic and social class as those who had hitherto predominated, and though class conflicts are to be found their pattern is confused, localized and obscured by the other emotions released during the period. Though mobs played their part they achieved little save when under upper-class leadership and control. The American Revolution is the revolt of men of property and it is among them that one must seek the fears and aspirations which led to conflict.

In 1763 loyalty to Britain seemed to be still the dominant political emotion in the colonies; based upon economic partnership, British prestige and a belief that liberty was the special characteristic of the British constitution, allegiance to the British Crown seemed paramount. Yet analysis of this loyalty shows how deceptive was the strength which Britain appeared to derive from it. If loyalty found support in material progress, it was also undermined by the growing divergence between British and Colonial interests, and the bonds were strained during the post-war depression. Exaltation of Britain's prestige might be a source of irritation rather than pride when her countrymen accused the colonists of failing in their duty during the war, and when the customary arrogance of the British upper classes offended

D

Americans who prided themselves upon their culture, their morals and their breeding. The defeat of the French removed the most powerful argument for subservience to British power. And, perhaps the most important, the British constitution had come to mean something in the colonies which it could not mean in Great Britain.

In Britain Parliament was still regarded less as a law-making authority (though Blackstone was shortly to emphasize its legal supremacy) than as a check upon executive power and a guarantee that the law would be observed. The ordinary subject looked to the courts of law rather than to Parliament for the protection of his personal rights, but because Parliament was itself composed of subjects with rights it was trusted to see that these were respected. The over-representation of landed property strengthened rather than weakened this argument, for the more a man had to lose the more anxious would he be to ensure its security under the law. Though no one pretended that Parliament represented the people it was maintained with some justice that it did represent their interests. Moreover the constitution was that of a 'mixed' government in which King, Lords and Commons had each the power to prevent the others from doing wrong; and if this meant that the government was often completely inactive in fields where activity is expected by modern men, it did leave to the citizen extensive personal freedom. Thus the harsh realities of an unrepresentative but sovereign assembly — in which the influence of the Crown could always carry the day provided that the co-operation of a sufficient number of territorial magnates was obtained — were veiled in a delicate system of checks and balances. Those who were nearest to the heart of things knew that the language of tyranny was a thing of the past and that what preoccupied 'the Court' was not a design to overthrow British liberty but the endless task of keeping together a Parliamentary majority among men who were independent, greedy, and not wholly insensitive to public opinion. But the further one moved from the centre the more Parliament looked like a despotic body moved by corrupt influences. In the colonies its unrepresentative character was clear because no

American interest was represented, (hence the extravagant praise heaped by Americans upon those such as Chatham, Camden, Wilkes and Barré, who appeared to be their spokesmen) and because American connection and influence lay with merchants, shipowners and nonconformists, not with the ruling class of landed proprietors. The will of Parliament appeared in America not as the final outcome of a subtle and complex process operating through all the channels of society but as the arbitrary fiat of despotic authority. This is the crux of all those factors described as causes of the Revolution; the fact that Parliament was not really like this does not remove the reality of the American grievance, nor does the nature of the grievance tell us much about the nature of Parliament. It was indeed one of those situations in which the differences between two societies ensure that they will talk nonsense about each other.

* * * *

Though there were sharp social divisions in the colonies they were not so sharp as those in Britain, and the extremes were less evident. If there were few very rich men by European standards there were also few who were without some property. The planter 'aristocracy' of the South was in fact no aristocracy, but a class of hard-working gentlemen farmers who lived in 'great houses' comparable in size and equipment to the modest manor houses of the lesser English gentry. There were rich merchants in the North with wide interests who compared favourably with the substantial tradesmen of London but whose wealth and influence was far removed from that of the great City magnates. At the other end there was no great class of landless white labourers, and no bestial lower stratum in the towns such as that which made the London mob one of the horrors of the world. There was also a high degree of social mobility and even among Virginian planters self-made men were more common than is sometimes believed.

It has already been noticed that the political institutions of the colonies reflected their social system and that hereditary privilege had been left out of their scheme of things. This made them anomalies in the eighteenth-century world, but Great Britain had never evolved a consistent policy for remedying the defect.[1] On the one hand the favour of the Crown was dispensed mainly to a few favoured families, but much of the patronage which might have been used to build up the influence of the Crown in the colonies was drawn into the net of home politics and used to reward the dependants of British magnates. Worst treated was the representative of imperial majesty himself, the colonial governor, who, between the claims of courtiers at home and favoured families in the colonies, found himself with very little patronage at all. Thus the influence of the Crown always rested upon too narrow a basis, the executive had little chance to broaden it, and the colonial oligarchies were to excite irritation without having the strength or numbers to stand against the storm.

At the other end of the scale the participation of the poorer people in politics was more real than in Britain. Small farmers, who composed the bulk of the electorate, have usually neither the leisure, the education, nor the inclination to take part in public life; members of the legislatures were therefore normally chosen from among the larger landowners, merchants, or lawyers; but most of the evidence seems to show that elections could be real battles in which the humble voter played an independent part. In New England the ordinary subject had also a good deal of experience in local government.[2]

---

[1] Many years later Lord Grenville argued that one of the fundamental causes of separation was that 'no care was taken to preserve the due mixture of the monarchical and aristocratical parts of the British constitution'. 'To the want of an intermediate power, to operate as a check, both on the misconduct of Governors and on the democratical spirit which prevailed in the Assemblies, the defection of the American provinces may perhaps be most justly ascribed' (*Historical MSS. Commission, Dropmore Papers*, I, 504).

[2] Robert E. Brown in *Middle Class Democracy and the Revolution in Massachusetts* effectively challenges the view that Massachusetts was dominated by a colonial 'aristocracy'. Almost any farm with a house, barn and twelve acres would qualify the owner for a vote; this would enfranchise the bulk of the rural male population. Most skilled artisans were enfranchised and propertyless and voteless labourers were comparatively few. The qualification for membership of town meetings was slightly higher, but in practice few resident males were excluded (pp. 78 ff.). 'The obstacle to colonial democracy was the British government, not a local "aristocracy" ' (p. 54). This argument should not however obscure the fact that there was a local oligarchy of favoured families, whose privileges were often as obnoxious to other members of the upper classes as to the people at large. See also Charles S. Sydnor, *Gentlemen Freeholders* and the same author's inaugural lecture at Oxford, *Political Leadership in Eighteenth Century Virginia*, in which he

The elected assemblies were the most lively elements in colonial life, and since they combined representation of the socially important with popular election, it was not surprising that they claimed and often exercised extensive privileges. Patterning themselves upon the House of Commons with free speech, freedom from arrest, and control of the purse as their salient characteristics, they could easily overreach the undistinguished men who were too often sent out as governors and whose salaries they controlled. The weakness of the executive on the spot meant that remote control had to be used to preserve imperial interests, and the disallowance of colonial acts was a source of annoyance which was increased by the long delay occasioned by slow sea voyages and the leisurely movements of government departments. The irritation might have been more easily borne if the colonial legislatures had really considered themselves as subordinate bodies on a par with the corporations of English boroughs (which was what they were according to one plausible interpretation of the imperial relationship). But, ridiculous as this might seem in England, these petty assemblies thought of themselves as co-equal in all but antiquity with the Parliament of Great Britain.[1]

This claim to equality was seldom made explicitly before the period of the final crisis, but it was implicit in much colonial thought. In the vital question of taxation it played an important part. The colonists were apt to find themselves arguing with logical inconsistency that Parliament had not the right to impose a direct tax, had not the right to tax for revenue, but could impose taxes indirectly and to regulate trade. The distinction was a difficult one to maintain so long as one argued that Parliament was omnicompetent; but it was easy to understand if one thought of a colonial assembly which had the sole power to tax but

observes that 'Democracy was a real and potent force in the political structure that brought the generation of great Virginians into power'.

[1] 'For even in the Provinces where the King appoints both Governors and Council, the authority of the Crown is not sufficiently supported against the licentiousness of a republican spirit in the people, whose extreme jealousy of any power not immediately derived from themselves, and whose affectation of considering England as an ally and friend than as a country to which they belong, and should be subordinate, dispose them generally to send as representatives the most artful and factious amongst them' (*Letter of Comptroller Weare, Massachusetts Historical Society Collections*, I, 1, 74).

permitted Parliament to impose certain taxes as a matter of expediency. It took many conservative Americans a long time to reach this position, and tactful radicals would not dare to express it too forcefully, yet it was the real nature of the claim made by Patrick Henry even before the struggle with Britain had begun.[1] It was also the position to which the majority of Americans would ultimately be led.

*   *   *   *

The mutual incompatibility of colonial autonomy with imperial interests was shrouded for several years by the American belief that the British constitution protected them against the actions which they disliked. They had long been accustomed to the idea of living under more than one law: under colonial charters, parliamentary statutes, laws of the assemblies, and the common law which normally drew directly upon British precedents; they had long been used to the idea of external authority intervening to disallow a colonial statute. Most American lawyers were bred upon Coke, and Coke had argued for the supremacy of the law; this had been reinforced by the Whiggish ideas of contract and consent derived mainly from Locke. It was therefore comparatively easy to slip into the idea that the actions of Parliament ought to be checked by a higher law, and to appeal from statute to the constitution.[2]

Unfortunately there could be no such appeal. The conflicts of the seventeenth century had produced two versions of the constitution which might, under certain circumstances, be in-

[1] In 1763 Patrick Henry argued the famous 'Parson's Case' which turned upon an act of the Virginian legislature which had been disallowed by the Crown. Henry is said to have argued 'that the act of 1758 had every characteristic of a good law; that it was a law of general utility', and could not, consistently with what he called the original compact between King and people, stipulating protection on the one hand and obedience on the other, be annulled'.

[2] 'The happiness of the people is the end, and, if the term is allowable, we would call it the body of the constitution. Freedom is the spirit or soul. As the soul, speaking of nature, has a right to prevent or relieve, if it can, any mischief to the body of the individual, and to keep it in the best of health; so the soul, speaking of the constitution, has a right to prevent or relieve, any mischief to the body of the society, and to keep that in the best of health' (John Dickinson, *Essay on the Constitutional Power of Great Britain over the Colonies*, Philadelphia, 1774).

compatible: the constitution existed to protect the liberty of the subject, but its cornerstone was the supremacy of Parliament. The ghost of Coke and the memory of Cromwellian constitutions might sustain the Americans, but logic and the law decreed that there was no act which a supreme legislature could not perform.[1] Yet if this was true every American might have to surrender something which he valued at the command of a sovereign Parliament over which he could have no control, and which was far more likely to be guided by British than by colonial interests. In this way the argument over rights ceased to be abstract and philosophical, and became a practical question of loss or gain. So much of American life had hinged upon the quest for social independence; in a world in which Parliament was really sovereign could independence ever be secure? Thus the version of the constitution in which Englishmen believed was one which the American could not accept and a clash was inevitable. But the form of that clash was determined by events between 1765 and 1776.

* * * *

Behind the façade of loyal fervour which Americans maintained at the conclusion of the Seven Years' War lurked a considerable disquiet, matched by a readiness in England to question the way in which the colonies fulfilled their role in the Empire. The disquiet was increased as 'the new imperial policy' — really a piecemeal reaction to problems and pressures — took shape.[2] To this

---

[1] Parliament 'hath sovereign and uncontrolable authority in making, confirming, enlarging, restraining, abrogating, repealing, reviving, and expounding of laws, concerning matters of all possible denominations, ecclesiastical, or temporal, civil, military, maritime, or criminal: this being the place where that absolute despotic power, which must in all governments reside somewhere, is entrusted by the constitution of these kingdoms' (Blackstone, *Laws of England*, Book I, Ch. 2, Sec. III).

[2] While the ministers do not seem to have pursued any grand imperial strategy their various measures did respond to the pressure exerted by a small number of men who took an interest in the colonies and pressed for imperial regeneration. Their spirit is expressed by Malachi Postlethwayt, a contemporary writer on commercial topics, in *Britain's Commercial Interest*, London, 1757, p. 427. 'Colonies become a strength to their mother country while they are under good discipline, while they are strictly made to observe the fundamental laws of their original country, and while they are kept dependent on it; but that, otherwise, they are worse than members lopped off from the body politic, being like offensive arms, wrested from a nation to be turned against it, as occasion shall serve.'

period belong the Proclamation of 1763, the considerable additions to the enumerated articles, a determined effort to stop the
illicit trade in foreign molasses, an overhaul of the customs system
which resulted in an unwelcome efficiency, and a general prohibition of colonial issues of paper currency. At the same time it was
becoming the talk of the day in England that the colonies had
grossly failed during the war to supply money, to equip men, or
to restrain themselves from trading with the enemy. Yet the sense
of crisis before 1765 should not be exaggerated. The effect of the
measures of 1763 and 1764 were local and confined to particular
groups; the importance of the 'new imperial policy' would be
seen only when a general grievance turned the claims of special
interests into popular causes; and on the British side, too few
were interested in the colonies for criticism of their actions to
have serious effect upon public opinion.

Even allowing for the disquiet among certain sections of the
colonial population, the violence of the reaction to the Stamp Act
of 1765 can still surprise us as it surprised contemporary Englishmen. It proposed to raise a very modest revenue — which would
be spent on American defence and civil government — by a tax
which had long been common in England, which was cheap and
easy to administer, and which was as equitable as an eighteenth-
century tax was likely to be. It was argued in England that a
colonial contribution to imperial revenue was necessary because
of the burden of debt and high taxation at home, that the colonies
had been given ample opportunity to make such a contribution of
their own free will, and that there was, after all, no logical
distinction between the indirect taxation which the colonies had
long accepted and the direct taxation which was now proposed.
It is therefore scarcely surprising that many Englishmen tended to
regard the opposition to the Stamp Act as the work of factious
trouble-makers. Appearances tended to confirm this impression.
In the two chief centres of disaffection — Virginia and Massachusetts — the movement against the Stamp Act was identified
with men who had a largely personal grievance against the
régime. In Virginia Patrick Henry led a group of Virginian gentry

who were dissatisfied with the monopoly of power enjoyed by a small 'in group' of large Eastern planters; in Massachusetts the opposition leaders were associated with the Otis family which had a personal quarrel with Governor Bernard and Lieutenant-Governor Hutchinson. In both of these important colonies the move to oust a local oligarchy played a vital part in the politics of the Stamp Act controversy. What was apt to escape notice at home was that even conservatives condemned the Stamp Act in principle as an encroachment upon the established conventions of local autonomy, and that they urged its withdrawal while deprecating the opposition attack upon the powers of Parliament. Indeed nothing could have been better calculated to undermine the position of the favoured families, upon whom Britain depended, so much as a policy which forced them to defend something which they could not approve and to rebut arguments which they respected though advanced by those whom they disliked and feared.

The gravest charge against George Grenville, who sponsored the Stamp Act, is not that he proposed a bad tax but that he made no provision against the consequences of opposition. Any form of novel taxation was likely to be resented by an eighteenth-century population, and British statesmen erred gravely in failing to ask how the tax was to be collected if colonists failed to co-operate. The grandiloquent claims of undivided and omni-competent sovereignty were not substantiated by regular and effective means of law enforcement; ultimately there could be only one way of executing an unpopular law and that was by armed force, but the statesmen who launched the Stamp Tax seem never to have asked themselves at what stage and in what manner they would use it.

Opposition to the Stamp Act was popular because the tax touched a comparatively large number of people, because it affected a broad cross-section of the population and not merely special or local interests, and because it brought to the fore easily understood constitutional principles. Most Americans could feel the force of the slogan 'no taxation without representation', and many were sufficiently well-informed to know how vital a part the power of the purse had played in the establishment of British liberties. It was as British subjects that they appealed against Great Britain; it was as the heirs of British constitutional liberties that they appealed from the sovereignty of Parliament to constitutional safeguards.

The resources of those who wished to oppose the Stamp Act were considerable and their employment in the autumn of 1765 laid down the pattern of revolutionary activity. The 'mob' of the towns was stirred up to protest and riot, directed mainly against the newly appointed distributors of stamps, but occasionally against officials in general and obnoxious members of the colonial upper classes. Merchants and consumers were persuaded to refuse British goods so that homespun and simple (though not necessarily sober) living became a mark of patriotism. Where colonial assemblies happened to be in session during the period of crisis a vigorous opposition developed, and in June 1765 the Massachusetts legislature invited the other colonies to send delegates to meet in Congress at New York. Revolutionary in concept and pregnant with future possibilities the Stamp Act Congress (attended by the representatives of nine colonies) was nevertheless dominated by conservative and moderate men, perturbed by disorder and attacks upon property, who preferred to proceed by humble petition rather than by overt defiance. Nevertheless the Stamp Act Congress did commit itself to declaring 'that it is inseparable to the freedom of a people, and the undoubted right of Englishmen, that no taxes should be imposed upon them, but with their own consent, given personally, or by their representatives', and that the Stamp Act had 'a manifest tendency to subvert the rights and liberties of the colonists'. The immediate effect of the Congress upon the crisis was less important than the precedent which had been created. In a later and greater crisis it would be natural to contemplate united colonial action.

The new ministry of Rockingham decided to repeal the Stamp Act in March 1766. Thanks to popular pressure, and the refusal of all classes to co-operate, the Act had remained inoperative, no stamps had been issued, and by the end of 1765 many colonial courts had re-opened in defiance of the law that all legal documents must be stamped. Resistance might have been overcome with military force or worn out by naval blockade; but insufficient troops were on hand in North America and non-importation was having too serious an effect to embark lightly upon a prolonged rupture of trade. In February 1766 an American merchant in London wrote, 'All the principal manufacturing towns have sent petitions for a repeal of the Stamp Act, a manufacturer from Leeds was ordered to the bar, who said since the stagnation of the American trade he has been constrained to turn off 300 families out of 600 he constantly employed. This fact will have great weight when added to many more evidences of the like kind. The country members are somewhat alarmed at so many people losing employ; if anything repeals the Act, it must be this.'[1] There were not wanting those who argued for 'firmness', and not least among them was King George III, but it was easier to advocate 'firmness' in general terms than to suggest the particular means which should be employed. If anyone had been able to suggest a speedy method of enforcing the Stamp Act it is probable that British opinion would have been prepared to back the use of force despite the vehement opposition of some Whigs and London agitators; it was the prospect of a long and inconclusive struggle, without definite prospect of success, and the certainty of expense and economic distress, which swayed British opinion towards concession and made possible the repeal of the Act.

The general trend of opinion in England, disregarding both the pro-American and the fire and sword extremists, was that a tactical blunder had been made, that the sovereignty of Parliament ought not to be diminished but that its use had been unwise, and that the Stamp Act though right in principle ought to be repealed as a matter of expediency. The colonists believed that the British surrender was the triumph of principle over unconstitutional wrong; the British believed that the use of a right, though not the

[1] Henry Cruger, Jr., to Henry Cruger, Sr., Feb. 14, 1766 (*Massachusetts Historical Society Collections*, 7th Series, IX, 139–43. Merrill Jensen (ed.), *English Historical Documents*, IX, 692).

right itself, had been abandoned to expediency. In the colonies rejoicing and expressions of renewed loyalty greeted the news of repeal; most chose to ignore the Declaratory Act which accompanied repeal and proclaimed the 'full power and authority [of Parliament] to make laws and statutes of sufficient force and validity to bind the colonies and people of America, subjects of the Crown of Great Britain, in all cases whatsoever'. Yet the Declaratory Act expressed the conviction not only of those who had fathered the Stamp Tax but also of those who had engineered its repeal; the basic conflict of Parliamentary supremacy with colonial right remained unaltered.

The movements of British and colonial opinion had thus set upon different courses; disagreement was more likely than agreement, and a minor disagreement might provoke a major clash. The decade which followed the repeal of the Stamp Act saw years of violent disturbance together with some years of calm which persuaded optimists that harmony was restored; but no period of reconciliation was likely to resolve the tension which now existed at the heart of the imperial system. The most favourable time for reconciliation was in fact that immediately following the repeal of the Stamp Act, and it is just possible that distinguished statesmanship in England might have led the way to a new relationship within the Empire. It was therefore a tragedy that political leadership was at a low ebb in England: Pitt, made first minister and Earl of Chatham in 1766, was soon incapacitated by mental disorder, Grafton, an amiable but not particularly able young peer, became caretaker head of a ministry dominated by the brilliant but unstatesmanlike Charles Townshend. North, who became first minister in 1770, was more shrewd and more popular, but he was too easy-going to determine a policy and at certain seasons became prey to nervous indecision and depression. The principal men in opposition, though more sympathetic to the Americans, had no solution to offer, and all the brilliance of Burke could not conceal his lame conclusion that time and tradition might heal the wounds if the colonists were left to enjoy the 'salutory neglect' of the years before 1760. Meanwhile on both sides of the Atlantic pamphleteers explored the differences and turned the limelight upon those which could not be resolved.

Charles Townshend, turning a debating point into a policy, seized upon the distinction made by colonists between direct and indirect taxation, and gave them indirect taxation in the form of duties upon tea and various British imports. This forced colonial spokesmen to a new distinction between taxes for revenue and taxes for the regulation of trade, fostered a new spate of non-importation agreements, and permitted the colonial radicals to keep their cause alive while improving their organization. By 1770 the committee of correspondence — a local or state group, usually selected on some representative principle, and remaining actively alive between the infrequent sessions of colonial legislatures — became the typical form of radical organization. A network of such committees soon covered the country and provided a standing means of communication and exchange between the discontented in the various colonies. In this may perhaps be seen an embryo form of the national political party.

Another feature of Townshend's policy was the reorganization of the American customs service and the establishment of a new administrative instrument, the American Board of Customs with its headquarters at Boston. It was the duty of the new customs commissioners to sweep with a clean broom, and one way of doing so was to impress upon subordinates that every American merchant and shipper was a potential law-breaker. Nothing is perhaps more likely to irritate a wealthy middle class than to be caught out in a piece of petty law evasion over which custom has cast the cloak of habitual approval. The New England merchants were men with high standards of personal morality and their close and complex association with British trade and industry ought to have made them one of the pillars on which to rest British power in America; it would have been politic to buy their support by major concessions; it was foolhardy to insist upon the letter of laws which they believed to be unjust and deleterious to their interests. In the same way, though the British won a tussle with the New York legislature over the right to quarter troops partly at the expense of the colony, this was the kind of victory which had better not have been won. That these and other disputes did not lead immediately to a new conflagration was because none of them touched so widely or so deeply as the Stamp Tax. In particular they hardly touched the planter gentry of Virginia where the local revolution which accompanied the Stamp Act controversy had placed the more radical groups in power. Virginians had their own grumbling grievance in the growing burden of debt to British merchants combined with the law of diminishing returns on hard-worked tobacco lands, but this was not the type of discontent which leads to revolt though it might provide an incentive for joining one.[1]

*   *   *   *

Historians have not ceased to wonder at the quality of the leaders who emerged in the colonies during these years and who subsequently guided the Revolution through its course. Virginia, a tiny state by European standards, produced during the course of a few years three men of outstanding talent — Washington, Jefferson, and Madison — and a great number of men of eminent ability among whom one might mention Patrick Henry, George Wythe, George Mason, Edmund Randolph, and the Lee family. Massachusetts produced Sam and John Adams, John Hancock, and James Bowdoin. From Pennsylvania came Benjamin Franklin, James Dickinson, and Robert Morris; from New York George Clinton and, in the younger generation, Alexander Hamilton. These were all men of wealth or professional distinction (Henry and Franklin, though born poor, became rich) and they were not

---

[1] Indebtedness might also, with scrupulous men, be an argument for restraint. In 1774 when a proposal was made to withhold remittances due to English merchants George Washington commented, 'Whilst we are accusing others of injustice, we should be just ourselves, and how can this be, whilst we owe a considerable debt, and refuse payment of it to Great Britain, is to me inconceivable. Nothing but the last extremity can justify it' (D. S. Freeman, *George Washington*, III, 360). Virginia instructed its delegates to Congress to oppose an immediate non-exportation agreement because of 'the earnest desire we have to make as quick and full payment as possible of our debts to Great Britain'. But it should also be noticed that non-exportation would have been a serious blow to tobacco planters with a crop on their hands. The debts were usually so long standing that men had learnt to live with them, but their existence did not lead Virginians to think more kindly of the British connection.

likely to become radicals in the social or economic sense. 'Life, liberty, *and property*' was the great slogan of the revolutionary movement. The revelation of economic motives for political action has however become too commonplace a pastime to tell us much about the character of men or movements. That the revolutionary leaders accepted the sanctity of property as a cornerstone of their political creed does not explain away the other elements in its structure; but their belief that liberty had an indissoluble connection with property was to have a profound effect upon the later development of American traditions.

A simple explanation of the quality of leadership is that the crisis had forced into public life men who might otherwise have stood aside. Without the Revolution Washington would have been no more than a rich planter, justice of the peace, and silent member of the elected assembly. Jefferson might have been a dilettante member of the planter class with a local reputation for scholarship. John Adams might have been a pious and successful lawyer, Sam Adams a disgruntled and unsuccessful businessman. Political training had also helped to equip them as leaders of a popular revolution. The Virginian gentry belonged by birth to a class which had been accustomed to public life while rendering account to an independent yeomanry. The Massachusetts town meeting extended political training down to the humblest free-holder. In every colony a substantial part of the upper class had experienced the give, take and manœuvre of election and debate. Social mobility also contributed to the strength of colonial leadership. The deadweight of privilege, which stifled so much ability in Europe, did not operate in America, and Franklin was only the most striking example of the way in which ability could prosper.

The education of the upper class, though narrow by modern standards, was extremely effective for the tasks which its members undertook. Most of them had some acquaintance with the law and the majority had been practising lawyers; they were well read in English political history, reasonably familiar with ancient history, and versed in political theory as expressed by Harrington, Sidney,

Locke and Montesquieu. The minds of New Englanders had also been moulded by the rigorous dialectic of Calvinist theology. They knew little of the Middle Ages, of scientific or economic theory, of the actual working of the British constitution, or of modern philosophy apart from the political theorists and excluding Hobbes. They were able to formulate the political ideas drawn from a particular stream of European thought and were not troubled by criticism from other sources. They were, moreover, preaching to men with the same educational background who shared most of their convictions. The great handicap of conservatism, already noticed in the Stamp Act controversy, lay in being forced to rebut arguments with which they were in sympathy; conservatives were in intellectual retreat throughout this period and loyalism had ultimately to depend upon emotion rather than upon reason as understood by the eighteenth century.

In the decade which followed the Stamp Act, American opinion gradually abandoned old ground. In 1765 membership of the Empire was a necessary condition for colonial well-being, by 1770 it is expedient but not essential, by 1776 it is an inconvenient burden. In 1765 the appeal is to colonial charters, the rights of British subjects, and the British constitution; by 1776 a majority are ready to go beyond written or customary law to universal principles of natural law. In 1765 George III was still the best of kings (misled perhaps by unwise ministers); in 1776 the complete incompatibility of British interests and colonial rights is symbolized by holding the king personally responsible for the misdeeds of his government. Radicals such as Sam Adams may have been convinced from the start that British rule must be mended or ended, but lawyers, planters and merchants would not break lightly with ideas of a lifetime. Years afterwards John Adams wrote, 'What do we mean by the American Revolution? Do we mean the American war? The Revolution was effected before the war commenced. The Revolution was in the minds and hearts of the people; a change in their religious sentiments of their duties and obligations.... This radical change in the principles, opinions, sentiments, and affections of the people was the real

American Revolution.'[1] At each stage in this Revolution some men felt that they could go no further and the body of conservatives who eventually became loyalists increased, but at the same time the convictions upon which the Revolution was based became more coherent, more widely disseminated, and more generally accepted. The ideas of constitutional right, of no taxation without representation, of trial by jury, and of colonial government for colonial affairs were not in themselves difficult to grasp, while the freedom of speech and of the press made them easy to popularize. And together with the positive teaching went the inculcation of a negative fear of the consequences of British policy, so that by 1774 inland farmers, who had been little affected by British policy, were ready to take up arms against British soldiers with whom they had no quarrel.

The final crisis came as the result of what the eighteenth century called a 'job' carried out by the British government to help the East India Company. In 1770 the Townshend duties were repealed except for that on tea; conscientious radicals refused to sell or drink tea imported from England, but a more serious threat to East India interests was the smuggling of large quantities of tea from Holland which undersold that supplied by the Company. In 1773 the East India Company (for other reasons besides this) was on the verge of bankruptcy and large quantities of tea were stored in its London warehouses. By a special act passed in 1773 the Company was permitted to export tea direct to America (hitherto it had been permitted only to auction tea in London) and to do so without payment of the normal export duties. By this means tea would reach the American consumer more cheaply but it would also pay the Townshend import duty. On both sides of the Atlantic it was charged that this was a bribe to induce the colonists to pay a tax imposed by Parliament; the charge has never been proved or disproved, but to American radicals it was clear that once the tea was on shore it might be impossible to prevent its sale, and they had already had experience with English precedent mongers. It therefore became their object to prevent the

---

[1] Adams to H. Niles, Feb. 13, 1818 (*Works*, X, 267).

landing of the tea. In this influential merchants were prepared to join them. Some had a special grievance in that their normal business as tea merchants had been by-passed; more disliked the idea that a great British privileged corporation should be allowed to set up a monopoly on American soil. Finally the secret intentions of the government seem to be revealed by the choice, as agents for the sale of Company tea, of men who had played a prominent part against the 'patriots'. The privileged oligarchy would get its share of the pickings at the expense of honest American merchants.

Radicals had plenty of time to organize for the reception of the tea, and in every port save one popular demonstrations were successful either in preventing the landing of the tea or in getting it shut up in warehouses without payment of duty. The one exception was the port of Boston where Governor Hutchinson, standing upon legal technicalities, asked for trouble and got it. Unlike most governors, Hutchinson had at his disposal troops, ships, and guns commanding the entrance to the harbour; this tempted him to show authority against the 'patriots', whom, as a member of the colony's oligarchy, he particularly disliked. The tea ships having entered Boston harbour were legally required to pay duty even if the goods were not landed, and Hutchinson refused them permission to depart without a clearance from the Customs. After twenty days the tea would become liable to seizure for non-payment of duty; the landing would then be carried out by the customs officials with the help of the military if necessary. To prevent this a party of Bostonians in disguise boarded the tea-ships and threw the tea into the harbour.

By itself the 'tea party' was more likely to provoke a conservative reaction than a radical outburst. However unwise the actions of the Parliament, the ministers and the Governor, property was still property, and the eighteenth-century mind recoiled in horror at the idea of its destruction. It was certain that the British government must ensure at least that compensation was paid; influential opinion in the colonies was likely to agree in principle and the government had the opportunity of putting radical agitators in the wrong. The agitation had seen a good deal of disturbance and terrorism instigated by self-appointed leaders of the people; colonial leaders were well aware of the dangers incipient in popular passions. But what measures could be taken in a country where juries would not convict, officials were unreliable, and men of influence had refused to co-operate with authority? This was the problem which faced the British government. The same sentiment which might in America have become the mainspring for a conservative reaction, gave the initiative in England to those who had always argued for stern disciplinary measures. Boston was to be punished, the execution of the law facilitated, and the diseases of the Massachusetts constitution remedied. By the first of what became known in American history as the 'Intolerable Acts' the port of Boston was closed until such time as the Company had been compensated and the duties paid; by the second the Governor could authorize the transference of trial to England when an official was placed on a capital charge alleged to have been committed in putting down riot or collecting the revenue; by the third the Council (hitherto elected by the lower house of the legislature) was to be appointed by the King, legal officers including justices of the peace were to be appointed by the Governor, and town meetings could not be held without the permission of the Governor or go beyond business which he had approved.

The alarm occasioned by the acts turned back the tide of conservative reaction before it had gathered force and caused a man as cautious as George Washington in far away Virginia to write, 'Does it not appear, as clear as the sun in its meridian brightness, that there is a regular, systematic plan formed to fix the right and practice of taxation upon us?'[1] The great danger of the Boston Port Act was that it could be made effective; however weak British authority might be in other respects the navy could easily cut off the life blood of any colonial port. The Administration of Justice Act implied that all officials might be placed under the protection of a special law and no longer restrained by the common law administered in colonial courts. The Massachusetts

[1] D. S. Freeman, *George Washington*, Scribner's; Eyre & Spottiswoode, III, 360.

Government Act constituted the most serious threat of all. Though many had not approved the extreme use of the elective principle in Massachusetts (other royal colonies had long enjoyed without complaint the type of government now imposed upon Massachusetts) these peculiarities of the constitution had nevertheless rested upon royal charter and had been sanctified by usage; now it seemed that the whole structure of colonial autonomy could be subverted by Act of Parliament, and the full implications of the claim of Parliament to legislate for the colonies in all cases whatsoever now became apparent. On its side the British government had now committed itself to a policy of coercion, without considering what would follow if firmness did not puncture colonial insubordination. The 'Intolerable Acts' might have succeeded in their aims if there had been an overwhelming military force ready to enforce them; events were to prove that the disposable military force was sufficient to hold the town of Boston and no more. The navy could close a port but it could not coerce a people, and the British ministers had committed the fatal error of embarking upon a policy of force without the immediate means of implementing it.

At this juncture British policy in the neighbouring colony of Canada aroused American fears to a still greater extent. The Quebec Act of 1774, which posterity is inclined to regard as a statesmanlike measure and the charter of French Canadian liberties, set up a centralized government in which legislative power was vested in an appointed council, the right to tax was reserved to Parliament, French civil law (which did not provide for jury trial) and the Roman Catholic Church were both given official recognition. In the excited state of American opinion it was not difficult to represent this as the pattern to which all colonies were to be moulded, and the supposed attack on American liberties was given greater point by a generous extension southward of Canada's boundaries. Even more far-fetched were colonial alarms at the still-born project of establishing an Anglican episcopate in America, which John Adams considered an important contributory cause of the Revolution.

Strong forces of opinion converged in the crisis. It was the aim of Massachusetts to obtain immediate aid from the other colonies in the coming struggle with Great Britain, and the not inconsiderable influence of her leaders was now wholly exerted to this end. At the same time other colonies were concerned to create general safeguards for colonial autonomy in the future. Certain conservatives, desperately alarmed at the threat of social disorder, hoped to retain the imperial factor in some form as the ultimate guarantee of property and law; but Virginian gentry, firmly in the social saddle and undisturbed by fears of revolt, were determined to be masters in their own house. In every colony a few men, growing stronger in popular esteem, saw the crisis as the heaven-sent opportunity for cutting adrift from the habits and ideas of the Old World. Merchants and planters in debt to England or irked by particular examples of British regulation, zealous Presbyterians and Congregationalists fearful of Popery and Episcopacy, and inland farmers who disliked government in any form, all played their parts in the struggle for America's destiny which now commenced.

Following the precedent of 1765 a Continental Congress met at Philadelphia. Though far from being a radical body, the Massachusetts politicians obtained from it almost everything which they asked. The Coercive Acts were formally condemned, and the attack was broadened to include thirteen other statutes enacted since 1763 which were said to violate colonial rights; it was no longer a measure but a system which was repudiated. After considerable debate on details an agreement was reached to end trade with Great Britain, that became known as 'the Association'. Its enforcement was entrusted to locally elected committees; this virtually meant Congressional endorsement of the radical organizations. The embryo national government had been fused with the embryo national party. Most significantly Congress refused by a small majority to adopt an imaginative proposal made by Joseph Galloway, a leading conservative, for an American Parliament to act within the Empire in association with the British Parliament. The majority, though not yet ready for independence, were unwilling to commit themselves to closer relations with the mother country.

In its second session in May 1775 Congress faced an altered situation. In Massachusetts a provincial Congress had ordered the people to prepare for resistance, established effective control over the whole colony save the town of Boston, and accumulated military stores at Concord. In April General Gage, recently appointed as Governor, was ordered to execute the Coercive Acts with force. Gage determined to take the initiative and to disrupt colonial preparations by destroying their supplies. On April 18 a strong detachment of troops moved out from Boston to march the twenty miles to Concord, but the Boston Committee of Safety sent Paul Revere to warn the countryside. In consequence the British found their way barred at Lexington by seventy militia men; the few shots which ensued before the Americans dispersed earned their place in history as the first in the war of the Revolution. The British troops reached Concord without great difficulty but failed to achieve anything of moment; gathering opposition forced them to withdraw to Boston through a hostile countryside, in which every farmer seemed to have seized a rifle, and they were pursued by American forces which were numerous if not well organized. Never again were the British able to make more than occasional forays beyond Boston and the colonial troops established a virtual siege. Militarily a stalemate developed. The British had insufficient force to subdue the country or indeed to venture far from the guns of their warships, while the Americans were unable to attack Boston and in June, after some extremely hard fighting, they were driven off two hills (Breed's Hill and Bunker Hill) which threatened the town.

Congress was therefore faced with a situation in which hostilities had broken out, and in which it must either organize for war or await the build up of British forces. There was now little doubt what the choice would be. Colonial solidarity was demonstrated by the appointment of Washington, a Virginian, to take command of all continental forces and to assume immediate responsibility for the operations before Boston. An expedition against Canada was ordered (which took Montreal, failed to take Quebec, and was abandoned a year later). Orders were given to raise a navy and privateering against British ships was authorized. At the end of 1775 local hostilities broke out in Virginia where the Governor, Lord Dunmore, raised a Loyalist army; but a promise of freedom to slaves who should desert their masters turned the whole planter class against him.

Even during this troubled year it was possible for Congress to agree to the so-called 'olive branch' petition which asserted that, 'The union between our mother country and these colonies, and the energy of mild and just government, produced benefits so remarkably important, and afforded such an assurance of their permanency and increase that the wonder and envy of other nations was excited, while they beheld Great Britain rising to a power the most extraordinary the world had ever known.' It went on to assure the King that the colonists were 'attached to your Majesty's person, family, and government, with all the devotion that principle and affection can inspire ... [and] not only most ardently desire the former harmony between [Great Britain] ... and these colonies may be restored, but that a concord may be established between them upon so firm a basis as to perpetuate its blessings. . . .' Despite the impatience of those who had already decided in their own minds for independence there is little doubt that a majority would still have agreed with these sentiments. Traditional ties were hard to break particularly when the cost of rupture would be a hard and doubtful war.

To bring the colonies from the twilight of uncertain aims into the daylight of independence two things were necessary: first, clear evidence of British intentions to pursue hostilities and then a decisive movement of popular opinion in favour of independence. The first was accomplished by George III and his ministers; in October 1775 George III's speech to Parliament asserted that 'The rebellious war now levied is become more general and is manifestly carried on for the purpose of establishing an independent empire. . . . It is now become the part of wisdom . . . to put a speedy end to these disorders by the most decisive exertions.' The second condition was supplied by *Commonsense*, a pamphlet appearing at the beginning of 1776 and written by Tom Paine, an English-born radical; it was Paine's object to tear aside the whole web of emotions which gathered round the symbols of monarchy, allegiance, and empire. The sentiments of this celebrated pamphlet have become a part of the substratum of American political thought. If all men were good, government would be unnecessary, but, 'Government, like dress, is the badge of lost innocence; the palaces of Kings are built upon the ruins of the bowers of paradise.' Governments are necessary evils whose sole function is to provide freedom and security, 'and however our eyes may be dazzled with show, or our ears deceived by sound; however prejudice may warp our wills, or interest dark our understanding, the simple voice of nature and reason will say, " 'tis right".' 'Government by Kings was first introduced into the world by the heathens, from whom the children of Israel copied the custom. It was the most preposterous invention the devil ever set on foot for the promotion of idolatry.' 'To the evil of monarchy we have added that of hereditary succession; and as the first is a degradation and lessening of ourselves, so the second, claimed as a matter of right, is an insult and imposition on posterity.' Paine went on to examine and discredit the arguments for reconciliation. 'The phrase *parent* or *mother* country hath been jesuitically adopted by the king and his parasites, with the low papistical design of gaining an unfair bias on the credulous weakness of our minds. Europe, and not England, is the parent country of America. This new world hath been the asylum for the persecuted lovers of civil and religious liberty from *every part* of Europe. Hither have they fled, not from the tender embraces of the mother, but from the cruelty of the monster; and it is so far true of England, that the same tyranny which drove the first emigrants from home, pursues their descendants still.' ' 'Tis repugnant to reason, to the universal order of things, to all examples from former ages, to suppose that this continent can long remain subject to any external power.' 'Small islands not capable of protecting themselves are the proper objects for kingdoms to take under their care; but there is something absurd in supposing a Continent to be perpetually governed by an island.' 'A government of our own is our own natural right: and when a man seriously reflects upon the precariousness of human affairs, he will become convinced, that it is infinitely wiser and safer, to form a Constitution of our own in a cool deliberate manner, while we have it in our power, than to trust such an interesting event to time and chance.'

Here were enunciated principles which found a ready response in the American mind and which have since supplied strong colours in the American self portrait. Hereditary government is barbarous, evil and absurd. The plain light of natural reason is the only sure guide. It is the destiny of America to remedy the oppression of the Old World with the freedom of the New. The government of peoples by an alien authority is unnatural and can be justified only when there is a need to protect the weak. Rational government can be set up; good laws can be framed; constitutions can be made to provide order, security, freedom, and justice.

In Congress the debate on independence began in June 1776. Recalcitrant defenders of the British connection had withdrawn, and the remaining conservatives no longer disputed the principle of independence while attacking its expediency. As late as July 1, John Dickinson, in earlier days a powerful anti-British pamphleteer, spoke for a retention of the imperial connection, but almost as he spoke a political upheaval in his own state of Pennsylvania gave control to the radicals; this, together with growing evidence of popular support, enabled Virginia and New England to lead the doubtful middle states to the Declaration of Independence, to which a majority finally agreed on July 4.[1]

The Declaration was largely the work of Thomas Jefferson

---

[1] John Adams in a letter to his wife (July 3, 1776. *Works*, I, 232) caught the sombre exhilaration of this historic moment: 'You will think me transported with enthusiasm, but I am not. I am well aware of the toil, and blood, and treasure that it will cost us to maintain this Declaration, and support and defend these States. Yet, through all the gloom, I can see the rays of ravishing light and glory. I can see that the end is more than worth all the means, and that posterity will triumph in that day's transaction, even although we should rue it, which I trust in God we shall not.'

then thirty-three years of age. The bulk of the document consisted of a long enumeration of grievances against George III — for since allegiance was a personal matter it was necessary to establish the personal wickedness of the sovereign — but it is the preamble to the Declaration which has made it immortal. 'Never', wrote a distinguished American historian, 'in the whole range of the writings of political theorists has the basis of government been stated so succinctly.'[1] It would be more accurate to describe it as the most succinct statement of the principles of American government, derived from Locke, and embodying the everyday assumptions of American people. 'We hold these truths to be self-evident, that all men are created equal, that they are endowed by their Creator with certain unalienable rights, that among these are Life, Liberty and the pursuit of happiness. That to secure these rights, Governments are instituted among man, deriving their just powers from the consent of the governed. That whenever any form of Government becomes destructive of these ends, it is the Right of the people to alter or abolish it, and to institute new Government, laying its foundation on such principles and organizing its powers in such form, as to them shall seem most likely to affect their Safety and Happiness.' There is much here to cause dismay to the modern philosopher — 'self-evident truths', 'natural equality', and 'unalienable rights' are not phrases likely to convince the European, weary though he may be with the round of metaphysical theories in a hierarchical society. Yet if its dogmatic utterances are turned into admonitions — 'Men ought to be treated as though they were equal . . . as though they were endowed with unalienable rights' — it is hard to imagine better precepts for sane government. Nor is it easy to avoid the common sense of the proposition that the functions of government ought to be those which people wish it to perform, and that when it ceases to perform them it ought to be changed. Thus the conflict with Great Britain which began as the defence of dimly conceived rights, derived from material interest rather than from abstract principles, ended with the claim to have discovered new principles

[1] Edward Channing, *History of the United States*, New York, Macmillan, III, 202.

of government and a new destiny for America. The ideas did not provoke the conflict, but evolved from it as 'self-evident truths', and provided a nucleus of thought and purpose around which a new nation could be formed.

[3]

Nationalism, Local Autonomy, and Democracy

Three great political forces emerged from the experience of the Revolution: loyalty to the union, loyalty to the separate states, and loyalty to the idea of government by the people. It was the hope of most Americans to serve all three, but as circumstances varied individuals might come to see one or another as central to their thought. From the outset of the revolutionary struggle very few Americans wanted to sacrifice the benefits of union, and a belief in its necessity is a mainspring of later political planning. But even those who were most impressed with the possibility of creating a nation, realized that tradition, with the need for decentralization, combined to make the loyalty to the states a necessity as well as a sentiment. Local autonomy did not however mean necessarily the separate existence of all the states; from an administrative point of view no great harm would have been done if Virginia had absorbed Maryland, if New York and Pennsylvania had partitioned New Jersey, or if Massachusetts had annexed Rhode Island. The small states might be even more fearful of powerful neighbours than they were of centralized national power, and the large states might have relatively more to lose if the power of the United States increased. All Americans believed that participation of the people in the business of government was the particular virtue of republican government, but there was considerable difference of opinion about the extent of this participation.[1] Some Americans had welcomed the idea of popular sovereignty as a new gospel, some had come to it

---

[1] 'A share in the sovereignty of the state, which is exercised by the citizens at large, in voting at elections, is one of the most important rights of the subject, and, in a republic,

64

reluctantly after a process of elimination during which all other sources of authority had been found unworkable. The latter desired a 'mixed government' incorporating 'checks and balances' upon all forms of authority, including that of the people, while others welcomed the direct rule of an elected majority as the logical outcome of popular sovereignty.[1]

In the half-century which followed the outbreak of the Revolution no one of the three great political traditions commanded a permanent allegiance from a fixed body of people; it was the very essence of the American situation that each tradition was attractive to the majority of the people, that the great mass of ordinary Americans attempted in their political thinking to reconcile the three. It was possible to attack nationalists without abandoning the union, deprecate local autonomy without wishing to destroy the states, and deplore the licentiousness of democrats without wishing to abolish popular representation. It is possible to see certain groups forming fairly consistent nuclei of support for each tradition, but this does not mean that the tradition was their exclusive possession or that it would have had no history without them. Thus the rising capitalists, the men who did well out of the war, the men whose assets were in public securities and most of

---

ought to stand foremost . . . . That portion of sovereignty to which each individual is entitled can never be too highly prized. It is that for which we have fought and bled; and we should cautiously guard against any precedents, however they may be immediately directed against those we hate, which, in their consequences, render our title to this great privilege precarious' (Alexander Hamilton, *Letters from Phocion. Works*, ed. Lodge, III, 486). Hamilton was arguing against the disenfranchisement in New York of former loyalists, so that these expressions have an element of special pleading, but it is in conformity with the thought of the man and his age.

'We may define a republic to be, or at least may bestow that name on, a government which derives all its powers directly or indirectly from the great body of the people, and is administered by persons holding their offices during pleasure, for a limited period, or during good behaviour' (James Madison, *The Federalist*, Number XXXIX).

[1] The following sentences from John Adams' Autobiography illustrate the scope of the arguments and the steps by which a radical revolutionary could be transformed into a conservative. 'Many members of Congress began . . . to ask me civil questions, "How can the people institute governments?" My answer was, "By conventions of representatives, freely, fairly, and proportionately chosen." . . . "But what plan of government would you advise?" "A plan as nearly resembling the government under which we were born, and have lived, as the circumstances of the country will admit . . . ." Every one of my friends . . . had at that time no idea of any other government but a contemptible legislature in one assembly, with committees for executive magistrates and judges . . . . I took care, however, always to bear my testimony against every plan of an unbalanced government' (*Works*, III, 19–22).

those who were dependent upon commerce saw that strong national power might preserve credit, establish a sound currency, and open to them the opportunity of exploiting the resources of the world's largest free trade area; but behind the activities of this minority can be seen the strong current of attachment to the union which the experience of war changed from expediency to conviction. The adherents of local autonomy included representatives of the great landed families of the South whose control of the local machinery of government and administration made them jealous of intrusion, and whose immunity from social revolt made them question the necessity of energetic national government; their influence was increased by the widespread belief that free government was possible only in comparatively small political units. Democracy appealed to the small farmers of the interior regions, whose society knew no ruling class and to whom danger came not from the propertyless but from men of wealth who controlled the sources of credit. Democracy appealed also to the artisans, shopkeepers and craftsmen of the towns where, unlike the rest of America, there was a real struggle for power between classes.

It is convenient and attractive to analyse the political conflicts of the age as between 'conservatives' and 'radicals'. Such a division may serve a purpose — for there are always men who are conservative by temperament and others who are radical by temperament — but it may also confuse. In America, where the orthodox statements of political belief are revolutionary slogans, the conservative could not appeal to the past in support of established institutions; he had to create the institutions and to popularize the ideas necessary for their support. Alexander Hamilton may be called a conservative but no man owed more to a vision of the future and less to experience of the past. By contrast radicals, having the traditions of the past on their side, are often concerned to preserve rather than to innovate. Urban radicalism may sometimes behave in a way which is familiar to Europeans, but agrarian radicalism was a reaction against threats to economic independence. The debtor farmer becomes a radical not because he wants to change the established order, but because he may lose his land; the gentleman planter of the South turns radical when the price of his crops fall, when the cost of manufactures rises, and when the law of diminishing returns is in the saddle. While most Americans were convinced that they must conserve what they had, they were also convinced that theirs was a new order of society, a system in which the vices of the Old World had been eradicated and in which Republican virtue was possible. Yet the assumption of virtue did not preclude the violence of faction and over it fell the long shadow of the former mother country. To many Americans it seemed that Republican virtue had most to fear from England whose example was likely to prove attractive to those who preferred wealth, security and genteel culture to the rigours of Republican life. On the other side many Americans were impressed by the conventional English theories, that republicanism was impractical, particularly in large countries, that licentiousness, violence and disorder would inevitably increase until salvation could be found only in military despotism, and that in this process of disintegration self-seeking demagogues would exploit the deluded people. During the period of the French revolution both groups seemed to see their worst fears realized by their enemies, and the violence of their reactions is not difficult to understand.

*   *   *   *

The progress of nationalism can be traced from the time when the Continental Congress assumed some powers over all colonies; weak as was the government instituted by Congress and later by the Articles of Confederation, it was nevertheless a standing reminder of the fact that the United States were greater than the separate states. Under the Confederation Congress could not impose a tax, regulate currency, credit or commerce nor exercise full control over the military forces; its members were not elected by the people and it had no means of enforcing any civil law against any citizen of any state; nominated by state legislatures the delegates voted in state units, the consent of more than a simple majority of the states was required for the more important measures of Congress and the consent of all the states was necessary for any amendment. Nevertheless this unwieldy and constitutionally ridiculous government conducted a great war, entered into treaties of alliance, borrowed large sums of money, and negotiated a triumphant peace. Its weaknesses became more apparent as the fever of war subsided, but the centrifugal effects of the system were now offset by great national interests — a public debt and merchants with nation-wide commercial dealings — which were the legacies of war. These great national interests played an important part in the drive for a stronger government, but the principal motive seems to have been a fear of social disorder, a desire for more effective relations with foreign powers, and distrust of the groups controlling some state governments.

The Federal Convention which met in 1787 to write a new Constitution was composed mainly of men committed to nationalism, and the document which they produced took the principles of national government as far as it was possible to take them at that period. It proposed a Congress composed of two houses: a Senate in which each state should have two members, and a House of Representatives in which representation was proportionate to population. Congress was to have increased powers which included those of taxation, control of currency and regulation of commerce among the states and with foreign nations. The old Congress had wielded both executive and legislative powers; the new Constitution followed the political fashion of the day — already anticipated in all the state constitutions — of having separate powers. The Executive power was in the hands of a President for whom an elaborate system of indirect election was provided. Compared with the formal powers of the King of England, those of the President seemed limited; he could not appoint senior officers in the administration without the consent of the Senate, he could not make a treaty without the consent of two-thirds of the Senate, he could veto a law but this could be overridden by two-thirds of both Houses; he could not spend a penny which had not been duly appropriated by Congress, was compelled to report to Congress on the state of the Union once a year, and together with all his subordinate officers was liable to impeachment. It required time and some curious constitutional twists before this comparatively weak chief magistrate emerged as a figure of great and commanding strength. The departments of government were completed by the judiciary which consisted of a Supreme Court and such inferior courts as Congress might appoint; in addition to some special cases such as those affecting diplomatic persons the jurisdiction of the Supreme Court extended to all cases arising under the Constitution, that is to all cases in which a private right was sustained or challenged by an appeal to the Constitution. It was not specifically stated (though some have held that it was inferred) that the Court could invalidate the laws of Congress, and for some years it remained doubtful whether this power, now regarded as a keystone of the American system, would be exercised.

It has often been argued that the essence of the new Constitution lay in the advantage which it conceded to certain types of economic interest, particularly to the holders of depreciated public securities who expected a rise, to other creditors whose paper assets had been adversely affected by overissues of legal tender state paper currency, and to merchants whose operations were hampered by unsound money, state obstruction, and weak foreign policy. It has been argued that the true meaning of the Constitution is to be found in the power to tax (which ensured a revenue to secure the public debt), in the power to regulate commerce, and in the removal from the states of the power to issue paper currency, make anything legal tender except gold and silver, or pass laws 'impairing the obligations of contracts'. If these provisions were all that really mattered in the Constitution a great many intelligent men spent a great deal of time to little purpose; these economic clauses passed with little debate and it was the political structure of the new government which kept the Convention delegates hard at work through the long summer days of 1787 in Philadelphia. Nor, apart from the power to tax, were these economic clauses attacked during the bitter controversy which followed before the new Constitution was ratified: indeed, in those records of the state ratifying conventions which have survived, there is no mention of the contract clause and only passing reference to the currency clauses.[1] While these facts may throw doubt upon the theory that the Constitution was the product of a conspiracy, they may give support to the idea that it reflected the needs and assumptions of a property-owning society. These were important matters, but they were secondary to the great design; the friends and the enemies of the new Constitution rightly concentrated upon the distribution of political authority, upon the definition and extent of the powers given to Congress, and upon the effect of the new government on individual freedom.[2] Opposition to the Constitution was strongest in those states which had fared well under the Confederation — that is in the large wealthy states — and least effective in the small weak states to which independence had proved an embarrassment.

The Constitution was not accepted without a severe struggle in some of the states; but the Convention had proposed that ratification by nine states would be sufficient to put it into operation and this was done by the spring of 1788. George Washington was chosen as the first President and the new government went into operation early in 1789. Upon the President and the first Congress lay the heavy responsibility of turning a blue-print into a working model. Laws had to be passed establishing the administrative departments, providing for a fiscal service and a revenue, setting up the judiciary, and deciding several minor points left uncertain in the Constitution. Among the latter the most important was the

[1] But a quotation from Hamilton may appear to support the argument of Charles Beard on these points. 'The Constitution of the United States interdicts the States individually from passing any law impairing the obligation of contracts. This, to the more enlightened part of the community, was not one of the least recommendations of that Constitution. The too frequent intermeddling of the State Legislatures, in relation to private contracts, were extensively felt, and seriously lamented; and a constitution which promises a preventative, was, by those who felt and thought in that manner, eagerly embraced' (May 28, 1790, *Works*, ed. Lodge, II, 142). A balanced view may be that some of those who were ardent supporters of the Constitution were influenced by such 'economic' clauses, but that these were not challenged by the opponents of ratification who concentrated upon the political implications of the Constitution.

[2] A product of the ratification struggle in New York was 'The Federalist'. Written jointly by Hamilton, Madison and Jay (the latter taking little part after the early numbers) this series of newspaper articles written by two young men in a polemical hurry forms a masterly discussion of the American constitutional system and of the principles of all free government.

question whether officers appointed by the President with the consent of the Senate could be dismissed by the President on his own volition, could not be dismissed without the consent of the Senate, or held their offices like the judges during good behaviour. It was decided that the President could dismiss without consulting the Senate, and the important argument was brought forward that he possessed all those powers classified as 'executive' which were not denied to him in the Constitution.[1] This decision made the President master of the administrative system, strengthened his control of Federal patronage, and made him the sole responsible officer for national administration. At the same time the attempt to build bridges across the formal separation of powers was defeated. It was decided that a departmental minister could not initiate a measure in Congress unless Congress asked him to do so, and early in 1790 that ministers could not present their programmes to Congress in person. Ministers who were denied seats in Congress under the Constitution would not be able to enter Congress in their official capacities (unless asked to attend committees), and presidential messages were left as the only recognized means of communication between the executive and legislative branches. Policy must be initiated somewhere, the Constitution had given no guidance where this should be, and the first Congress decided that a void should exist at the centre of government which might be filled by the strongest competitor.[2]

[1] 'The enumeration [of executive powers in the Constitution] ought therefore to be considered as intended merely to specify the principal articles implied in the definition of executive power; leaving the rest to flow from the general grant of that power, interpreted in conformity with other parts of the Constitution, and with the principles of free government' (Hamilton, *Pacificus. Works*, ed. Lodge, IV, 141). Madison took the same line in the important debate in the First Congress over the right of the President to dismiss Federal officers.

[2] William Findley, one of the most consistent of the anti-Federalists, said, 'The gentleman has . . . observed, that there is independence and good sense in this House to examine, alter or reject a Report of the Secretary of the Treasury. . . . What does this argument amount to? Why, it amounts to giving the peculiar trust of originating to the Secretary, and reserving that power to ourselves which the Constitution rests in the other branch.' (*Annals of Congress*, 2nd Congress, 2nd Session, 446). And also Page of Virginia: 'Every subject should come before the members of this house unaccompanied with the opinions of any individual whatever; this was consonant to the general practice of the House; this would divide the responsibility of public measures' (*ibid.*, 4th Congress, 1st Session, 249). These arguments represent the majority opinion in the House; had they not prevailed the House of Representatives might today be more like the House of Commons, more subject to ministerial initiative, and more significant in the life of the nation.

The difficulty was brought to the fore when Alexander Hamilton became Secretary of the Treasury; for Hamilton had a policy which he meant to initiate. Hamilton was of obscure West Indian birth and had made his way by his talents alone, but unlike other self-made men seldom referred to these facts; he acquired the manners of the upper class, into which he married and which he dominated by his intellect. He was a small vigorous man with red hair. Inspired by an ardent nationalism he intended to use financial measures, in the first instance, both to restore the national credit and to secure backing for the new government. His creation of a national debt and a national bank incidentally, but not unintentionally, enriched the capitalists who had come to hold the major part of national and state securities and gave the same group control over the country's credit system. Hamilton relied too much upon English examples both in the details of his financial policy and in the belief that government influence, combined with that of interested parties, could provide the support and make possible the energy which he believed to be necessary in government. He was attracted by the stability which British merchant interests provided for their government, but he failed to appreciate that the real stability in Great Britain was provided by a massive land-owning class able to control the representative system. In a country where few white men lived in economic subjection to other white men, influence of this type and on this scale was impossible. In fact Hamilton came dangerously near to alienating the mass of the people from the national government, and it was saved not by his efforts but because his opponents were equally committed to the continuance of the union. In spite of this political failure Hamilton's analysis of America's needs was remarkably prescient, and his vision of a great nation, exploiting the resources of a continent under the guidance of an active government and through the initiative of individual capitalists, with the general welfare constantly raised by these efforts, anticipated with accuracy one side of American development since his day. If the concept of nationalism was weakened by the attacks which Hamilton's policy engendered, it had also become embedded in the hopes and aspirations of many Americans.[1] Whereas most of the 'founding fathers' had thought of national government as necessary to effect a harmony between conflicting interests, Hamilton propounded the idea that national government should play a positive role in national life. Though unacceptable to a majority of his contemporaries and often misunderstood by posterity, the concept was grafted upon the nationalist tradition for future use.

A less spectacular though essential contribution to the nationalist principles was made by John Marshall, Chief Justice of the Supreme Court for no less than thirty-three years (1801–34). In his first great case (*Marbury* v. *Madison*, 1803) Marshall established to his own satisfaction and to that of future generations (though not to that of all contemporaries) the right of the Supreme Court to invalidate acts of Congress which conflicted with the Constitution.[2] More than ten years later he began the great series of decisions which extended and consolidated the constitutional powers of the national government by denying the

[1] 'I can scarcely contemplate a more incalculable evil than the breaking of the Union into two or more parts.' Thomas Jefferson to Washington, May 23, 1792 (from the letter which he wrote to persuade Washington to seek re-election). 'Your being at the helm will be more than an answer to every argument which can be used to alarm and lead people in any quarter into violence and secession.'

[2] 'All those who have framed written constitutions contemplate them as forming the fundamental and paramount law of the nation, and consequently the theory of every such government must be that an act of the legislature repugnant to the Constitution is void. This theory is essentially attached to a written constitution, and is consequently to be considered, by this court as one of the fundamental principles of our society.... It is emphatically the province and duty of the judicial department to say what the law is.... If two laws conflict with each other, the courts must decide on the operation of each' (from Marshall's judgement in *Marbury* v. *Madison*, 1803). Compare the argument of Breckinridge (a prominent western Republican) in the same year: 'To make the Constitution a practical system, this pretended power of the courts to annul the laws of Congress cannot possibly exist. My idea of the subject in a few words is, that the Constitution intended a separation of powers vested in the three great departments, giving to each exclusive authority on the subjects committed to it.... That the construction of one department of the powers vested in it, is of higher authority than the construction of any other department ... that therefore the Legislature have the exclusive right to interpret the Constitution, in what regards the law-making power, and the judges are bound to execute the laws they make' (*Annals of Congress*, 7th Congress, 1st Session, 178 ff.). And John Randolph of Roanoke: 'The decision of a Constitutional question must rest somewhere. Shall it be confided to men immediately responsible to the people, or to those who are irresponsible.... To me it appears that the power which has the right of passing, without appeal, on the validity of your laws, is your sovereign' (*ibid.*, 645). The arguments against Marshall have been swamped or even unrecorded by most constitutional historians but have recently been restated with considerable vigour in W. W. Crosskey, *Politics and the Constitution*, Chicago, 1953, Chs. XXVII–XXIX.

right of states to obstruct the operation of laws enacted by Congress or of corporations chartered by it, by extending congressional regulation of commerce to the widest limits compatible with federal government, and by enforcing the right of appeal, when the Constitution was invoked, from state to Federal courts. While Marshall strengthened by interpretation the powers of the national government, he also helped to deliver private business from interference by state legislatures. His interpretation of the commerce clause not only meant that Congress need not stop at state boundaries and might reach out to regulate the sources of interstate commerce, but also implied that men engaged upon interstate or foreign commerce were immune from regulation by the separate states. His interpretation of the contract clause meant that business contracts and privileges established by incorporation could not be altered or voided by state enactments. When Marshall came to the Supreme Court its prestige was low and its powers uncertain, by the time he left it the Court was far advanced towards the extraordinary repute and power which it now enjoys; and while it claimed to judge the acts of the national government it was also a national institution which was likely to decide disputed points in a national sense.

The war of 1812 with Great Britain provided further fuel for nationalism. Though its causes have been disputed (and will be noticed later) it was for most Americans a war to establish the right of the United States to be treated as an independent power and not as a client state. Its military history provided little which could contribute to the growing national tradition, for American performance in the campaigns on the Canadian frontier was at the worst humiliating and at the best pedestrian. At sea the United States did add some picturesque incidents and personalities to her national mythology, though failing to make any impress upon the overwhelming naval strength of Great Britain. A British force actually landed in Maryland, swept away the militia forces opposing them, forced President Madison and his government to fly to the interior, and burnt the Capitol. These setbacks were somewhat redeemed by Andrew Jackson's victory at New

Orleans over a British regular army; this battle made Jackson President fifteen years later and established the Westerner — the hunters of Kentucky — as a new and powerful figure in American folk lore.[1] In spite of the disappointments of the war, most Americans continued under the curious belief that they had won it, and in retrospect it is not unremarkable that a nation so weak in military power, so lacking in wealth, and so loosely organized could avoid total defeat at the hands of a great power organized for war. The war was unpopular with many Americans, but in the history of nationalism its importance lies not in the bid for local autonomy in the New England centres of earlier nationalism, but in its popularity in precisely those areas — the farming South and the pioneering West — where nationalist doctrines had been most suspect.

The emotional commitment of the West to nationalism, and the laying of English bogies, help to explain the new atmosphere apparent in American politics. There was a growing conviction that the future of the country depended upon exploitation of her own resources, upon the extension of American power over the continent, and upon divorcing herself from the conflicts of Europe. Because the conflicts of Europe were in fact stilled during the next generation and because the British navy was prepared to act as the policeman of the North Atlantic, the United States were able to develop an ardent and isolated national spirit. In politics and economics this took the form of a revival of Hamilton's ideas of government's role in developing economic life; a new generation of nationalists, prominent among whom was Henry Clay, sponsored a new national bank (the charter of the first bank having expired in 1811), agitated for high tariffs to foster American industry, and proposed to use the revenue for ambitious schemes of improvement in internal communications.[2] This programme

---

[1] 'But Jackson he was wide awake, and wasn't scared of trifles,
  For well he knew what aim we'd take with our Kentucky rifles;
  So he led us down to Cypress Swamp, the ground was low and mucky;
  There stood John Bull in martial pomp: but here was old Kentucky.'
For a brief and penetrating review of the evolution of the western hero (with special reference to Davy Crockett) see Constance Rourke, *American Humor*, Ch. II, and for the political implications see J. W. Ward, *Andrew Jackson: symbol for an age.*
[2] An eloquent expression of this new nationalism was given in 1817 by John C. Calhoun, later to be its most severe critic, 'We are great, and rapidly — I was about to say fearfully

was described by Clay as 'The American System' and is usually known by this name. From President John Quincy Adams (1825–9) this new nationalism received its most elevated expression when he envisaged not only economic but also cultural and scientific development under the aegis of national authority.[1]

Thus, by the 1820's, the United States had moved far along the nationalist road. Predictions of an early dissolution for the Union, which had been the common currency of British comment in 1783, were no longer uttered; the administration of the national governments and the authority of the national courts were firmly established; an allegiance to the Union, celebrated in splendid oratory by Daniel Webster during the year 1830, had come to supplement and in some instance to supplant loyalty to the separate states. If the state was more intimately bound up with the lives of most citizens than the remote national government, the latter had become a powerful symbol in the minds of all Americans. One might hope for good from national union, one might fear that its effects would be evil, but it was no longer possible to ignore the fact that for good or evil the destinies of America would be determined by the national authority. But while

— growing. This is our pride and our danger; our weakness and our strength. Little does he deserve to be intrusted with the liberties of this people, who does not raise his mind to these truths. We are under the most imperious obligation to counteract every tendency to disunion. The strongest of all cements is, undoubtedly, the wisdom, justice, and above all, the moderation of this House; yet the great subject which we are now deliberating [internal improvements] in this respect deserves the most serious consideration. . . . Let us bind the republic together with a perfect system of roads and canals. Let us conquer space' (*Works of John C. Calhoun*, ed. Crallé, II. 190).

[1] 'The great object of the institution of civil government is the improvement of the condition of those who are parties to the social compact. . . . For the fulfillment of those duties governments are invested with power, and to the attainment of the end — the progressive improvement of the condition of the governed — the exercise of delegated powers is a duty as sacred and indispensable as the usurpation of powers not granted is criminal and odious' (*First Annual Message of President J. Q. Adams*, Dec. 1825). The hostility aroused by the American system is summarized by James K. Polk. 'The American System, as it is falsely called, consists of three things. . . . One is high prices for the public lands to prevent emigration to the West, that a population of paupers may be kept in the East, and forced to work for low wages in factories. Another is high duties and high taxes to protect the manufacturer and produce a surplus revenue taken from the people. The third is the great system of internal improvements which is the sponge to suck up the excess revenue taken from the people. . . . There has been a constant tendency to accumulate power in the Federal head, and to encroach upon the legitimate and reserved rights of the states; to use doubtful constructive powers and to build up a splendid government differing only in name from a consolidated empire' (*Annals of Congress*, 21st Congress, 1st Session, 692).

the rise and progress of nationalism seems a clear and emphatic theme throughout this period of American history, it had not won its victories without substantial concessions to local autonomy and to democracy, and it is now necessary to sketch the parallel development of these two traditions.

* * * *

Geography and tradition determined that a large measure of authority would remain with the states, though not necessarily with the states as they were constituted in 1776. To many observers it seemed self-evident that independence would bring with it interstate struggles, and that the greater states would come to dominate their weaker neighbours. The problem of local autonomy is more than the problem of states' rights, which has in practice nearly always meant the rights of powerful states; it is also adherence to the proposition that the separate states have co-ordinate and equal powers. Nationalism and local autonomy do not stand at two poles of political argument; while nationalism has often had the power to destroy, it has also preserved the weaker states. As the union spread westward across the continent this became more apparent; the poor and thinly populated states of the West entered the union as equals of the older states because and only because they were creations of the national law.

At the outbreak of the Revolution it was clear that the colonies, become independent states, would have to surrender something to central authority; it was not to be expected that they would surrender very much, and they actually surrendered less than expediency or tradition might have demanded. It was certain that they would not surrender the right to tax or responsibility for law and order; for the exclusive right of colonial legislature over the life, liberty and property of their subjects had been the crucial point of the revolutionary debate. But even on the eve of independence the necessity for some centralized regulation of commerce had been admitted, and in refusing this to Congress the states took more than they had ever claimed from Great Britain. The degree of autonomy enjoyed by the new states was highly satisfactory to most Americans; it was widely believed that the government of a large country must be despotic, while the remote control from Westminster, under which Americans had grown up, had seemed neither efficient nor just. Moreover a good many Americans did well under their state governments, and the agrarian majority of the people had an instinctive dislike of any government which might interfere effectively with their pursuits. By contrast the small governments gave numerous opportunities for small men to gain positions of authority and profit, and thus a not inconsiderable number came to have vested interests in the state governments. Finally the state legislatures seemed to offer the best opportunity for realizing the demands of debtors, and in Rhode Island to protect themselves they passed laws forcing creditors to take the state's depreciated paper currency in settlement of debts. Thus geography, tradition, vested interests, and democratic aspirations combined to create a powerful body of attachment to the states, and for many it was difficult to see why these governments required any external control.

Against these state interests there grew, from 1781 onwards, a nation-wide alliance working for a stronger central government. The emergence during the war of certain national interests has already been noticed, and so, too, has the sentiment of attachment to the idea of union. In the states many of the more wealthy and better educated feared for social order; they had already fought, with general success, for constitutions which incorporated checks upon the elected majority, but these might not be indefinitely maintained. In 1787 a revolt broke out in the western counties of Massachusetts, led by a Captain Shays, in which debtor farmers challenged the state government, and though suppressed without great difficulty this raised alarm throughout the United States, and created an atmosphere in which the making of the Constitution was possible.

The balance achieved in the Constitution between nationalism and local autonomy was likely to be disturbed if either were too vigorously asserted. The economic programme and political philosophy of Alexander Hamilton raised the alarm. He attempted to use the national debt to enrich a monied *élite* and to give it a vested interest in national government; opposition ran through two channels, fear for the liberty of individuals and fear for the rights of states. Around Hamilton grouped the first recognizable political party, known to history as the Federalists, led by men of large property and widely supported by men of conservative instincts and with an interest in national stability; in opposition the Anti-Federalists or Republicans, whose architect was Madison and whose leader was Jefferson, fused together the fears of democrats and alarm from the states. The first clear division occurred over Hamilton's proposal to fund the national debt at its face value; as it had greatly depreciated, this would make a handsome profit for those who had bought public securities at low prices. The second great controversy came over the proposal to take over the debts of the states, and the third over the setting up of a national bank. The assumption of state debts raised two questions; in the first place the states with small debts, led by Virginia, held that the increase of national taxation to pay the debts of the heavily indebted states would be unfair; in the second place the assumption would mean the transference of a great deal of power and influence from the states to the national government. The National Bank would be a national agency capable of influencing economic life in the states and it would also represent an accumulation of power in the hands of those who had already profited by funding and assumption.

Hamilton was successful in all three of his major proposals, but the opposition aroused prevented the further development of his policy of positive government, and gave birth to a rival theory of government. Hamilton claimed that the National Government was sovereign over all those functions of government which had been assigned to it by the Constitution and must be allowed discretion to choose the means by which it would exercise that sovereignty. Thus, though the power to charter a bank was not mentioned in the Constitution, it was implied by the power to tax and the power to pay the debts of the United States. The Bank was as much a reasonable instrument of this sovereignty as the

Treasury or the Customs service, on both of which the Constitution was silent. Against this Jefferson argued that the wording of the Constitution ought to be strictly construed in exactly the same way as a judge would regard the precise letter of a statute when the life or liberty of a subject was at stake. Those who were imperilled by the law ought to be allowed every advantage which its wording would give them, and one ought to assume that legislators meant exactly what they said and no more. The approach is indicative of Jefferson's approach to government as a necessary evil which would inevitably encroach upon liberty if permitted to do so. The Constitution empowers Congress to enact all laws which are 'necessary and proper' for the execution of the powers entrusted to it, and the whole constitutional debate between Hamilton and Jefferson turned upon the meaning of the word 'necessary'; did it mean something without which a power could not be exercised at all (as the revenue service was necessary for the collection of taxes), or did it mean anything which facilitated the operations of a power (as the Bank facilitated the management of national finances)? The great weakness in Jefferson's theory was that the judgment of what was necessary would inevitably be a matter of opinion, and a factor of arbitrary decision would be introduced at the heart of the constitutional system; the great danger in Hamilton's theory was that implied powers recognized no boundary. Jefferson would have confused and Hamilton would have consolidated the powers of the national government.[1]

In 1798 the problem of how to decide what was constitutional came to the fore when, during the Presidency of John Adams,

---

[1] Jefferson: 'I consider the foundation of the Constitution as laid on this ground — that all powers not delegated to the United States, by the Constitution, nor prohibited by it to the states, are reserved to the states, or to the people (10th amend.). To take a single step beyond the boundaries thus specially drawn around the powers of Congress, is to take possession of a boundless field of power, no longer susceptible of any definition.' But it must be allowed that *some* powers not mentioned in the Constitution are necessary. Hamilton: 'The doctrine which is contended for is not chargeable with the consequences imputed to it. . . . It leaves . . . a criterion of what is constitutional and of what is not so. This criterion is the end, to which the measure relates as a mean. If the end be clearly comprehended within any of the specified powers, and if the measure have an obvious relation to that end, and is not forbidden by any particular provision of the Constitution, it may safely be deemed to come within the compass of the national authority.'

Congress passed the Alien and Sedition Acts, designed to restrain criticism of the government and the activities of recent immigrants. The restrictions upon the freedom of the press, and the arbitrary power of deporting foreign born given to the President, roused strong opposition. The legislatures of Virginia and Kentucky determined to protest and applied respectively to Madison and Jefferson for draft resolutions which they might pass. Both sets of resolutions argued at length that the acts were unconstitutional, and, in the words of the Virginia resolutions, asked other states to concur with them 'in declaring ... that the aforesaid acts are unconstitutional; and that the necessary and proper measures will be taken by each for co-operating with this state in maintaining unimpaired the authorities, rights, and liberties reserved to the states respectively or to the people ...'. Every Northern state condemned the doctrine advanced and said (in the words of the New Hampshire reply) 'that the state legislatures are not the proper tribunals to determine the constitutionality of the laws of the general government; that the duty of such decision is properly and exclusively confided to the judicial department'. Jefferson, having the last word through the Kentucky legislature, replied 'that the several states who formed [the Constitution] ... being sovereign and independent, have the unquestionable right to judge of the infraction; and, that a nullification by those sovereignties of all unauthorized acts done under the color of that instrument is the rightful remedy'. As an academic proposition this may seem satisfactory, but what could it mean in practice? Could any government exist when its constituent parts had the right to decide which laws were to be obeyed? If Jefferson's doctrine was to be taken literally it meant that the powers reserved to the states must paralyse the national government by giving every local legislature a veto upon its actions.

*   *   *   *

Contemporaries believed that a revolution occurred at the election of 1800 when Jefferson won the Presidency by a small margin, and the Republicans won a decisive majority in the House of Representatives.[1] Historians have found it hard to distinguish between the policy of the Republicans in office and that of their Federalist predecessors. The fears of the time were real fears — of monarchy, aristocracy and oppression on the one side, of atheism, violence and 'levelling' on the other — but leaders on neither side conformed to the stereotype made by their enemies. Jefferson, born and bred in America's closest approach to an aristocracy, confined his radicalism to speculative flights in private correspondence; in political behaviour he was cautious, realistic and conservative; Madison was even less likely to disturb the balance of the Constitution which he had helped to frame. Both believed that the Constitution had established as satisfactory a balance as was possible between local and national authority, and both believed that their opponents had been the dangerous innovators threatening this balance. What was called for was not activity but lack of activity on the part of the national government, and they regarded it as a mark of merit when few subjects could be found for legislation or executive recommendation. The guiding light for the people, in their self-development, would be found not in the national government but in the states. Few governments have made a more self-conscious effort to provide the negative without the positive aspects of national authority, and yet few left more tangible marks of positive action. Without constitutional authority Jefferson, whose commonsense usually outweighed his legal scruples, committed the United States to the purchase of the vast Louisiana territory; without much regard for the wishes of states he forced the reluctant New England states to accept an economic breach with Great Britain; with even less regard for the economic interests of the commercial states Madison took the country into war with Great Britain in 1812. In

[1] 'Dec. 31, 1800. Here ends the 18th century. The 19th begins with a fine clear morning wind at S.W.; and the political horizon affords as fine a prospect under Jefferson's administration, with returning harmony with France — with the irresistible propagation of the Rights of Man, the eradication of hierarchy, oppression, superstition and tyranny over the world, by means of that soul-improving genius-polisher — that palladium of all our National joys — the printing press — whose value tho' unknown by the vulgar savage slave, cannot be sufficiently appreciated by those who would disdain to fetter the image of God.' From the diary of Dr Nathaniel Ames (Charles Warren, *Jacobin and Junto*, Harvard University Press, 158).

coercing the Northern states the government had the full support of Southerners who had formerly championed states' rights, and the New Englanders, formerly ardent nationalists, planned secession and used the language of the Virginia and Kentucky resolutions. Under the aegis of Jeffersonian republicanism there also grew up that second wave of nationalism which has already been noticed; a national road was built across the Alleghenies, a second national bank was chartered, a tariff was passed to protect manufactures, and a further programme of national aid for internal communications was planned.

The rhythm of American history might lead one to expect new nationalism to be followed by a new appeal to local autonomy. This time the storm centre was not Virginia, but South Carolina, which had produced some noted Federalist leaders in the earlier period. The key to the new movement is cotton. Demand from Europe and particularly from Lancashire had led to an enormous growth in cotton culture; this produced an era of prosperity in the lower Southern states, fostered an expansionist movement which carried cotton and Southern culture into the Southwest, and provided a new and persuasive argument for slavery without which the recruitment of a large labour force would have been difficult. Riding the crest of the cotton boom in 1816 South Carolina, the leading cotton state, produced in John C. Calhoun a leader of the new nationalism; with cotton prices high and manufactures cheap (thanks to superabundant British importations), the South Carolinians could think of themselves as the dominant state in the Union and afford the generosity of a tariff to save infant industries. The situation changed dramatically in 1819 when a confluence between over-expansion and unsound banking brought depression and failure to many agricultural areas. Credit recovered from the panic of 1819 but cotton prices sagged even lower while manufactures grew slowly but perceptibly dearer. At the same time the division between North and South was sharply and bitterly emphasized in 1820 during the debate over slavery west of the Mississippi. The controversy led to the celebrated Missouri Compromise under which Missouri was admitted to the Union with a constitution permitting slavery, but elsewhere in the territories north of latitude 36° 30′ slavery was forbidden. Constitutionally it had emphasized a situation of great significance for the future: a majority in the House of Representatives wished to prohibit the adoption of slavery in Missouri, but a solid block of Southern Senators with a handful of Northern Senators held firm against the proposal. In 1824 an attempt to raise the tariff on manufactures seemed directly inimical to the interests of South Carolina; in 1828 the success of a high tariff policy seemed to mark the real beginning of exploitation by Northern capital of Southern needs. In England as in America there was a clash between the landed and manufacturing interests; there, too, was a clash between protection and free trade; in both countries the interest concerned with the home market was protectionist and that concerned with foreign markets was free trade. South Carolina and the Manchester school talked the same economic theories and both flattered themselves that they stood on the side of the angels of light; American and British industry both pressed for policy to facilitate their expansion and seemed to represent forces which were dynamic and new. In the Northern states there had been a significant shift of capital away from commerce into industry, and by 1828 manufactures were no longer conducted only by small masters.

The clash of interest was clear; what is characteristic of America is the translation of this clash into a constitutional argument. Logically South Carolina might have had some difficulty in showing that a tariff, imposed by a Congress with the power to tax and to regulate foreign commerce, was unconstitutional; but did so to her own satisfaction. More significantly the South Carolina Exposition of 1828, written by Calhoun the former nationalist, proposed a method for dealing with unconstitutional national acts. This was 'nullification', by which a single state could refuse to allow the operation of an act within her borders. There was a beautiful simplicity about nullification which compels admiration; once a nullification ordinance was passed no state official could assist a Federal officer in executing the act, the state courts would regard the act as void and automatically punish those who attempted to enforce it, the state militia (the only sizeable armed force normally on the spot) would protect citizens and ensure that punishments were carried out. Yet nullification did not contemplate secession from the Union; it left a state free to take all the advantages from a national union while refusing obedience to any act which it disliked. Local autonomy could hardly be carried further, and had nullification been in operation since the formation of the national government it was hard to imagine any act of national importance which would not have been rendered futile by the act of at least one state.

Nullification was posed as a threat in 1828, and its execution was deferred until Andrew Jackson, elected President in that year and believed in the South to favour states' rights and a low tariff, had had an opportunity of remedying South Carolina's grievances. In 1832, four years having passed without a revision of the tariff, the threat was carried into execution and a state convention formally nullified the Tariff Act. Andrew Jackson's concept of duty was entangled with no constitutional niceties; he had sworn faithfully to execute the laws of the United States and execute them he would. South Carolina found herself faced by a determination to carry out the Tariff Act with national forces mobilized for the purpose; but at the same time a compromise tariff was hurried through Congress by Henry Clay who, nationalist and high tariff man though he was, preferred peace to civil war. South Carolina then rescinded the nullification ordinance. National authority had been preserved but a Southern threat had forced the abandonment of a policy approved by a national majority, and the traditions of local autonomy had been hardened into a specific demand that a state should be judge of its own interest.

During 1830 the two traditions of nationalism and local autonomy received emotional and oratorical expression in the famous debate between Senator Daniel Webster and Senator Robert Hayne. Webster dignified the sentiment of nationalism, too often in the past defended by an appeal to special interests, as a great principle of strength and security to which the American

G

people owed their progress from weak colonial societies to a nation able to speak on equal terms with any in the world. Webster's splendid language had a pervasive and persuasive effect upon the rising generation in America, but it smothered rather than confuted Hayne's contention that a state must have the right to choose her own destiny. Another possibility emerged: a single state might be unable to withstand national pressure, but what if a group of states resisted? The rights of a single state might mingle with those of like-minded states, and the idea of a new allegiance to a 'section', to 'the South', might emerge.

* * * *

By 1832 local autonomy had therefore reached the stage at which it must either admit the superior force of nationalist argument and power, or it must go forward to merge its doctrines into a larger unit capable of challenging national authority. The logic of the situation was to wait for nearly thirty years before it moved forward to the ultimate conclusion; the long delay was the result of numerous factors but chief among them was the rise of democracy, the third of the great forces released by the Revolution.

An incidental part of Paine's *Commonsense*, published in 1776, had argued against the supposed virtues of 'mixed government'. 'I draw my idea of the form of government from a principle in nature which no art can overturn, viz. that the more simple anything is, the less liable it is to be disordered, and the easier repaired when disordered.' What could be simpler or more just than unicameral government by an elected assembly? This was the question which inspired democrats and shocked John Adams into taking the first long step away from radicalism in his 'Thoughts on Government', which is one of seminal documents of American constitutionalism. 'I think', he wrote, 'a people cannot long be free, nor ever happy, whose government is in one assembly. . . . A single assembly is liable to all the vices, follies, and frailties of an individual.' The want of 'secrecy and despatch' makes an assembly unfit for the exercise of executive power; it 'is still less qualified for judicial power because it is too numerous, too slow, and too little skilled in the laws'. The need for separate powers follows; but ought an assembly to have even undivided control over legislation? An independent assembly and an omnicompetent executive would be sure to clash, and the remedy lay in giving the executive a veto and in making a 'distinct assembly . . . as a mediator between the two extreme branches of the legislature, that which represents the people, and that which is vested with the executive power'.[1] Adams suggested the election of his upper house by the lower house, others were to prefer its election by an electorate restricted by a high property qualification, but the principle of bi-cameralism was the same. Here then were two alternative systems of government: one which was novel and unorthodox, the other which reframed the familiar pattern of colonial government without the hereditary monarchy. Between the two the issue was joined in every state during the Revolutionary period, and in every state save Pennsylvania the conservatives were triumphant, and even in Pennsylvania unicameral government with a weak executive lasted only until 1789. Thwarted in their original aim the democrats had nevertheless a profound influence upon American development. Nothing, for instance, is more evident in the deliberations of the patricians who wrote the Constitution of 1787, than their awareness that their work must be approved by the people. They wrote democracy into the Constitution by making the House of Representatives directly elective by the people, and by leaving franchise to the states, where it was more likely to be lowered than raised. They realized that an intelligently designed government had more to fear from the vested interests of local autonomy than from the democracy, and they knew that a strong government must rest upon popular approval. Though the checks and balances of mixed government are incorporated in the Constitution, popular sovereignty flows through each of its several channels, and after its acceptance the authors of the Constitution

[1] Adams, *Works*, IV, 193–200.

sought to increase its strength with the people by adding a Bill of Rights (the first ten amendments) consisting mainly of guarantees of personal freedom. It shows a very inadequate understanding of the period to represent the Constitution as an undemocratic document or even as a reaction against democracy. A remark by Elbridge Gerry in the Constitutional Convention that 'the evils we experience flow from the excess of democracy' has been too often quoted without noticing that the context of Gerry's remarks referred to the election of the House of Representatives, which he wished to see in the hands of State Legislatures, and that in the vote on this question six states were against Gerry, two were divided, and only two supported him. A much truer indication of the mind of the delegates is given in Madison's remark in the same debate that 'the great fabric to be raised would be more stable and durable, if it should stand on the solid foundation of the people themselves, than if it should stand merely on the pillars of the Legislatures'. In this connection it is worth noticing that the 'founding fathers' expected the House of Representatives to be the dominant part of the national government and did not anticipate the later rise of the Senate.

*　　*　　*　　*

It was improbable that the democratic tide would be held back by artificially imposed property qualifications. The early years of the nineteenth century saw battles over the franchise which invariably resulted in its extension. As the general qualification was lowered the special qualifications for Senates were mitigated or abandoned. And even before the end of the eighteenth century the elaborate system for the indirect election of the President through an electoral College had been turned into a straight party vote and in most states the electorate voted directly upon the choice for President. These changes were by no means uniform throughout the country and though, by 1830, most white males could vote, a bewildering variety of minor property or tax-paying qualifications remained, the character of the state Senates varied, and so did the means by which Presidential electors were chosen.[1]

For some years after the turn of the century national government remained in the hands of upper-class Easterners, but with the increasing influence of the democracy in the states and with the rise of new Western states, there was a growing resentment at the narrow confines within which power revolved. This was accentuated by the economic troubles of the year 1819.[2] Between 1822 and 1828 the democratic forces gradually gathered behind Andrew Jackson, a landowner of Tennessee with a national reputation as the victor of New Orleans. The Jackson movement was not entirely the homespun democracy which some then, and others since, have believed it to be; like other successful American political movements it was complex and diverse in its alliances, ranging from old Federalists to Western demagogues, from Southern gentlemen to astute professional politicians, from debtor Western farmers to small Eastern manufacturers, and from dour defenders of states' rights to ardent nationalists. Its psychological impact was simpler and more significant; for the majority it was

[1] An epic debate upon the character of popular government took place in the Constitutional Convention of the State of New York in 1821. There was little opposition to a wide extension of the elective franchise (to almost complete male suffrage) so far as the Assembly was concerned; strenuous opposition developed over the senate and over an attempt to impose a property qualification in voting for that body. Chief Justice Spencer said, 'Are we jealous of property that we should leave it unprotected? To the beneficence and liberality of those who have property, we owe all the embellishments and the comforts and blessings of life. Who build our churches, who erect our hospitals, who raise our school houses? Those who have property. Are they not entitled to the regard and fostering protection of our laws and constitution?' Chancellor Kent said, 'The apprehended danger from the experiment of universal suffrage applied to the whole legislative department, is no dream of the imagination. It is too mighty an excitement for the moral constitution of man to endure . . . . Liberty rightly understood is an inestimable blessing, but liberty without wisdom and without justice, is no better than wild and savage licentiousness. The danger which we have to apprehend, is not the want, but the abuse of liberty. We have to apprehend the oppression of minorities, and a disposition to encroach upon private right — to disturb chartered privileges — and to weaken, degrade, and overawe the administration of justice . . .' (*Report of the Proceedings and Debates of the Constitutional Convention*, Albany, 1821, 218, 221. The second quotation also in H. S. Commager, *Documents of American History*, No. 124).

[2] In May 1820 John Quincy Adams found John C. Calhoun in a gloomy mood. 'He says that there has been within these two years an immense revolution of fortunes in every part of the Union; enormous numbers of persons utterly ruined; multitudes in deep distress; and a general mass of disaffection to the Government, not concentrated in any particular direction, but ready to seize upon any event and looking out anywhere for a leader. The Missouri question and the debates on the tariff were merely incidental to this state of things' (*Diary of J. Q. Adams*, May 22, 1820).

the triumph of democracy and it is no accident that the Jackson party assumed and retained the name 'Democratic'.

Controversy is ever likely to play around Jackson. The champion of democracy was, in his own state, a large and conservative plantation owner; the simple soldier proved to be one of the most successful political leaders in American history; the elderly and ignorant Westerner proved to be a man of iron will, who dominated his administration, the country, and triumphantly asserted his views on such technical questions as banking and currency. Actually Jackson had been a planter-magistrate, a Senator and the governor of a territory as well as a military commander; while his range of information was limited his mind was powerful, and despite errors in spelling he wrote voluminously and vigorously; detached observers found his manners excellent and his bearing dignified. A man of violent temper he had learnt control and could use a rage when it suited him without letting it distort his judgment; but the temperament of a duellist remained, he would not forgive an insult, and he saw his political opponents as personal enemies. He believed that it was the function of government to deny privilege and to insist upon equal rights under the law; it was this which made him the fit leader of the resurgent democracy. America must be returned to the pure and simple principles of the past, and the power to corrupt must be resisted; this power was an attribute of the privileged rich and the manipulation of currency one of their most deadly instruments. He summed up his political testament in old age as 'Keep us from temptation! This is the text'. The national debt, prolific source of corruption, must be paid off by careful husbanding of the public land, and when this was done the same source could be used to support education and improvements. 'To protect your morals and to cap the climax of your prosperity, and protect the labor of your country, you must provide in your constitution, by a *positive provision*, that your legislature never shall establish a bank or corporation whatever, with power to issue paper.'[1] A younger follower and future

---

[1] Jackson to Houston, March 12, 1845.

President added, 'I would keep no surplus revenue to scramble for, either for internal improvements, or for anything else. I would bring the Government back to what it was intended to be — a plain economical Government.'[1] The radical wing of the Jacksonian party — the Equal rights or Loco-foco movement, which flourished for a time in New York City and in other urban areas — attacked wealth and privilege in language which shocked conservative men; but their remedy was unlimited free enterprise and equal opportunity, not government action, to redress economic inequalities.[2] It was of great significance for the future of America that the tumultuous forces of democracy were led along this negative road; it was also of significance that under Jackson democracy became wedded to nationalism.

The occasion of Jackson's most significant conflict was an attempt, in 1832, to recharter the Bank of the United States (a successor to Hamilton's Bank, which had been chartered by Congress in 1816). Jackson vetoed the recharter Bill with a message which was a political manifesto rather than a constitutional argument, and which made opposition to the concentration of economic power the main theme of his own campaign for reelection in 1832 and of the Democratic Party for the future. Against Jackson the former National Republicans, led by Henry Clay, offered the so-called 'American system' (the phrase had been coined by Clay in 1824) under which a National Bank provided stable currency and elastic credit, a protective tariff fostered American industry, and Federal revenues were used to aid and promote the development of internal communications. In addition, the Clay Republicans, or Whigs as they came to be called after 1834, challenged the new authority which Jackson claimed

---

[1] James K. Polk, Charles Sellers, *James K. Polk: Jacksonian,* Princeton University Press, 152.

[2] At an early meeting of the Equal Rights movement in New York the rival Democrats attempted to disrupt their proceedings by turning off the gas lights; the Equal Rights men foiled this by providing themselves with candles and with loco-focos — the sulphur matches of the day — and thus earned a nickname which stuck. Some people may have associated the name with a Spanish word meaning 'insane'. Other radical Democrats in the same state were called 'Barnburners' from an old story about a farmer who burnt down his barn to kill the rats in it.

for the President as the supreme representative of the people. Clay was decisively defeated in 1832, and subsequent historians had often echoed the Democratic inference that his 'American system' was tailored merely to suit the needs of the wealthy. But a vision of the national government as the agent of economic development could become popular wherever men or regions felt that they were not sharing to the full in the benefits of expansion. The depression which began in 1837 seemed to demonstrate the inadequacy of Democratic policies, and by the end of the decade the Whigs, supplemented by many individuals and groups antagonised by Jacksonian ascendancy, had gathered popular support and were poised for electoral victory. For the next twelve years the two parties were to fight neck and neck in most states of the Union.

A minor obstacle in the path of Jacksonian democracy had been the method of nominating candidates for office. Until about 1820 the normal method was by caucus, that is by the party leaders acting as a kind of unofficial committee. The Republican caucus for nominating candidates for President consisted, for instance, of all Republican members of Congress who chose to attend or were not unacceptable to the majority; the procedure by caucus was less oligarchic than might seem at first sight for Congressmen were susceptible to public opinion and knew the interests of their constituents. But after 1820 there was an increasing demand for the nominating procedure to be more broad-based; in 1824, when the caucus operated for the last time, its candidate was acceptable only to a minority of the party, and three other candidates were nominated by state legislatures and unofficial state conventions. A system was required which would satisfy the democratic desire to have a hand in nomination while preserving some means of choosing between the too numerous choices of the people before they were committed to the election campaign. The answer was found in the National Nominating Convention, first used by the major parties in 1832, and ever since the keystone of the party system. The Convention consists of delegates sent by the members of the party in each state with the object of nominating a candidate for the Presidency and approving a party programme (or platform). In this great, excited and often unruly assembly the real issues of American politics are often decided; here the great men of the party take their chance with the rank and file, here sectional and other differences must be reconciled, and from here must emerge a single man upon whom the hopes of the party are pinned.

The American political party is itself largely a consequence of the democratic drive. The first party — the Hamiltonian Federalists — was a party on the English model: a group of leaders associated loosely in a common policy expecting to command votes partly by their policy and partly by their influence. It failed to develop any rank and file organization and for this very reason its career as a national party was short-lived. Their Republican opponents, without control of the government and at most times before 1800 without a majority in Congress, were forced to make use of popular organization. Building upon Democratic Societies, which seem to have arisen spontaneously but which may trace their descent to organizations of the revolutionary period, the Republicans developed a party in which the life came from local units, while the central direction did little more than guide, co-ordinate, and fight congressional battles. Under Jackson this type of broad-based and decentralized party achieved an organization which was to endure until the Civil War. Jackson's opponents, who became the Whigs, imitated Democratic methods but never with the same success; while they could win an election the elements which they were forced to combine stretched too far even the elastic bonds of an American party. While a party may generate an emotional appeal which brings immediate success, long term success comes only to the party which can build an organization which will carry it through slack times. The Democrats combined a strong popular appeal with an army of professional politicians who maintained the momentum of the party.

*   *   *   *

A final reflection may be made upon the long and complex phase of American history which has been surveyed in this chapter. In the early national period men were convinced that a purified society bred political virtue; while fully aware of the possibility of corruption they believed that republican virtue would preserve America from the vices of Europe. In government this promise was fulfilled to a remarkable degree. Perhaps no administration in history has a better record for public spirit than that of Washington, and though the President took care not to give office to known opponents of the Constitution, public appointments were not dictated by party needs. Some removals on political grounds followed Jefferson's victory in 1801, but the majority of public servants continued undisturbed.[1] By the 1820's the civil service was probably a little overweighted with elderly men but the country had an administration which was by far the best in the world. The coming of Jacksonian democracy brought a sad change. The professional politician was the backbone of the party and the professional is in politics for its rewards. It is no bad thing to make men have a material interest in politics, but a weakness of the American system is that its decentralized organization requires an enormous number of professionals. In consequence political appointments tend to spread and ramify; when there are so many sheep to be fed there is a standing temptation to discover that a public office would be better filled by a faithful party man than by some hangover from the previous régime. In Jacksonian democracy the convenient doctrine of rotation in office came as a blessing to patronage managers; since the public duties in a republic ought to be simple it followed that no special talents were required, and as men were liable to develop aristocratic notions if they held office for too long, it followed that their tenure ought to be short. The falling standard of public life infected Congress whose members became more and more shameless in seeking special, local and personal favours. The

---

[1] 'The purpose has been to remove some of the least deserving officers, but generally to prefer the milder measure of waiting till accidental vacancies should furnish opportunity of giving to Republicans their due proportion of office. To this we have steadily adhered.' Draft of a letter to J. Duane from Jefferson (*Writings of Gallatin*, ed. Adams, I, 130).

nature of democratic politics tended to deter men of education and first-rate talents from running for office and the second-rate became the rule in public life; the exception was the South where the gentry continued to act as natural political leaders (which helps to explain the extraordinary dominance of Southerners in national affairs between 1828 and 1860). The decline in the tone of public life is even sadder to record when one remembers that it was at this very period that the reform movement was taking hold in England, sweeping away old abuses, and finally building upon the ruins of aristocratic culture the finest civil service in history.

[4]

The United States in a World of Growth and Change

The formative period of the American nation was the most extraordinary in the history of the Western World. An enormous and sustained increase in population; a scientific revolution which dissolved the old frontiers of knowledge, equipped man with new techniques for the control of his environment, and had deep philosophical implications; a political revolution which shook and eventually destroyed the old social order set up gigantic reverberations which are not yet stilled: these were the dominant forces of the age in which the new nation had to find its place and by which its destiny was to be moulded. This chapter is concerned with the extension of political control over the territory of the United States, without which the rewards won by the application of new techniques to the inland empire of virgin land might have been reaped by others; with the effects of the powerful influences emanating from Europe upon the growing people; and finally with the increasing tension between the receptive Northern and Western states and the less receptive Southern states as a by-product of these changes.

The political independence gained in 1783 could not conceal the weakness of the country in a world of competing colonial empires.[1] With Great Britain to the north, in the Atlantic and in

---

[1] Lord Sheffield, an influential advocate of the retention of the Navigation Laws after 1783, wrote, 'It will not be an easy matter to bring the American states to act as a nation; they are not to be feared as such by us. . . . We might as reasonably dread the effects of combination among the German as among the American states, and deprecate the resolves of the Diet, as those of Congress' (*Commerce of the United States*, 4th ed., 198).
Twelve years later Hamilton could still write, 'A very powerful state may frequently

the Caribbean; with Spain in Florida, along the Gulf coast, and ruling vast territories west of the Mississippi; with France not far away in Hispaniola and not yet reconciled to the loss of North America, the new nation was encircled by potential and powerful enemies. With few and unimportant manufactures, desperately short of capital, dependent upon European markets for the sale of their staple products, the Americans could hardly escape dependence upon one or more of the great powers. While the rivalries of the powers might preserve a balance in which the integrity of the United States was one of the conditions, their conflicts might also embroil and divide the people of America. Too great a dependence upon one power would make America a client state but to hold aloof from all would render her desperately weak; the emotional commitment to France — the ally of 1778 and after 1789 the apostle of revolution — might be hard to reconcile with the economic necessity for close relations with Great Britain; and while American sea power was negligible her western frontiers were also vulnerable to any determined enemy in alliance with the Indian tribes.

The fundamental problem of American foreign policy was therefore to break through the encircling barriers, and this was true whether its application was found in the western wilderness, along the Canadian frontier, at the mouth of the Mississippi, or on the waters of the Atlantic. Then, and often since, men have failed to appreciate the unity of the problem and have played West against East, North against South, agriculture against commerce, Indians against commercial difficulties, and Francophiles against Anglophiles. It was fortunate for the United States that her first President under the new Constitution showed a firm grasp of essentials. Washington's policy was summed up in his Farewell Address, embodying his ideas though owing some detail to Hamilton and Madison. The case established by the Farewell Address was that a weak power, threatened by competing imperial

hazard a high and haughty tone with good policy; but a weak state can scarcely ever do it without imprudence. The last is yet our character; though we are the embryo of a great empire' ('*Camillus*' *1795. Works*, ed. Lodge, IV, 384).

powers, must commit its political interests to no one power. Binding alliances would necessarily transfer European conflicts to American shores and set Americans against each other in order to maintain foreign interests. But as material growth was the road which would eventually lead America out of her position of weakness, commercial links should be as numerous and as untrammelled as possible. 'The great rule of conduct for us in regard to foreign nations is, in extending our commercial relations to have with them as little political connection as possible.' Behind the formal language of the Farewell was the unwritten and shrewd advice: play one's cards carefully, get what one can if the price is not too high, give nothing away even to a friend save for value received, and remember the repercussions of foreign entanglements upon domestic emotions. So powerful was the language and the advice that it was still dominating American thought on foreign affairs in the twentieth century, when America was powerful, impregnable, and rich.

The great European war which began in 1792 brought complexities and passionate disagreements to American life, but it also brought some compensating advantages. Playing upon the needs of the belligerents for neutral shipping, the United States found in her large merchant marine an asset which was entirely her own. It was not quite so strong a weapon as Jefferson tried to make it, when he embarked upon economic warfare in 1806 to make belligerents respect neutral American rights, but it was the first great economic interest for which the United States did not depend upon Europe. As American shipping grew it brought with it problems of policy; the freedom of the seas had always been an American interest, and it now became doubly important. Though Republican presidents after 1801 can be criticized for some aspects of their policy they were surely right in regarding the rights of neutral shipping as an American interest for which they must fight if necessary.

An indirect and unexpected result of the European conflict was the acquisition of Louisiana which brought about a vast change in America's world position. At one moment France thought to bolster her position in Europe by the acquisition of new power in America, and a secret negotiation transferred from Spain to France the whole of Louisiana forming a great triangle with its apex at New Orleans, its east side the Mississippi, its west side the Rockies, and its base the undetermined Canadian frontier. News of this secret deal created consternation in Washington (recently occupied as the Federal Capital) for an aggressive France was a very different neighbour from Spain in decline. Jefferson immediately countered with the threat of an Anglo-American alliance. But some obscure calculation in the mind of Napoleon brought about a change and persuaded him to offer American emissaries not New Orleans and West Florida which they had come to buy, but the whole of Louisiana for fifteen million dollars. By this purchase Spain was forced back to desert and mountain, the Mississippi became American on both shores throughout the whole of its course, and France had definitely written off her North American projects. The problem of encirclement was radically changed and the most pressing barrier now became the power of Great Britain to the north and on the sea.

This is the background to the war of 1812 between Great Britain and the United States. The complex train of diplomatic manœuvre and economic coercion on both sides of the Atlantic, the doubt as to whether the Americans suffered more from English or from French attempts to impose a pattern of trade in the Atlantic, the American indignation at high-handed British naval actions and at supposed intrigues with the Indians, all serve to obscure the essential simplicity of this war. Its aims were to conquer Canada, to secure favourable treatment for American ships, and thus to strike at the two most threatening barriers of encirclement. Neither aim was achieved and — apart from heroic but minor naval episodes and the defeat of a British regular army at New Orleans — the American record was unimpressive, and the peace of Ghent which ended the war settled none of the outstanding issues. Yet the war had its significance: for the first time Great Britain was driven to treat the United States as a fully independent power and not as a would-be client state. Faced with the prospect of a long war and doubtful gains, Great Britain had preferred to give tacit approval to an Atlantic balance of power under which the Americans would be supreme on the continent, the British supreme at sea, and British North America would become a hostage for British good behaviour not a base for offensive operations.

Although the war of 1812 was the last armed conflict between Great Britain and the United States, and although it was succeeded by an era of growing cultural and business contacts, the old animosities remained. England was, for Americans, the most hated nation, while the English upper class continued to denigrate all things American. American contacts were mainly with merchants, bankers, manufacturers, writers, and middle-class radicals; the nobility and gentry who still ruled England remained aloof and for the most part unfriendly. And indeed America had only to be held out as the epitome of the radical dream to be damned by upper-class Englishmen, and the majority of travellers who published accounts of their American experiences did so to demonstrate that the Americans were crude, uncultured, violent, careless of the public duties, and not too eminent for private virtues. For the American the typical Englishman remained, despite the corrective of frequent contact with humble members of the race, an arrogant, upper-class gentleman, who indicated with an offensive accent the full measure of his contempt for all who did not belong to his race and his caste.

These lingering animosities could not inflict more than superficial damage upon a relationship which developed out of the complementary needs of the two countries. Neither wished to see European powers advancing their interests in the New World; the United States for obvious reasons, Great Britain because of her enormous and growing commercial interests in North and South America and because of the military weakness of Canada and the West Indies. America still needed to import manufactures in large quantities (though also attempting after 1816 to shield young industries against British competition), and the accumulated savings of the British middle class was the largest single source of capital for the expansion of American economy. Shortly after the end of the war several American states began to raise loans on the British money market, and these bonds, offering high rates of interest combined with government guarantees, were attractive to British investors.[1] The capital so raised was used to finance roads, canals, and later railways. The most spectacular operation of this type was the building of the Erie Canal, linking New York with the Great Lakes, with money which was largely raised in London by the state of New York. In a later generation the British investor discovered that the good faith of a weak state government was not quite the same thing as that of the British Treasury.[2] While Britain was giving these aids to the growth of the American nation, the United States made their contribution to the rise of industrial civilization in the Western World. The rise of cotton culture in the South linked the rural economy of that region with the factory towns of Lancashire, and allied Southern planters with Manchester men in a free trade alliance which was to fail in America but to triumph in England in the mid-century. Thus the United States found in the British navy, British capital, and British industry powerful aids to American development, which were usually overlooked in the mythology which passed for national history, and Great Britain's most profitable industry depended upon an American raw material.

It is therefore more gratifying than surprising to find the outstanding disagreements between the two countries settled quietly by diplomatic negotiation. Boundary agreements in 1818, 1842 and

[1] Between 1815 and 1830, five or six million pounds found their way 'very quietly' to the United States; at this time investments in Europe and Latin America were much larger (L. H. Jenks, *Migration of British Capital*, 64). By 1841, 197,551 shares out of 350,000 in the United States Bank were held in Europe (*ibid.*, 95). In 1835 an estimate gives $66,000,000 of British capital invested in the separate states and approximately the same in United States securities (*ibid.*, 85). This increased rapidly during the next two years; new investment was checked sharply by the economic crisis of 1837 but revived during the 1840's.
[2] Sidney Smith, the Whig parson and polemic writer, lost money and retaliated with a *'Humble Petition to the House of Congress at Washington'*. 'The fraud is committed in profound peace, by Pennsylvania, the richest state in the Union.... It is an act of bad faith which ... has no parallel, and no excuse.... The Americans who boast to have improved the institutions of the Old World have at least equalled its crimes.'

H

1846 finally determined the frontier between the United States and British North America, leaving it lightly held and ultimately undefended. The government of the United States refused to exploit British difficulties in Canada in 1837 and ignored demands for annexation which came from Montreal in 1849.

In 1830 one of the hoariest disputes between the United States and Great Britain — going back to the year 1783 — was settled when trade between America and the British West Indies was opened on a basis of full reciprocity. In 1846 the repeal of the Corn Laws permitted American grain to enter England free of duty, though high transport costs still gave some protection to British agriculture. In 1849 the Navigation Acts — for two hundred years the axis around which British commercial policy revolved — were finally abolished and American ships could trade without restriction in all British-owned ports. Of more historic importance was the British contribution to the Monroe Doctrine of 1823; having discovered a common interest in preventing the French from aiding Spain to recover her South American empire, the British government was prepared for joint diplomatic action. Acceptance of the offer by America would have raised reconciliation based on common interests to the higher plane of an official *entente*, but prejudices against the ancient enemy were still too strong and, having been assured that the British navy would be employed to prevent the movement of French or Spanish troops across the Atlantic, President Monroe declared that the United States had a special interest in the Americas and that they would regard any extension of European colonies North or South as a hostile act. To the basic doctrine of Washington's Farewell Address — that of freedom from entanglement in the affairs of the Old World — was added an assertion of the United States' special interest in all that concerned the New World.

The main casualty in what has been called 'the sleeping partnership' between Great Britain and the United States was the power of Spain. Though it was argued that maintenance of Spanish power in North America was a subsidiary British interest,

British statesmen showed that they would not intervene to save it. American raids on Spanish territory (sometimes unofficial but usually backed by public opinion), combined with a diplomatic offensive, gained Florida in three stages (1810, 1813, 1819) and a boundary in the West which was highly favourable to the United States. Mexico, the successor state to the Spanish North American empire, was left to bear the full weight of American aggression. Americans who had settled over the boundary revolted in 1835 to set up the independent republic of Texas; in 1845 Texas was annexed by the United States with inflated territorial claims and out of this grew the war with Mexico in 1846. In that year Americans in California staged their own local revolt and set up the Bear Flag Republic, but, before the success of this movement could be gauged, an American squadron arrived and declared the occupation of the country. At the end of the war California, together with the modern states of New Mexico, Arizona, Colorado, Utah and Nevada, passed under American rule. When the Mexican war began the United States were still uncertain of the outcome of a dispute with Great Britain over the Oregon Territory; but this was concluded in 1846 with an agreement which extended the boundary along the 49th parallel (with a southward deviation to leave all Vancouver island under British rule). Seventy-two years after the thirteen tiny commonwealths on the Atlantic coast had rebelled against British rule, the nation which they had formed stretched west to the Pacific and had become one of the largest countries in the world.

*   *   *   *

Behind the superficial record of territorial expansion lie great forces which were transforming the whole Western World. An old aristocratic society in which status was related to land was being replaced by a middle-class culture in which right was dependent upon contract and status was determined by wealth. This new culture was far from simple, and the dynamic forces which explain its creation flowed into many different channels: materialist and humanitarian, scientific and evangelical; mingling the fiery doctrine of the rights of man with staid constitutionalism on the English model, fiercely nationalistic while trying to replace the cosmopolitanism of aristocracy with the internationalism of business, and combining (occasionally in the same person) simple avarice with idealism of a high order. The world of 1850 was wholly different from the world of 1750 and still presents a tangle of contradictions to the modern historian. If one theme seems to unite all it is a belief in the betterment of man; this at least provides a common factor between adulation of hard-headed businessmen and the heroism of missionaries dying for their faith in remote regions.

In America many landmarks of the old régime had been obliterated during the era of the Revolution. The civilization upon which broke the dynamic influences emanating from Europe was already middle class, democratic, and equally captivated by material progress and political idealism. There was little to obstruct or modify the operation of these powerful forces, there was no old hieratic order to be conciliated or copied, no aristocratic culture to be undermined or assimilated, and American religion, without a national establishment, was easily adapted to the religion of progress. If modern America illustrates both the superb qualities and much which is unlovely in the civilization of the Western World, it is because the United States have no Middle Ages. The lineaments of the modern world were painted upon a clean canvas.

*   *   *   *

The first census of 1790 showed that the United States contained fewer than four million people; this doubled by 1815, doubled again by 1837, and reached thirty-one and a half million by 1860. At some momentous but little-noticed date between 1840 and 1850 the population passed that of Great Britain and henceforward the most numerous exponents of Anglo-Saxon civilization would be found in America. Much of this growth was caused by a high natural rate of increase in a rural land where children were an economic asset and the incidence of disease was low, but the United States were also reaping the harvest of Atlantic migration. Immigration boomed between 1783 and 1793, slackened as war tightened its grip upon European populations, and was beginning to revive by 1820 when the first official record shows under 8,500 immigrants. 22,600 came in during 1831 and over 60,000 in 1832. Fleeing from famine, political oppression and the petty tyranny of landlords, attracted by American opportunities and American democracy, the swelling tide rose to 104,500 in 1842, 379,500 in 1851 and 427,800 in 1854. These were peak years but they were reached by a fairly smooth upward movement. It is difficult to imagine what it meant to deliver an average of 82,000 immigrants a week during 1854 to American ports in the small ships of the day, few of which were powered by steam, and on many of which travelling conditions were abominable.

Immigrants tended to come from those areas of Europe where social and economic upheaval was most marked; they were more likely to be drawn from peasant stock with small savings and from the older type of craftsmen than from the destitute poor or the new factory proletariat. In 1830 the largest single group of immigrants came from England, by 1854 Irish and Germans were by far the most numerous; the country which had been moulded by Protestantism and representative institutions now received a great influx of Roman Catholics and of men who had never known what it was to cast a vote.

English and German immigrants usually made land ownership the object of their ambitions, but the Irish (perhaps because they were poorer) tended to congregate in the growing towns of the nation. In 1790 the urban population was only 200,000, but by 1860 it was 6,000,000. The alien character of the new cities, with their teeming population of foreign born, added a distinct American twist to the familiar problem of country versus town. Nowhere was the lack of medieval heritage more noticeable than in the towns where few civic traditions or patrician groups provided nuclei around which a new urban civilization could grow. It was as though the dominant pattern in English urban life had been set, not by the old-established corporate towns, but by the raw and overgrown villages of the industrial North. Rural America had its traditions which though recent were firmly established; the independent farmer had been idealized by the Republicans, provided the voting strength for the Democrats, and had been conciliated by the Whigs. In the 1850's there was a revolt by the old and rural Americans against the growing influence of the new and urban, and a good many of the well-to-do in the towns were receptive to arguments advanced by the American or 'Know Nothing' party, the first nativist political movement which polled nearly one-quarter of the votes cast in the Presidential election of 1856. This conflict was to be overlaid by the greater struggle between North and South, but the problem of the city and of the foreign born remained.

American industry often grew in a rural rather than an urban environment. The small entrepreneur set up his mill near water in rural isolation; the skilful mechanic turned small capitalist was often a farmer's son, making his way by hard work and initiative, and defending his interests against interference in exactly the same way as the agrarian debtor. It is a common error to suppose that American industry was already 'big business' in 1830; in fact the small masters predominated and many of them were found battling for economic freedom in the ranks of Jacksonian democracy. The protective tariff was a political necessity not because of large pressure groups but because in New England and Pennsylvania a great many small men and voters were concerned.

The twenty years between 1830 and 1850 saw the most important phase of the American industrial revolution. Railways opened the way to markets and raw materials, the successful manufacturer at the head of a moderate sized business emerged from the mass of small master mechanics, English factory techniques and power machinery were fully mastered, and the enormous possibilities in the expanding continental market were beginning to dawn upon bold spirits. Even so the role of Northern capitalist manufacturers is often exaggerated; the United States were still predominantly rural and comparatively thinly populated. Though the manufacturers were learning to use the language of Jeffersonian agrarianism they could not hope to rival the influence of rural leaders. Congress, the administration and the state governments were all heavily dominated by landowners; the great debates preceding the Civil War were carried between different types of farmer not between farmer and industrialist; and if the manufacturers entered the new Republican party its voting strength was agrarian.

The nineteenth century saw the penetration of the great land masses, so long closed to market economy, by new means of communication which changed the geo-political map of the world. Nowhere were the effects more dramatic than in America. The national road from Baltimore to Wheeling (Ohio) and the Erie Canal opened the West to settlement and to limited commerce. Railways got away to a good start, but by 1850 a wide gap still separated the fairly well-developed railway network of the East from the few lines of the Mississippi valley. During the next decade it became possible to travel from New York to Chicago by three different routes, the upper Mississippi valley had its web of lines, and a transcontinental line was being seriously discussed.

The coming of the railways to the West changed the pattern of development. Without the railways it would have been natural to look south down the great rivers to New Orleans, or north-west to the Great Lakes and the St Lawrence, with New York via the Erie Canal as an outlet of secondary importance. Railway connections with New York, Philadelphia and Baltimore ensured the West would look along the shortest routes to Europe and the Eastern urban markets.

The great expansion took place in an age which had not yet adopted *laissez-faire* dogma. The role of the states in raising funds and using them for internal improvements had already been mentioned, but the states interfered in economic life in numerous other ways, ranging from the archaic assize of bread (regulating the size and quality of loaves) to labour laws, public education, and the use of the chartered corporation to ensure that certain economic tasks were done as they ought to be done. The railways were built by private enterprise, but usually obtained help in raising capital and public ownership was seriously discussed. The decline of state activity, and the rise of the notion that it was prima facie harmful, came partly as a result of the financial difficulties in which several states found themselves after the panic of 1837, partly because the calibre of state politicians did not often encourage confidence in their ability or honesty, but most often because of the ebullience and growing confidence of the business-man. Experience and success, prestige as a pioneer, and the absence of a hereditary upper class secured for the businessman a substantial measure of support when he claimed that his judg-ment of economic opportunities must serve the public best. It was partly the evaporation of the old restraints upon economic activity which absolved the businessman from the necessity of fighting his own battles in politics, and since his social prestige depended upon his business success he had neither the time nor the leisure to devote his time to public affairs. By the time of the Civil War a new *élite* could be discerned in the North which would not rule in the accepted and traditional way of ruling classes; they would not be magistrates and legislators, and public life would fall generally into the hands of second-rate; they would not become patrons of the intelligentsia, and art and letters would flourish only in narrowly circumscribed areas where older tradi-tions survived; they were concerned mainly with the home market, developed few cosmopolitan links with foreigners, and ignorance of the rest of the world would be regarded almost as a virtue. The full impact of this new class upon America would be felt after the Civil War, but its pre-war origins are not without significance and demand more investigation.[1]

In a 'government of laws not men' the lawyer must play an essential part; in the growing civilization of the United States he played a dominant part. From the august pronouncements of the Supreme Court, down through all the courts of the land, judges

---

[1] De Tocqueville, of course, noticed this as he noticed almost everything else and made an interesting comment. 'Je pense, qu'à tout prendre, l'aristocratie manufacturière que nous voyons s'élever sous nos yeux est une des plus dures qui aient paru sur la terre; mais elle est en même temps une des plus restreintes et des moins dangereuses' (*De la Démo-cratie en Amérique*, ed. André Gain, 2ᵐᵉ Partie, Ch. XX, 217–18).

were required to interpret not only the Constitution of the United States but also those of the several states. If they sometimes obstructed the will of the people by strained interpretations of the law, they also protected the liberty of the subject and rendered workable the more obscure statutes of the state legislatures. The profession of law was the natural approach to public life and lawyers provided the great majority of congressmen and most of the presidents. Again, the lack of an established upper class meant that there were no social barriers and no privileged interests to hinder the rise of successful lawyers to the highest positions, while the reluctance of most businessmen to enter politics meant that the lawyers had to act as intermediaries between the world of business and public life. The great exception to these generalizations was of course the South. Here lawyers were important and legal training was often a part of a gentleman's education, but there was an upper class which combined economic, social and political leadership; lawyers tended to be auxiliaries of this class rather than leaders in their own right.

American society was expansive, often crude, and ruthless in its attitude toward failure. It had nothing but contempt for decadent aristocracies and little use for the weak, the destitute and the unemployable. No public responsibility was admitted for poverty, disease, or the care of the aged. Yet this age of materialistic drive was also the age of humanitarian endeavour, while private charity supplied some of the gaps left in the social services. From quite another quarter the lot of the urban poor was mitigated as politicians realized the possibility of a city vote which could be won by comparatively small favours. By the middle of the century the Irish figured prominently in Northern city 'machines' and local political activity had become an instrument both for the assimilation of the alien and for remedying in a haphazard but genial way the material evils of urban life. The new immigrants profited by the wave of democratic reform which had displaced older ruling groups and introduced virtual manhood suffrage; five years were required for naturalization but it was comparatively easy for the corrupt politician to find a judge who would accept false evidence or no evidence at all, and permit naturalization and voting rights to recently arrived immigrants. The result was that the immigrant found almost at the outset someone who was interested in his welfare, his difficulties, his opinions, and his vote.

One social service made marked progress during the first half of the nineteenth century. Education as a public responsibility was part of the old Puritan tradition, though a wide gulf might be fixed between the provision of a school by the community and making it free and compulsory. A turning-point in the great controversy over public elementary schools came in Pennsylvania in 1834; a state law setting up a free system had been passed, a strong agitation was made for its repeal, but it was retained after a stirring debate in which the free school was championed by Thaddeus Stevens, later to earn fame and notoriety as the author of 'radical' reconstruction after the Civil War. With local variations most of the Northern states and of the new Western states made it possible for all poor children to obtain elementary education, several made it free and compulsory for all. The progress of public education was less hampered than in England by religious disputes, though considerable difficulty was encountered over the Roman Catholic objection to having the English Bible read in public schools; in the long run the effect of this was to diminish and finally to drive out religious instruction from the tax-supported schools.[1]

---

[1] 'Celui qui veut juger quel est l'état des lumières parmi les Anglo-Américains est donc exposé à voir le même objet sous deux différents aspects. S'il ne fait attention qu'aux savants, il s'étonnera de leur petit nombre; et, s'il compte les ignorants, le peuple américain lui semblera le plus éclairé da la terre' (De Tocqueville, *De la Démocratie en Amérique*, ed. André Gain, I, 2ᵐᵉ Partie, Ch. IX, 462).

J. S. Buckingham, an English radical, observed that in Massachusetts 'there is not a single child . . . for whom gratuitous instruction may not be secured . . . . Within a few years the single city of Boston alone is said to have expended upwards of two millions of dollars in support of her literary, religious, and benevolent institutions, in addition to an annual amount of $200,000, or £40,000, per annum, for the support of public schools alone; while the utmost amount that could be obtained from the British government, a few years ago, for the whole kingdom of Great Britain, was only £20,000, not for a single year, but for an indefinite period' (J. S. Buckingham, *America*, London, 1841, III, 285). New England did however present an exceptionally favourable picture; in Pennsylvania it was said that only one in three of the children between five and fifteen were attending school, and that of the 250,000 who were not receiving instruction many never went to school at all (*ibid.*, II, 64).

Enthusiasm for education was one example of the urge for reform which infected the middle-class culture of the Northern and Middle states during this period. The movements were diverse, ranging from religious revivalism to purely secular schemes for social betterment. Most of them contrived to blend religious motives with secular purposes. In this the temperance movement was typical; the American Temperance Union held its first national convention in 1836, the state of Maine passed a prohibition law in 1846 and was followed by twelve other states and one territory before 1855. The societies for the Abolition of Slavery did not stand alone but were representative of a whole group of movements run by men who fervently believed that evil could be driven out by good laws. On an intellectual plane the philosophy of the age was provided by Emerson's Transcendentalism which provided the uplift of Christian ethics without the inconvenience of Christian dogma. It was a feature of these reform movements that many were operating on both sides of the Atlantic; the bustling, moralistic and mechanistic outlook of the American reformers was very like that of contemporary radicals in England, and there was a good deal of cross-fertilization between the two countries. Some of these movements were absurdly limited in their aims, some were advanced with ludicrous pomposity, and some produced grave errors of judgment, but together they created a new climate of opinion which was more sensitive to evil, more responsive to idealistic arguments, and more convinced of man's power to control his environment and his destiny than any which the world had known.[1]

*   *   *   *

[1] In old age Emerson looked back upon New England at this period and wrote: 'There are always two parties, the party of the Past and the Party of the Future; the Establishment and the Movement. At times the resistance is reanimated, the schism runs under the world and appears in Literature, Philosophy, Church, State, and social customs. It is not easy to date these eras of activity with any precision, but in this region one made itself remarked, say in 1820 and the twenty years following. It seemed a war between intellect and affection; a crack in nature, which split every Church in Christendom into Papal and Protestant; Calvinism into Old and New schools; Quakerism into Old and New; brought new divisions in politics; as the new conscience touching temperance and slavery. The key to the period appeared to be that the mind had become aware of itself. Men grew reflective and intellectual. There was a new consciousness' (*Historic Notes of Life and Letters in New England*).

From all this ferment the South stood somewhat apart. It was true that the plantation economy had marched into the Southwest, that the Southern way of life had been profoundly influenced by the demands of industrial change, and that cotton was vital to the American economy; but still the Southern states retained the archaic flavour of an eighteenth-century rural society, and the one nineteenth-century influence to which the Southern planter class gave an enthusiastic welcome was the romanticism of Sir Walter Scott with its glorification of an age of chivalry. Cotton provided the economic justification for the great plantation employing slave labour, it continually tempted the small independent farmer to raise that crop alone, the substantial profits in good years attracted capital which might otherwise have been used for more general development. And since capital invested in cotton was sunk in land and slaves it was comparatively immobile, especially in the bad years when no one wished to buy either. In spite of the proximity of raw material very few cotton mills had developed in the South; other industry hardly existed despite extensive coal and iron deposits. The South had lagged behind the North and Midwest in railway building, and its banking system was dependent upon that of the North. The South imported manufactures and even food, exported cotton, tobacco, rice and money, and saw her carrying trade fall into the hands of Northern merchants. The South was in fact a striking example in the nineteenth century of the specialization of function.

Like most peoples the Southerners wanted the best of all worlds. They were grateful for their rural way of life and considered it superior to any other; yet they were not prepared to pay the price by surrendering to others economic control of the nation. When cotton prices fell their resentment rose and they were ready to believe in Northern conspiracies to oppress the South. According to the free trade model the South, North and West had complementary economies and a good deal of America's material success might be explained by the neat way in which the sections supplied each other's needs; but the unfortunate paradox was that the more intertwined the sectional economies became the more sectional jealousy increased. The tariff was treated as a sectional grievance, though some Southerners supported it and there were many Northern free traders.[1] Any expenditure of federal funds was likely to set the Southern defence mechanism at work, as it appeared that Northern roads, canals or railways would get the immediate benefit. The disposal of public lands became a chronic cause for controversy. Any measures giving strength to the national government were opposed because in local autonomy lay the South's best chance of preserving its own interests.

Though archaic, the Southern society was also expansive. Though very few immigrants went to the South, the pressure of population upon poor or exhausted land caused chronic land hunger. During the early part of the century Southerners in search of land settled the Southwest, crossed the Mississippi into Arkansas, settled in Texas, pressed north into Missouri and the southern parts of Indiana and Illinois. Southerners were the main beneficiaries of the collapse of Spanish power in Florida, enthusiastically supported the war with Mexico in 1846, and dreamed of the annexation of Cuba as a new home for themselves and their slaves. The accidents of history which had blunted the drive against Canada meant that save for remote Oregon the Southerners had almost monopolized the fruits of territorial expansion; they could also claim to have supplied most of the inspiration and perhaps a majority of the fighting men. Southern enthusiasm for expansion had its counterpart in Northern doubts. There were heirs of the Puritan tradition and believers in 'Republican virtue' who deprecated acquisitive war, or doubted the wisdom of extending the Republic until it became unwieldy or ungovernable;

[1] What annoyed Southerners as much as the principle of the tariff was the means by which it was obtained. After the passage of a low tariff measure in 1846 President Polk, himself a Southerner, wrote, 'The capitalists and monopolists have not surrendered the immense advantages which they possessed, and the enormous profits which they derived under the tariff of 1842, until after a fierce and mighty struggle. This city has swarmed with them for weeks. They have spared no effort within their power to sway and control Congress, but all has proved to be unavailing and they have been at length vanquished. Their effort will probably now be to raise a panic (such as they have already attempted) by means of their combined wealth, so as to induce a repeal of the act' (*Diary of Polk*, ed. Nevins, Longmans, 134).

other Northerners could see in the great westward movement economic advantages and land to supply the needs of unborn generations; but both could unite in deploring the prospect that the new west might be opened to plantation slavery. Whether because they believed that it would strengthen and perpetuate slavery, or because they did not want the Negro slave or free, a majority of Northerners could agree that in the new lands, as in the old North-West, slavery should be prohibited. This hostility to the extension of slavery came as a profound shock to Southerners. On the one hand Southerners would be prevented from taking their characteristic social structure into the new lands, on the other they would find themselves encircled by free soil with increased opportunities for fugitive slaves and increased difficulties in maintaining plantation discipline. Beyond these practical considerations was the psychological fact that prohibition of slavery in the territories implied a condemnation of the whole Southern way of life, and Southerners, aware that they alone among civilized peoples adhered to slavery, became ever more sensitive to any criticism of their 'peculiar institution'.

Historians have differed on the relationship of slavery to the Civil War. Some have written of that conflict as one between an agrarian and a capitalist society; some have seen it as a war of independence; some have seen it primarily as an attempt to solve the perennial problem of the relationship between local and central power. Everywhere in the western world agrarian and industrial societies clashed; only in America did the conflict lead to the battlefield. Other nations fought for independence, but the South had known only one nation — the American nation — and only after hostilities had begun did loyalty develop to a new entity, the Confederacy. The American Constitution had been designed to reconcile central with local authority; there was no power in the Constitution to interfere with the most important aspects of the states. The thing which made these conflicts bitter, extraordinary and disastrous was the existence of slavery. Slavery was so entwined with Southern society that every other problem was conditioned by it. Between the belief that slavery was right and the belief that it was wrong there was no possible compromise; argument was useless, and at the heart of the whole controversy between North and South was a great area in which rational argument was both useless and impossible.

Partly because it adhered to slavery, partly because it was a rural society in which the mass of the population was barely literate, the South had been little affected by the tides of intellectual debate which flowed across the Atlantic. Scientists, social reformers, and literary men were conspicuous by their absence from the South; and since most of the things with which scientists, social reformers and writers were concerned implied criticism of slavery, Southerners grew not more but less receptive. On slavery itself rational discussion was still possible in 1830, but by 1850 social pressure prevented any expression of doubt. Nor was this conformity imposed from above; it was spontaneously sought by the mass of the white people.

The great conflict which was preparing was not one between an agrarian and a capitalist society — this is a most misleading simplification — but a conflict between a society in which the ferment of nineteenth-century change had worked to the full and one in which it had remained inert or become stagnant. The problem of its origin is not solely domestic, and it can only be understood when one has appreciated America's place in a world of growth and change.

[5]

The Approach to Civil War

In 1844 the philosopher Emerson declared that, 'The development of our American resources, the extension to the utmost of our commercial system, and the appearance of new moral causes which are to modify the state, are giving an aspect of greatness to the Future, which the imagination fears to open. One thing is plain for all men of common sense and common conscience, that here, here in America, is the home of man. After all the deductions which are to be made for our pitiful politics, which stake every grave national question on the silly die, whether James or Jonathan shall sit in the chair; after all deduction is made for our frivolities and insanities, there still remains an organic simplicity and liberty, which, when it loses its balance, redresses itself presently, which offers opportunity to the human mind not known in any other region.' Countless ordinary Americans would have echoed these sentiments with less eloquence but with equal sincerity. By the mid-century America seemed an outstanding success, and if visitors such as Dickens found it difficult to understand and even harder to excuse the presumption of the common man, the American saw in it his hope for the future. It is in these aspirations that the real tragedy of the Civil War lies; whatever else was lost or gained they were its principal casualty. After the war the old slogans would be taken up and Americans would believe once more that their country was the world's best hope, but the old confidence would be sadly shaken.

Yet anyone who could ignore the political frustrations of the 1850's might have cause for renewed confidence. When Emerson wrote the passage just quoted, the population of the United States was about nineteen and a half million; in 1860 it was nearly thirty-one and a half million. Soaring immigration figures demonstrated the enormous attraction of America for Europeans of the peasant and working classes. The value of manufactured goods doubled during this single decade and the railway network of the North-east reached out to link with that of the Mid-west while long tentacles were thrown out over all the rich farming lands of the Mississippi valley. There were still men living who had been among the two and a half million colonial subjects of King George, and in every community west of the old piedmont there were ancient men who had seen their district pass from frontier settlement to thriving farms, market towns, or manufacturing centres. This new civilization had made few and insignificant original contributions to philosophy, science or literature, but the leaders of American life had had an unexampled success in diffusing the elements of Western civilization both horizontally across the continent and vertically from the top to the bottom of society. Mid-nineteenth-century thought had been moulded by the need to cast one's ideas in a form which could be readily understood by men who were quick and practical rather than highly educated, and men who in other civilizations might have turned their energies to scholarship, scientific discovery or public administration preferred to make their mark as orators, newspaper editors, or popular lecturers.

Highly bred European contemporaries found in this culture neither grace nor penetration, and what they missed most was a forum in which men of ideas could hammer out their views with intellectual equals without being overheard by the public. In America there were few private worlds, and though in several states an old-established *élite* tried to maintain a spirit of intellectual exclusiveness, their small cliques were stamped with provincialism and defeat. There was no great metropolitan culture in which the crudities of popular opinion were transmuted into something which could be more elegant, more powerful and more flexible. This lack of a metropolitan *élite* had more than a cultural importance, for while such an *élite* may be overthrown and dispersed by upheaval from below, it is less likely to be split by internal rifts. Between the various leading groups in America there was surprisingly little communication; the most obvious and most striking gulf was fixed between Southern and Northern leaders who met hardly at all save in the artificial atmosphere of Washington, but in addition the hierarchy in each state was autonomous and often suspicious of external influences. To establish any community of action and belief it was necessary to simplify what ought to have been subtle, to play upon familiar themes rather than to examine their ultimate consequences, and to appeal to the past rather than to the future. The paradox of American life was that while the economy was dynamic and society fluid, political argument was static and barren. Though a majority in all states regarded the Union as one of God's great blessings the meaning of this grand concept was narrowed down to legalistic argument over special points. Year after year the orators covered the same ground, made the same points, and sought the same abstractions; and all the while the storm clouds of sectional rivalry grew more ominous.

From these generalizations his admirers then and now have sought to rescue John C. Calhoun. Originally a strong nationalist he became so impressed with the danger to Southern interests that he ended his life as the architect of secession. His extreme sensitivity to regional wrongs often blinded him to the value of individual rights. His much praised logic consisted in seeing the most unfavourable consequences of a situation, treating them as its inevitable results, and deducing that the least concession would be a disaster.[1] A man of powerful intellect his practical experience was limited to Washington and his own state of South Carolina, and while the coarser side of Clay and Webster was redeemed by their vision of the American future the purer intellect of Calhoun saw only the dangers which lay ahead. Capitalism, immigration,

---

[1] 'I would at no period make the least sacrifice of principle for any temporary advantage (Calhoun, *Works*, II, 486). In 1836 Calhoun asked how the abolitionist threat could be met and answered, 'There is but one way: we must meet the enemy on the frontier . . . . The power of resistence, by an universal law of nature, is on the exterior. Break through the shell, and there is no resistance within' (*Works*, II, 484).

westward expansion, humanitarian movements and scientific advance meant evils which threatened the South. This refusal to come to grips with the facts of modern civilization has won him admirers by whom he is regarded as a significant political theorist. Calhoun had one important contribution: he saw the dangers which lay in a naïve faith in the majority, he saw how minorities might be oppressed, and characteristically inferred that minorities must always be oppressed. Against the sovereignty of the majority Calhoun set the principle of concurrent majority, that is the idea that the will of the numerical majority should be legally effective only when accepted by minority interests or regions. The mechanism by which this would be effected was left uncertain but it would seem that at one pole would lie the right of a state to nullify Federal laws and at the other a dual executive — one Southern and one Northern President — with a separate power of veto over national acts to prevent the coercion of a nullifying state. Calhoun did not specify whether his idea was capable of infinite multiplication, whether each region, each state, each district might not claim similar protection; in fact he was not concerned to protect all minorities but a particular minority, that of the Southerners who appeared about to lose their long predominance in the national councils.

Calhoun's demand for a perpetual constitutional guarantee of minority interests might commend itself to those who believed that the best government was that which governed least, but not to Northerners already restive under the obstructive and negative weight of Southern political ideas. The grand scheme of national internal improvements had been killed. The national bank had been killed. The tariff, which manufacturing interests believed essential to their progress, had been pared down until it ceased to afford protection.[1] The price of public lands had been held up and access to them rendered more difficult. And lately the Southerners had shown a taste for an aggressive imperialism which was un-

[1] The tariff of 1828 was highly protective. The so-called Compromise Tariff of 1833 planned a successive reduction to a maximum of 20% by 1842. In 1842 the Whigs raised duties and restored protection; but in 1846 the Democrats went back to the low tariff, and the duties were lowered again in 1857.

popular in the North because it spread slavery, offered no returns, and offended well-grounded prejudices against colonialism. Yet the South never lacked friends in the North; there were powerful banking and commercial interests who depended upon cotton, there was the urban democracy of the larger cities, and there were Western farmers of Southern descent. The irritation against the South was concentrated first in New England and (more strongly) in the Western areas settled by New Englanders such as northern Ohio, and then in the small towns and commercial farms of the Mid-west. Here a kind of intense decency mingled with a robust materialism, here politics were more than phrases and became the manipulative process by which the interests of a community could be promoted. There were so many contributions which politics could make to the growing network of commercial endeavour, and it was the business of the politician to obtain them; but between him and attainment there stood too often the symbolic and monumental figure of a Southern statesman.

Southern politics belonged to a simpler order of things; with an established social hierarchy, with the plantation as an established economic institution, and with slavery supplying heavy ballast to the social system, the main object was to hold authority at a distance and to confine its activity. The small Southern farmer was frequently at odds with the greater planters and local battles could be fierce and prolonged, but the aim of the farmer was to get a fair deal, to maintain his independence, to be left alone. Thus even the fiercest struggles between Whigs and Democrats ended with negative results, with minor shifts in power, and with the basic social facts unchanged and unchallenged. The South had, in general, sent better men to Washington than the North, yet their qualities made it harder for Southerners to understand the bustling men of the North for whom they would express the same distaste as did their English counterparts for men 'in trade'.

Geographical separation helps to explain why annoyance and disdain culminated in civil war. Elsewhere the rural and the business societies lived in a proximity which forced compromise; in

America it was possible to develop their separate characteristics in isolation. Yet it is doubtful whether the gulf would have been so wide, nor the catastrophe more severe, had not the South clung to its peculiar institution of slavery. One can ignore slavery in explaining the difference between a rural hierarchical society and a business society; one can explain the timing of the Civil War by other factors; but it is necessary to emphasize slavery in order to explain why the war took place at all.

Slavery encouraged men to think in absolute terms and it could not be ignored. The Negro had to be either slave or free and there was no intermediate status upon which compromise could fasten. Even gradual emancipation must end in total emancipation, and with emancipation neither the discipline of the plantation nor the independence of the white farmer would be possible; for the Southerner abolitionism was no mere attack upon Southern manners but aimed at the subversion of his society.[1] Northerners might ignore slavery in the South, but the expansion of slavery into the unoccupied West, which had been marked down by the Northern farmer as a promised land, was another matter. Experience proved that a rural society must either be that of the plantation, in which the poorer whites were deprived of opportunities, or that of the small farm in which opportunity was equal and classes were not supposed to exist. And every boatload of immigrants, drawn from Europe by the splendid prospect of owning land, reinforced the opposition to the westward expansion of slavery. Material calculations did not complete the picture; most Northerners believed that slavery was morally wrong and an abolitionist minority was determined to right this wrong, and the further Northerners veered towards a conviction that slaveholding was a sin, the more inclined were Southerners to defend slavery as a moral institution. In the late eighteenth century

[1] In 1836 Calhoun asked his fellow Southerners whether they expected the abolitionists to 'commence a crusade to liberate our slaves by force? ... The war which the abolitionists wage against us is of a very different character, and far more effective. It is a war of religious and political fanaticism, mingled on the part of the leaders, with ambition and the love of notoriety — and waged, not against our lives, but our character. The object is to humble and debase us in our own estimation, and that of the world in general; to blast our reputation, while they overthrow our domestic institutions' (*Works*, II, 484).

leading Southerners believed that it was wrong and ought to be abolished, in the early nineteenth century they believed that it was a necessary evil, by mid-century they believed that it was a positive good.[1] Beyond this latter extravagance lay awkward questions about racial relations which slavery made it unnecessary to ask.

The Southerner found it necessary to insist that slavery was not only good where it existed but also to demand its expansion. With a rising population and an agriculture which was wasteful of soil, with the risk of increasing slave escapes with every addition to free territory along the Western borders, and with the political need to maintain an equality of slave and free states in the Senate, the South had strong inducements to insist that slavery should follow the flag. And as the argument developed the expansion of slavery came to have a symbolic meaning for the South; if granted the South might feel that its interests were assured, if refused the price of Union would be thought too high.

In August 1846, during the opening stages of the Mexican war, David Wilmot, a Pennsylvania Democrat, proposed that 'as an express and fundamental condition' for the acquisition of land from Mexico 'neither slavery nor involuntary servitude shall ever exist in any part of the said territory'. Easily passed by a Northern majority in the House and rejected by the Senate, the Wilmot Proviso initiated a debate which was to drag its way through fifteen weary years until it had ruptured two great parties, buried countless reputations, ruined a nation, and raised a new party and

[1] As early as 1837 Calhoun said that the abolitionist agitation 'has produced one happy effect, at least — it has compelled us of the South to look into the nature and character of this great institution, and to correct many false impressions that even we had entertained in relation to it. Many in the South once believed that it was a moral and political evil. That folly and delusion are gone. We see it now in its true light, and regard it as the most safe and stable basis for free institutions in the world' (*Works*, III, 179–80). The Southern view in the early nineteenth century was well expressed by Early of Georgia in 1806. 'A large majority of the people in the Southern States do not consider slavery as a crime. They do not believe it immoral to hold human flesh in bondage.... Reflecting men apprehend, at some future day, evils, incalculable evils, from it; but it is a fact that few, very few, consider it as a crime.... A large majority of people in the Southern States do not consider slavery even as an evil' (*Annals of Congress*, 9th Congress, 2nd Session, Dec. 31, 1806). One is apt to generalize too much from the opinions of 'reflecting men' and to forget that for generations the majority had accepted slavery as one of the facts of life productive of more good than harm.

a new nation upon the ruins of the old. One immediate effect was to raise a Free Soil Party in the North, which absorbed the older Liberty Party of the abolitionists; it made a striking debut in 1848, but its result was to rouse Southern fears rather than to advance the anti-slavery cause. Were Northerners wrong, at this stage, to oppose the extension of slavery? If the preservation of the Union was the greatest good they were clearly wrong. North and South, the wisest heads predicted that the slave states must resist and that in resisting they would discover a community of interest against the rest of the United States. Calhoun argued that the Union was a compact, that the compact could not be kept without the will to keep it, that a separation of interest must destroy the will to remain in Union, and that without guarantees which would restore Southern faith in the Union it must dissolve as the Protestant denominations had already dissolved into Northern and Southern elements. By the ordinary rules of political calculation there was therefore little to be said for anti-slavery tactics; but slavery was not a normal political problem any more than slaves were normal pieces of property, and it was the Southern refusal to recognize either fact which made the situation explosive.

In 1850 it was still possible to compromise when the controversy over the Mexican acquisition came to a crisis. The measures of 1850, proposed by the veteran Henry Clay, and carried by an alliance of moderate men from both sections, gave something to both without pronouncing upon any of the fundamental questions which had been raised. California, which had written itself an anti-slavery constitution in a somewhat irregular manner, was admitted as a free state. The Wilmot Proviso was dropped and in the new territories of New Mexico and Utah the decision on slavery was left to the people on the spot, with a promise to admit them when ready as either slave or free States (this was the principle of popular sovereignty of which more was to be heard hereafter). To conciliate the North the slave trade was abolished in the city of Washington which had long been an important slave mart. To conciliate the South a new Fugitive Slave Law made it possible to invoke Federal aid for the recovery of runaways when the state authorities could not or would not act. In the South the compromises strengthened the hand of Unionists, but it was Unionism based on the premise that the North would now cease its attack upon Southern interests. In the North the compromise was accepted in most quarters with relief, but Webster, who had come to the support of Clay, was bitterly condemned by certain sections of New England opinion for having admitted that popular sovereignty might spread the sin of slavery, and the Fugitive Slave Law — which carried the least attractive aspects of slavery to the doorsteps of Northern men — brought an enormous accession of strength to anti-slavery opinion.

* * * *

The political parties had been amongst the principal instruments of national union. Since a nation-wide alliance was necessary for national success, the parties strove to moderate sectional jealousies and to seek formulae of agreement rather than points of dissension. If party platforms often seemed vacuous their very lack of meaning was a contribution to national strength. The Democratic party was the alliance created by Jackson and his followers; by origin a party of small property owners, both rural and urban, of superior artisans, and of New York Irish, it had ramified among a great variety of interests and employed an incomparable army of professional politicians. It could be many different things to many different men; the party of national expansion and of equal rights, of executive authority and of states' rights, of political reform and of Tammany; the party which had crushed nullification but had a tenderness for Southern interests, which could be for low tariffs in a free trade area and for a judicious tariff among Pennsylvania protectionists, and which, while continuing its claim to be the party of the common man, could become also the chief hope of the Southern gentry. During the debates of 1850 it became apparent that, when a small number of free soil democrats had been shed, the party's main voting strength in the North and West — the lower classes in the cities and the farmers of Southern descent in the West — were indifferent about slavery, and were still more concerned with their traditional struggle against commercial and business domination. Thus the party as a whole might play an important part in Southern defence; in consequence the long standing rivalry between the planters and 'the democracy' subsided, conservative Southern gentlemen began to appear in the councils of the party and were to be heavily represented in its cabinets during the coming decade. The party was to choose two Northern Presidents, Franklin Pierce and James Buchanan, but both were markedly sympathetic to the South.

For fifteen years the opponents of the Democrats had been the Whigs; a party whose architect was Henry Clay but which made him only once its nominee for President. Indeed a failure to unite, a top weight of men of talent, and ineffective party machinery had been the party's leading weaknesses. Formed as a party of opposition to Jackson it tried to combine a Hamiltonian nationalism — tariffs, internal improvements, and central banking — with hostility to executive authority, and to join Northern businessmen with Southern planters and rural voters. The Whigs were unfortunate in their Presidents: Harrison, elected in 1840 died a month after inauguration, and Tyler, who succeeded him, broke with his party and ruined with his veto several of their favourite measures. Clay lost by the narrowest possible margin in 1844, and Zachary Taylor, who won in 1848 and confronted the crisis of 1850, had made a good record as a general but knew little of politics, was obstinate and uncertain in his judgment, and (surprisingly for a Southern slave-owner) leaned heavily for advice upon the extreme anti-slavery men in his party. When Taylor died at the height of the crisis he was succeeded by Millard Fillmore, who performed a notable service by placing his supple and conciliatory skill behind the compromise, but who made little impression upon the public. Clay and Webster were both old men nearing their end and as a result the party lacked the decisive leadership which might have restored the dangerous rift which developed between pro-slave and anti-slave Whigs. In the years after 1850 the party began to disintegrate rapidly, leaving a void in politics which was difficult to fill.

The Whigs had been the party of property, North and South; it was the party of the respectable middle class and it was strong along the line of New England migration to the West; most men of wealth, intellect and breeding had a natural affinity for the Whigs and Whiggish doctrine was preached from many a pulpit. Where would such men now find their political haven? Wealthy Southerners tended towards the Democrats or remained in unhappy isolation as old-line Whigs. Northerners clung to the party organization so long as it existed, but seemed to lack the will to revive it. For a short time it seemed that a new conservative alliance might form around a virulent anti-Catholic and anti-foreign movement nicknamed the 'Know Nothings'. The cause was more attractive than first appeared: it was robustly nationalistic, its particular enemies were the corrupt Catholic and Irish city machines, and it turned men away from sectional controversy. During its brief career the 'Know Nothing' movement raised animosities which were to continue far into the future, but as the axis for a national party it was too weak and too disreputable. In 1854 it scored striking electoral successes but in 1856, when Fillmore ran as its candidate, it carried only one state and soon disappeared from the national stage. But as the 'Know Nothings' declined and the embers of Whiggism smouldered to a finish a new star arose on the horizon; in February 1854 a diverse group of old Whigs, anti-slavery Democrats and free soilers joined to form the new Republican party; the reason for its spontaneous and spectacular success must be sought in the further development of the sectional controversy.

*   *   *   *

In 1854 Stephen Douglas, Democrat from Illinois and the most dynamic figure among the rising generation of politicians, proposed to organize a territorial government in Nebraska. Its purpose was to open the land for settlers, create a new sphere of operations for Chicago businessmen, and clear the ground for a

Pacific railway. The southern part of this territory, later to be separately known as Kansas, bordered upon the state of Missouri where a somewhat isolated group of slave-owners were uncomfortably aware of the growing majority of non-slaveholding farmers in the state. If the slave enclave should be bounded on the west by a free state this outlying bastion of the Southern system might be lost. Further south men looked hopefully for land into which Southern migrants might move. It was therefore likely that Southern members of Congress would obstruct any measure which prohibited slavery in the new territory. Northern opinion might be equally sensitive; the migratory pressure was even stronger from the Mid-west and East, businessmen did not fancy their chances in a slave economy, a slave wedge once inserted might open a wider gap in the great West, and Kansas lay north of 36° 30′ which the Missouri compromise had laid down as the boundary between slave and free. Faced with this dilemma Douglas decided upon a bold move: he would repeal the Missouri compromise, and apply to the region the principle of popular sovereignty. He believed (rightly) that Southern support would be attracted by the possibility of spreading slavery in the West and that the superior numbers of anti-slave settlers would ultimately prevail.[1] Nothing in Douglas's calculations could have indicated the clamour which was aroused by his proposal; the persuasive argument for popular sovereignty (surely a good American

---

[1] One of the most forceful attacks upon the Douglas bill came from Senator Thomas Hart Benton, of Missouri, a redoubtable veteran of Jacksonian democracy. Benton pointed out that Congress could not evade responsibility by passing decision to the settlers themselves. 'What is the object of this movement, which so disturbs Congress and the country? . . . To settle a principle is the answer — the principle of non-intervention, and the right of the people of the Territory to decide the question of slavery for themselves. Sir, there is no such principle. The Territories are the children of the States. They are minors, under age, and it is the business of the States, through their delegations in Congress, to take care of them until they are of age — until they are ripe for State government.' He argued that popular sovereignty was a sham because it 'extends only to the subject of slavery, and that only' (*Congressional Globe*, 33rd Congress, 1st Session, Appendix 560).

A typical Northern defence of Douglas comes from Senator English of Indiana. 'In voting for this bill, I do not vote to extend slavery. I do not vote to give it legal existence where it is not. The people of these Territories will never adopt the institution; but if they should, it is their fault and not mine — it is their right with which I cannot justly interfere any more than slave holders could interfere to force slavery into the community where I reside' (*Congressional Globe*, 33rd Congress, 1st Session, Appendix 609).

principle) was drowned by the conviction that this was a great betrayal, that the long established birthright of the free North to a free West was being bartered away in a dark conspiracy. But once the matter had been opened Douglas could hardly withdraw, for the Southerners were now in full cry after the measure and prepared to regard its passage as a matter of principle. Backed by the administration of Franklin Pierce the Kansas–Nebraska Act was forced through Congress; its consequences were disastrous for the Democratic party, for Kansas, and for the nation.[1]

It was never quite clear whether Douglas meant popular sovereignty to operate when the territory was ready for statehood (as in New Mexico) or when the first settlers had mustered sufficient numbers to form a territorial legislature. The first settlers on the ground were pro-slavery men from Missouri the Southerners and the Administration seized upon the latter interpretation.[2] First Pierce and then Buchanan held that the action of the first legislature in permitting slavery must bind the territory despite a growing number of anti-slavery settlers. Civil war broke out in Kansas between pro-slave and free with the latter setting up their own illegal government, but when the pro-slavery men presented a pro-slave constitution for admission as a state Buchanan attempted to force it upon Congress. This threw Douglas, who had always declared against legislating slavery into a territory where it was not desired by a majority of the inhabitants, into opposition and Kansas subsided into uneasy calm without statehood. The whole episode had been the kind of tragic

---

[1] 'I see a cloud, a little bigger now than a man's hand, gathering in the north, and in the west, and all around, and soon the whole northern heavens will be lighted up with a fire that you cannot quench. The indications of it are rife now in the heavens, and any man who is not blind can see it. There are meetings of the people in all quarters; they express their alarm, their dismay, their horror at the proposition which has been made here.... You of the South, all of you.... Do you not see that you are about to bring slavery and freedom face to face, to grapple for the victory, and that one or the other must die?' (Senator Ben Wade, Feb. 6, 1854. Speaking on the Kansas–Nebraska Bill, *Congressional Globe*, 33rd Congress, 1st Session, 340).

[2] Benton had pointed out that popular sovereignty in the territories and no decision by Congress on slavery must exaggerate dissension. 'This principle of non-intervention is but the principle of contention — a bone given to the people to quarrel and fight over at every election, and at every meeting of their Legislature, until they become a State government. Then, and only then, can they settle the question' (*Congressional Globe*, 33rd Congress, 1st Session, Appendix 560).

farce which can only occur when politicians lose grip with reality.

It was the Kansas–Nebraska question which provided the stimulus for the formation of the Republican party. Its success was explained by its concentration upon one point — prevention of the expansion of slavery — which happened to interest a great many people more than anything else. But the party also gained momentum because it provided a rallying point for many of those who had been dispossessed by the demise of the Whig party, for small businessmen restive under Southern rule, and for many minor groups of reforming tendencies. Conservative German settlers of the Mid-west and restive urban working men were equally attracted. The adhesion of these various groups and interests did not make the party forget its dominant aim, the containment of slavery. In its first Presidential Election it did not win but its candidate, Frémont, carried all the free states save five and in these he was a good second. A minor shift would give these five states to the Republicans and make a President — without a single vote from the South!

The readiness of President Buchanan to force a pro-slavery decision in Kansas may be explained by his knowledge — perhaps foreknowledge — of the Supreme Court's decision in the fateful case of *Dred Scott* v. *Sandford* which had been making its slow way through the courts since 1846. Dred Scott, a Negro, sued for his freedom on the ground that he had been taken by his master to live on soil where slavery was prohibited; on free soil he would probably have been freed by the state courts but having been brought back to the slave state of Missouri he began his suit there. In March 1857 the Supreme Court decided by a majority vote that a slave was not a citizen of the United States and could not therefore sue in the Federal courts; and that the Missouri Compromise, which prohibited a slaveholder from taking his property north of 36° 30′, being contrary to the fifth amendment — by which Congress could not deprive any person of his property without due process of law — was therefore invalid. The Missouri Compromise was already repealed but the Supreme Court now forbade Congress from prohibiting slavery anywhere in the

United States, and what stood against Congress stood against the territorial legislatures which derived their authority from Congress.

In 1846 it had been the South which raised the alarm against aggression by the Wilmot Proviso; in 1857 the South was well satisfied with the constitutional right to carry slavery into all the Territories of the United States and it was the turn of the North to be alarmed. Not only might the whole vast area west of the Mississippi be dedicated to slavery but it was confidently predicted that a further twist in constitutional interpretation might deny to free states the right to prohibit slavery. No one was more hardly hit by the Dred Scott decision than Douglas who had striven manfully to make popular sovereignty the bridge by which Southern and Mid-western interests might be joined; but popular sovereignty now lay in ruins. The rejoinder of Douglas was ingenious but laid up more trouble for himself: he now argued that while a territorial legislature could not prohibit slavery neither could it be forced to protect it. Slavery could not exist without a slave code, and if a territory refused to exercise its police power to make such a code it could effectively exclude slavery. This satisfied the Northern adherents of Douglas but it led the Southern extremists to demand a Federal slave code to protect a Federal right. Douglas had done more than any other man to earn the Democratic nomination to the Presidency and he came to the party convention in 1860 with the majority of Northern and Western delegates committed to him; but Southern extremists would not accept his nomination without a positive promise to give Federal protection to slavery in the Territories. When Douglas refused, many Southern delegates withdrew and later nominated their own candidate. The slavery question had driven remorselessly forward to disrupt the one remaining instrument of national union — the Democratic party — and with the party split, victory for the Republicans was certain.

*   *   *   *

One cannot understand the spirit of these years without realizing that there was madness in the air. On the Southern side this madness took the form of a withdrawal from reality. Though the cotton economy prospered in the 1850's and the development of railways and commercial institutions seemed at last to be taking a step forward, the Southerners lived in growing intellectual isolation from the rest of the world; for many of them imagination was bounded by the plantation or by the genteel culture of Charleston where Southern society seemed impregnable and Southern ideas unassailable. Those who contemplated secession — and an increasing number did so, though still a minority in 1860 — could not realize how weak a purely rural nation would be in an industrialized world. They could not understand that a society of primary producers, harnessed to industrial economies, must pay the price for economic well-being in a degree of dependence upon others. Implicit in the Southern madness were also the symbols of honour for which so many Southern gentlemen had died in duels. They would demand from the North not only tolerance and tacit connivance at what they believed to be wrong, but 'satisfaction' in the form of an explicit statement that wrong was right. Indeed the satisfaction could never be complete until Northerners declared from their pulpits, in their newspapers, and through their majority in Congress that slavery was divinely ordained for perpetuity; any qualification would be an insult to Southern Honour, as would also be any tolerance for abolitionist agitation. It was this withdrawal from reality and this exaggerated notion of honour which enabled the secessionists to take command in the South as anti-slavery victory became (by their own action) inevitable.

Northern madness was of a different form, less pervasive but more concentrated. It took the form of a monomania which regarded slave-ownership as a sin which outweighed all virtues. Ignoring the historical circumstances which had produced slavery and the perplexing problem of race relations, believing only the atrocity stories from the worst plantations and refusing to believe that master and slave relationships could ever be kindly and humane, the extreme abolitionists would sanction any means to attain their end. This fanaticism was demonstrated in its most violent form by the determination of John Brown, a patriarchal figure of Old Testament proportions, whose career in Kansas had been marked by the deliberate murder of five pro-slavery settlers, to strike a blow against the heart of slavery. His raid in 1859 on the small Virginian town of Harper's Ferry was intended to stimulate a slave revolt and to set on its way a tidal wave which would destroy slavery in America. As the armed prophet of abolitionism Brown was a failure; his raid was a fiasco, he was arrested, tried and hanged by the state of Virginia. As a symbol of Northern aggression, substantiated by the magnetic attraction which he had undoubtedly had for some high-minded abolitionists, he magnified Southern fears and confirmed them in their belief that an overthrow of Southern society was the real object of Northern policy. As the martyr dying on the scaffold for the sake of enslaved millions he transformed abolitionism from a creed for cranks into an heroic endeavour and it was no accident that his soul went marching on in the most famous of all soldier's songs.[1] The raid also took the conflict beyond the realm of constitutional argument into a phase in which any action which would relieve the tension might be welcome.

If John Brown represented Northern madness, Abraham Lincoln of Illinois seemed to speak for Northern sanity. With a Southern wife, Southern ancestry, and a conservative and conciliatory disposition no man was better fitted to bridge the sectional gulf. Yet Lincoln saw, what Calhoun had also seen, that a nation could not contain two separate societies. He saw also that it was slavery which made them different, and he saw what Calhoun had always refused to see — that the stronger society would not voluntarily relinquish its hold upon the Union, but would seek to impose its own way of life upon all. In a speech which became famous he declared that 'A house divided against itself cannot stand. I believe this government cannot endure

[1] 'I am not a little surprised at the easy effrontery with which political gentlemen, in and out of Congress, take it upon them to say that there are not a thousand men in the North who sympathize with John Brown. It would be far safer and nearer the truth to say that all people, in proportion to their sensibility and self-respect, sympathize with him. For it is impossible to see courage, and disinterestedness, and the love that casts out fear without sympathy' (R. W. Emerson, *Speech at Salem, Massachusetts*, Jan. 6, 1860).

permanently half slave and half free. I do not expect the Union to be dissolved; I do not expect the house to fall; but I do expect it will cease to be divided. It will become all one thing, or all the other.' Should the Union be, ultimately, all slave or all free? When the choice was expressed in this way only one answer could be given. Slavery was 'a moral, social, and political wrong' and it should be treated as a wrong 'and one of the methods of treating it as a wrong is to make provision that it shall grow no larger'. Thus Lincoln, who established a national reputation in 1858 when he contested the senatorial election in Illinois with Douglas, defined the Republican position. There was no constitutional power or political necessity to interfere with slavery where it existed, but slavery should not expand and was doomed to eventual extinction. Selected as the Republican candidate for President in 1860 he fought and won his campaign on this simple programme. He made it clear that the South had no cause for immediate alarm; but the South was right in seeing his election as a vote against slavery in the abstract, against its concrete expansion, and ultimately for a Union which would be all free.

That Lincoln was a great man none would deny, but it is sometimes difficult to believe that he was quite so great as Americans think him to have been. No hero of antiquity has a memorial so magnificent or so moving as that of Lincoln at Washington. Seated in a vast temple reached by a noble flight of steps the great brooding figure seems to epitomize both the dignity and the tragedy of human endeavour. For it is the tragedy in Lincoln which appeals as well as his achievement: the poor boy who sought to make himself a great public man, the small-town lawyer who aspired to the Presidency, the self-made man who reached the zenith of his ambition only to find himself confronted with problems which would have defeated the long-matured wisdom of ancient aristocracies; the harassed and inexperienced President, unsure of himself, of his subordinates, or even of the people whom he served, forced to make decisions which would determine the destiny of the nation and the life or death of thousands; the blundering war leader served by unimpressive generals,

Parties and Sectionalism 1848–1860

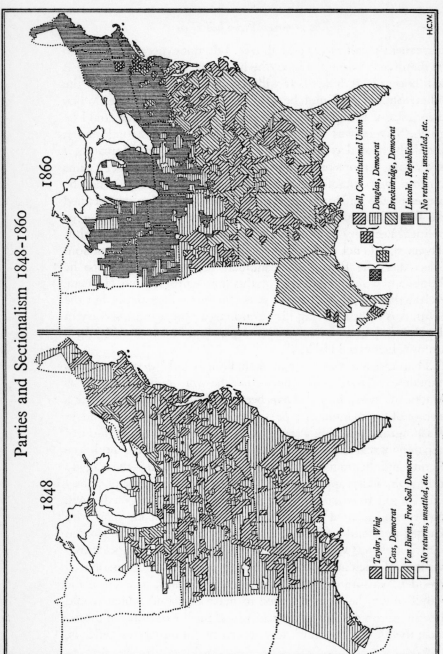

1860

1848

Taylor, Whig

Cass, Democrat

Van Buren, Free Soil Democrat

No returns, unsettled, etc.

Bell, Constitutional Union

Douglas, Democrat

Breckinridge, Democrat

Lincoln, Republican

No returns, unsettled, etc.

H.C.W.

1848: both major parties draw support from all parts of the nation.
1860: the Republicans get no support in the South; the Democrats are divided and the Northern Democrat (Douglas) gets little support in

enduring defeat yet refusing to relax his confidence and seeing the great war machine over which he presided gradually forge its way to victory; the man who believed in justice, humanity and tolerance forced to administer the harsh powers of a war-time government and to instigate the destruction of a society which he respected even while he rejected one of its fundamental institutions; the man of war yearning for the constructive tasks of peace, slain by a deranged creature at the moment of victory and in the hour when his depth of understanding might have contributed most to the future. Here is a man who seems to lie in the hands of a sinister and cynical destiny determined to expose the vanity of human wishes. Yet the greatness of Lincoln lies in the fact that while he seems to stand at the vortex of events there is never a doubt that he is meeting them with an extraordinary depth of wisdom. Nor is there ever a doubt that he stands for the ordinary human virtues of decency and forbearance combined with an adherence to principle. The symbolism of the great memorial at Washington is that America's man of destiny, in her most tragic hour, epitomized the virtues upon which the survival of civilization depends.

*　　*　　*　　*

The impact of Lincoln's election upon the South was certain to be profound, and by a cruel chance the initiative passed to the State of South Carolina where secessionists were most rabid and the withdrawal from reality was most complete. For secessionists the hour had now arrived; old men who had endured the humiliation of the nullification crisis, young men who had seen moderate men desert them when the compromises of 1850 gave new hope to the Union, ardent spirits who would risk all for honour, and prophets who saw Southern independence laid up in the storehouse of history, all rejoiced at the presentation of an unequivocal question: could South Carolina endure the rule of a Northern President and of a Northern majority elected upon a programme of hostility to slavery? One factor which distinguished the situation of 1860 from that of 1832 or 1850 was the near certainty that other states of the lower South would follow the initiative of

South Carolina. Though a majority of votes in the South had been cast for those who believed in the maintenance of the Union in some form or other, the secessionists knew what they wanted, and were strong in high places; the Unionists were uncertain in their aims, demoralized by the course of events, and had their main voting strength in the more remote hill regions. This expectation was fulfilled; when the convention in South Carolina unanimously decided to secede from the Union, six other states followed suit and early in 1861 created a new political association, the Confederate States of America. So was accomplished 'the glorious act of secession, which is to make the Southern States the greatest people under the sun, and South Carolina the greatest state of them all'. Rhett, one of the keenest advocates of secession, imagined an historian of A.D. 2000 writing of the Southerners throwing off oppression, 'and in extending their empire across this continent to the Pacific, and down through Mexico to the other side of the great gulf and over the isles of the sea they established an empire and wrought out a civilization which has never been equalled or surpassed — a civilization teeming with orators, poets, philosophers, statesmen and historians equal to those of Greece and Rome — and presented to the world the glorious spectacle of a free, prosperous and illustrious people.'[1] In this manner self-deception became a way of life.

* * * *

The fact of secession created a new situation. Once it had taken place the argument over slavery and its extension was succeeded by the yet more momentous question of the character and destiny of the United States. Men who would never have fought to end slavery would fight to save the Union; men who would never have fought to defend slavery would now fight for the right of a people to establish their independence. And was it only the future of America which was at stake? Lincoln enlarged the question to see in it the whole future of democratic government: if a legally

[1] The first extract is quoted by Harold S. Schultz, *Nationalism and Sectionalism in South Carolina*, Duke University Press, 230, from a contemporary South Carolinian newspaper; the second by Allan Nevins, *The Emergence of Lincoln*, II, Scribner's, 334.

constituted majority was to be defied as soon as its decisions were unpalatable to a minority, then government by the people could not endure. When the ground for offence was not policy but the choice of a government this applied with even more force, and the failure of a Constitution — which even the secessionists agreed was the best in the world — meant the failure of the constitutional and democratic experiments upon which the nineteenth century had embarked. Against this it might be asked what meaning could be attached to the proposition that government derived its just powers from the consent of the governed if consent could not be withheld.

Four possibilities followed upon the fact of secession: the North might recognize secession, the North might attempt to coerce the seceding states to rejoin the Union, the South might then hold a defensive position long enough to compel recognition of its independence, or the North might win in the armed conflict and then be confronted with the problem of subduing and conciliating a rebellious people. In the North there was some support for the recognition of secession; years before some abolitionists had favoured the expulsion of slave states from the Union and in 1861 many more moderate men were prepared 'to let the erring sisters go in peace'.[1] Against this the plan of coercion was favoured by the emotional attachment to the Union and by material interests which would be damaged by its disruption. The Mid-western states would not readily contemplate the existence of a foreign power in the lower Mississippi valley and business interests, which had, on the whole, been conciliatory towards the South, now regarded with disquiet the loss of markets, opportunities and invested capital.

On the Southern side not all was guided by emotion. The possibility that the South could gain its objectives even without great victories was apparent, and most Southerners expected victories. The formation of a new Southern Union among the seceded states — to be known as the Confederate States of

---

[1] The phrase was coined by Horace Greeley, the celebrated Republican editor of the *New York Tribune*.

America — meant that the North would be opposed by a new power which would rapidly develop the attributes of nationality and the bonds of loyalty. It would be a war for Southern independence and the Confederacy could draw to itself sentiment similar to that which supported and inspired the struggles of subject nationalities in Europe. Moreover the fact of coercion would almost certainly add to the Confederacy some or all of the border states and in particular the key state of Virginia where states' rights was still a living creed. In all, the prospect of Southern independence even in the face of Northern coercion was good. But even Northern victory in a coercive war would leave unsolved the problems which had occasioned it, and a defeated South might still extract from the North a large measure of autonomy which might extend even to a separate government within the formal bonds of Union. As in the North, personal ambition and material calculation contributed towards the decision. Politicians envisaged a wider scope and new opportunities; planters felt that they would get a better deal if the Northern intermediaries between Europe and themselves were removed; merchants believed that secession might improve their status from agent to principal.

The American Constitution laid down that a President elected in November was not inaugurated until March. The immediate responsibility for dealing with secession rested therefore with the repudiated President Buchanan. It is possible that an immediate appeal to force, following the precedent set by Andrew Jackson in 1832, might have frightened enough Southerners to wreck the secession movement; but it was more likely to throw the border states into the arms of the Confederacy and precipitate conflict. In 1832 Jackson had had to deal with one state and had been able to play upon a very real attachment to Union throughout the South; in 1861 Buchanan had to deal with a new political power which grew daily in strength. There was no easy solution and Buchanan has perhaps received more than his fair share of blame for the policy which he pursued. He refused either to recognize secession or to take active steps to combat it; he continued to take advice from Southern sympathizers and refused to throw himself wholly upon the North; he hoped — and the hope was not altogether impracticable — to allow time for passions to cool, to rally the Union sentiment which was still strong in the Southern states, and to avoid counter-measures which would inevitably make the breach permanent. In a rational world Buchanan's policy might have had some success, but in the mad world of 1861 it allowed the Confederacy to build up its strength, seize Federal arsenals in the South, organize government, and generally to prepare for the conflict which they expected Lincoln to begin unless he could be deterred from doing so by a show of superior force.

The decision rested upon Lincoln. In the months before inauguration he instructed Republicans to refuse any compromise proposals which included the territorial expansion of slavery; after inauguration he faced the bitter realities of power. Though the government of the United States was one of separate powers it was upon the executive alone that the decision rested, to take or to avoid actions which might precipitate or avert the conflict. Executive responsibility was emphasized by the peculiar situation which had developed by March 1861, for the whole problem of relations between the National Government and the Confederacy had become concentrated upon the fate of a tiny island in the mouth of Charleston harbour. On this island was Fort Sumter, garrisoned by a handful of Federal troops. If the island were surrendered to the state authorities this would symbolize acceptance of secession as a *fait accompli*; if retained it would stand as representative of Federal authority in a position where it could command the Confederacy's second port. Was South Carolina a sovereign state, was the Confederacy an independent government? These were the questions which hung upon the decision to hold or abandon Fort Sumter.

The new President was inexperienced, regarded by his detractors as a figure of fun, and beset by all the problems of a new party anxious to enjoy the spoils of office. Most people knew of him only his humble origins, his vote-getting capacity among Western farmers, and certain publicized speeches which were characterized by directness and simplicity rather than by the florid oratory favoured in that age. Lincoln's strength of character, his masterly opportunism, and his underlying idealism were as yet hidden from the public. Against the advice of a majority of his cabinet Lincoln decided to send provisions to Fort Sumter which would enable the garrison to subsist without supplies from the mainland. It has never been decided whether this decision was an ill-considered compromise or a masterly move to throw the onus of decision upon the South. No action was taken against the South, yet this fragmentary reminder of lawful authority would be kept in being and could be displaced only by armed force. If a bait had been offered it was taken by South Carolina; Sumter was bombarded and surrendered, the secessionist forces had been used against the flag of the Union, Lincoln was able to declare that an insurrection existed and to call for troops to subdue it. It is probably incorrect to infer that Lincoln had set a trap for the Confederates with the intention of bringing on the war; yet any statesman who believes that war may come has a duty to ensure that its immediate occasion will unite rather than divide his own people. By ensuring that the Confederacy would be forced either to accept a symbol of Federal authority or to fire upon the flag of the United States Lincoln set a course which must strengthen Northern morale whatever happened. In the event no sequence of events could have had a more stimulating effect upon Northern opinion; beyond any doubt the Southerners had shown their intention of destroying the Union and against this threat Northerners rallied as they would have done against foreign invasion. Yet the price was also high; Lincoln's call to arms was immediately followed by the secession of Virginia, North Carolina, Tennessee and Arkansas.[1]

* * * *

[1] The dilemma of patriotic Virginians received its supreme illustration in the case of Robert E. Lee. He had earned distinction as a soldier of the United States and in April 1861 was offered command of the Union armies; he refused and subsequently became the leading General of the Confederacy. He had written in 1856 that 'In this enlightened age there are few, I believe, but will acknowledge that slavery as an institution is a moral and political evil in any country'. In January 1861 he wrote, 'I can anticipate no greater calamity for the country than a dissolution of the Union. It would be an accumulation of all the evils we complain of, and I am willing to sacrifice everything but honour for its pre-servation. . . . Secession is nothing but revolution.' In April he wrote, 'In my own person

The wisdom of the decision to treat secession as rebellion will long be debated. The subsequent greatness of the United States, the fact that its territory has not become divided among several nations, and the emancipation of the slaves provided powerful arguments in support of Lincoln. Against this may be set the heavy casualties (over 600,000 dead from the two armies), the failure to solve the race problem, and the bitter feelings which long outlived the war and are ever ready to revive. It may well be argued that the South, freed from Northern pressure, would have soon been led to abolish slavery in conformity with the rest of the world, and that the subsequent history of the American Negro would have been happier than it has been. It is possible that the lapse of time would have produced an atmosphere in which reunion would have become feasible, just as the intensity of local autonomy had given way in 1787; the victory of the secessionists in 1861 was the product of circumstances and many Southerners would have gladly returned in calmer times to the Union which Southerners had so largely helped to make. The war which was begun had to be long if the North was to be victorious and victory could not solve the problems which had occasioned it. The secession of the border states gave to the Confederacy a very considerable increase in manpower and resources, included the areas on which Southern military defence was later to hinge, and greatly improved, both psychologically and strategically, the Southern chances of survival.

At its most favourable interpretation therefore Lincoln's decision saved the Union, preserved America from the rampant nationalism of Europe, and ensured the future greatness of the United States. Seen in its worst light it precipitated a war which caused immense suffering, discredited the American experiment in government, attempted to remedy by force problems which could only be solved if men recovered their calm, and drove millions to reluctant repudiation of the Union.

I had to meet the question whether I should take part against my native state. With all my devotion to the Union and the feeling of loyalty and duty of an American citizen, I have not been able to make up my mind to raise my hand against my relatives, my children, my home.'

[6]

The Civil War and its Aftermath

Military history does not lend itself readily to summary. The details are too important and the bald account of strategic factors flatters too much the prescience of the victors. A search for lucidity must exclude muddle, and muddle is an inevitable part of war. It is true that modern warfare often seems to make the battlefield ancillary to the resources, administration and morale of the belligerent nations. The day has passed in which a weak power could defeat a strong one in a single battle, because a large and industrial nation can repair losses, throw in new supplies, and raise new armies; but mass and mobility carry their own weaknesses because mouths have to be fed, men armed, and communications preserved. If the cumbrous machinery of war can mitigate the consequences of tactical defeat it can also prevent the exploitation of success, and amid an organization of unparalleled complexity success is often the reward of improvisation. War is still a contest of skill, resourcefulness and courage, but it is no longer fought as a tournament but as a struggle between peoples in which every factor counts.

The American Civil War was a modern war, but many, particularly in the South, thought of it as a tournament, believed that the great victory could win the war, and hoped that victories could be won by the heroism of massed infantry and the skill of brilliant leaders. If this type of warfare could have succeeded the Confederates would have won the war. Until the battle of Antietam on September 17, 1862 the South won all the great battles, but at the end of this period the Northern armies outnumbered the Southern, were better clad, better armed, and had the resources of a great industrial state behind them. The supreme tactical skill and dominant personality of Robert E. Lee prolonged the struggle far beyond the point at which Northern superiority began to tell, but the heroism of the Confederates in their latter days merely extended the war to a point at which Northern supremacy was so overwhelming that total defeat was inevitable.

The management of the industrial-military machine of the North was not however so efficient that it might not have been thrown out of gear at an early stage. The South did not have to conquer territory in order to win its independence; the North would have to occupy and subdue. It is not surprising that many in the South went optimistically into the war, and that many in the North doubted that it could ever be won. Anything short of complete victory would make it impossible for the North to attain its objective, the preservation of the Union; anything short of complete defeat might leave the South with independence. And if a military stalemate developed the South might well expect the intervention of foreign powers, of France and of England, who for various reasons would not be sorry to see the United States partitioned and the control of the cotton trade wrested from Northern hands. In the early stages of the war the South was therefore likely to achieve its objectives if it could persuade the North that it could not win, and foreigners that an independent South would be an asset. This the South nearly achieved.

The first battle of Bull Run (July 21, 1861) taught the North not to expect a quick victory. The battle of Antietam ended the Southern hopes of winning the war. The campaign of Gettysburg and the attack on Vicksburg (both concluded on July 4, 1863) ensured ultimate victory for the North. Sherman's capture of Atlanta (September 2, 1864) and Grant's persistence in Virginia, despite great losses and Lee's tactical superiority, ended the Southern chance of a negotiated peace. Each of these great events owed much to chance and personality. Bull Run was almost a Federal victory and was turned to defeat by Stonewall Jackson's stand. Lee was within sight of victory at Antietam, and Gettysburg was decisive, apparently because the Federal troops showed unexpected determination in the face of Southern attacks, but really because Lee had risked too much without reserves, with inadequate supplies, and with a threatened line of communications. Vicksburg was Grant's own success won by a bold movement which few commanders would have attempted. Sherman's march through the South was again a personal triumph which owed something to Confederate errors. Would the outcome of the war have been different if the Confederates and not the Federals had been routed at Bull Run; if Lee had prevailed at Antietam, if the Federal lines had broken at Gettysburg or if Meade had pursued Lee after that battle; if Sherman had stayed in Tennessee or if Grant had withdrawn after the terrible losses which he suffered in the final campaign in Virginia? These battles certainly altered the timing of the war, but, provided that the Northern will to fight was sustained it is improbable that an agrarian state with few industries and a smaller population could ever have achieved permanent victory against the North. The proviso was important. Grant's great contribution as a military leader was his realization that a populous and industrialized nation could not lose if it did not falter. Between May and June 1864 Grant lost 18,000 men in the Wilderness, 12,000 at Spotsylvania, 12,000 at Cold Harbor, 8,000 at Petersburg and 10,000 in minor engagements. A greater general would have avoided such casualties, a lesser man would have retired. Grant remained where he was before Petersburg and so demonstrated that success in the field could not give victory to the South.

While the history of the Civil War tends to concentrate upon the military episodes, the naval and diplomatic war was almost as important. Unlike the officers of the army most of those in the navy remained loyal to the Union and from the first the North had naval superiority which was only shaken temporarily when the South, driven by necessity, evolved an ironclad ship capable of breaking through the wooden Federal fleet. The paucity of good harbours in the South made it comparatively easy to establish a blockade, and command of the sea made possible the amphibious operations which captured New Orleans at an early stage in the war. The South hoped that this blockade would rebound upon the North by rousing the hostility of European nations starved of cotton and markets for manufactures.[1] Mid-western wheat was however almost as important as cotton and the Northern consumer market was much more important than that of the South. The emotional sympathy of mid-Victorian Englishmen for nations struggling to be free was clouded by the fact of slavery; the upper classes were divided though predominantly sympathetic to the South, the middle classes were generally sympathetic to the North save where they had strong material interests in Southern victory, the working classes identified the Northern cause as that of radical democracy. More realistically it was seen that intervention in favour of the South could only be effective if backed with naval force, and by the commitment of a major force to the defence of Canada at a time when the British army was small and widely dispersed. No vital British interest demanded such an effort. The French might have been more disposed to give immediate aid, but would not act without Great Britain, and preferred to use the opportunity of breaking through the Monroe doctrine and launching an adventure in Mexico. The European powers would not even recognize the Confederacy as a belligerent power. Thus the South was isolated economically by the blockade, and diplomatically by converging forces which can be traced back to the superior resources and moral appeal of the North.

*   *   *   *

The long period of Federal reverses (July 1861–September 1862) imposed problems of political leadership of a formidable character. Lincoln had to work out the implications of his constitutional authority as Commander-in-Chief during a great war, to hold a delicate balance between the enthusiastic and the reluctant supporters of the war, and to assume executive powers which alarmed even those who sympathized with his objectives. As late as the summer of 1862 there were a great many Northerners

[1] Southern confidence in the power of 'King Cotton' was such that, in the first year of the war, the Confederate Government prohibited the export of cotton in the hope that Great Britain would be forced to intervene.

who believed secretly or openly that Southern independence must be recognized, and as late as 1864 there were many who argued for a negotiated peace because victory could not hope to solve the problems posed by the clash. At all times there were those who argued, from both sides of the fence, that the war was a failure because it had been so badly conducted. Lincoln's great strength lay in his conviction that the justice of his cause must lead to eventual victory. For Lincoln the war had been fought to preserve the Union, which meant the triumph of sane and ordered government over disruptive and anti-democratic tendencies which must reduce the American nation to a collection of weak and quarrelsome states manipulated by European powers. Lincoln's handicap was lack of military experience, which made it difficult for him either to organize victory or to present a coherent explanation for the necessary delays and early reverses. Nor did Lincoln find it easy to impress contemporaries with his aims and purpose; in retrospect Lincoln's appreciation of the meaning of the Union and of its future seems just and realistic; to contemporaries it often seemed abstract and speculative, to offer too many imponderables and an insufficient number of clearly expressed objectives. The age in which Italy and Ireland, Hungary and Poland were struggling to be free was not conducive to the philosophy of the great state. The preservation of the Union had to be supplemented by more tangible aims such as the abolition of slavery and the overthrow of the Southern ruling class, identified as the enemy of democracy. Lincoln had always believed that slavery was wrong and must end, but he had not gone to war to abolish slavery and he was reluctant to introduce it as a war aim at a late stage; nor, as a conservative statesman, did he wish to precipitate a social revolution with unpredictable consequences. He came to accept the emancipation of slaves as a military necessity reinforced by abstract justice; he never accepted the need for any radical change in the structure of Southern society, and as he looked forward to the reconstruction of the Union this conservatism became more and more apparent.

As a military leader Lincoln began with an inadequate appreciation of his role. In a modern war the civilian command should determine overall strategy, organize the nation for war, ensure that the armies in the field are supplied, pick the military chiefs and interfere as little as possible in minor strategy and individual commands. Lincoln committed most of the mistakes which could be made. In the early days he interfered too much with commanders in the field, failed to organize the nation for a long war, hovered unpredictably in the choice of generals and in the support which he gave to them. His relations with the ablest of his early generals were uniformly unfortunate. McClellan was an annoying man but he was a good soldier who appreciated the disastrous consequences of over-reaching Federal strength in the initial stages of the conflict, realized that training and preparation were more important than combat in the first months, and achieved wonders in making an efficient army out of the raw levies which had already experienced a major defeat at Bull Run. He was also popular with his troops. What more could be required of a general? Fully supported, McClellan might have won the war through his Peninsular campaign, and, even without the troops he had expected, his withdrawal inflicted crippling losses on the Confederates. The men with whom he had to share responsibility or by whom he was supplanted — Pope, Burnside and Hooker — all met crushing disaster, and he was able to stop the most hopeful of all Confederate counter-offensives at Antietam. Yet what McClellan failed to deliver was the decisive victory which Lincoln and the Northern people so ardently desired, and mutual recrimination developed between President and General. By contrast Lincoln's relations with Grant in the later stages of the war were a model of those between the civil and military command. Undeterred by Grant's heavy losses and disappointingly slow progress in Virginia Lincoln organized victory behind the lines, resisted ignorant criticism, and did not interfere with the campaign in the field.

In dealing with his political problems Lincoln was throughout more successful. He showed himself a master of his government, played off the various political elements with masterly skill, and impressed the country with the slow wisdom which was his abiding strength. Chief criticism came from the group of extreme anti-slavery or radical Republicans, led by Charles Sumner and Thaddeus Stevens, who represented the same impulse for middle-class reform which found its English outlet in Gladstonian liberalism. Posterity has not been kind to the radicals yet it is still hard to resist their contention that the war was not being handled efficiently and that the end of slavery must become one of its objectives; in the emotional atmosphere of war they offered action and idealism in place of confusion and caution. They also appealed to the inbred suspicion of executive power in their attempt to seize the initiative for Congress. As early as December 1861 they set up a Joint Congressional Committee on the Conduct of the War and a year later tried to force a dismissal of the Cabinet ministers (accused of being moderate, half-hearted or inefficient) and their replacement by sound radicals. Lincoln was well aware of the deficiencies of some of his ministers, but he was also aware that an outright radical policy might alienate more support than it gained and would render more difficult the subsequent restoration of the Union. Yet the radicals pressed him hard and support for their policies increased in the country. The crucial question was the future of slavery. Lincoln had begun by offering the South a constitutional amendment which would have guaranteed slavery in the states; he still insisted that slavery was subordinate to the security of the Union.[1] Three slave states — Maryland, Delaware, and Kentucky — remained in the Union, and a fourth, Missouri, was won for the Union by a local civil war. Lincoln

---

[1] Compare the following:
  Lincoln to Horace Greeley, Aug. 22, 1862. 'I would save the Union. I would save it the shortest way under the Constitution. The sooner the National authority can be restored, the nearer the Union will be "the Union as it was." If there be those who would not save the Union unless they could at the same time *save* slavery, I do not agree with them. If there be those who would not save the Union unless they could at the same time *destroy* Slavery, I do not agree with them. My paramount object in this struggle *is* to save the Union, and it is *not* either to save or destroy Slavery. If I could save the Union without freeing *any* slave I would do it; and if I could do it by freeing *all* the slaves I would do it; and if I could do it by freeing some and leaving others alone, I would also do that.'
  Charles Sumner to the Duchess of Argyll, April 7, 1863. 'Remember . . . I am no idolater of the Union; I have never put our cause on this ground. But I hate slavery. . . .' (*Memoirs and Letters of C.S.*, ed. Pierce, Vol. IV, 133.)

argued unsuccessfully for voluntary emancipation in these states, and without agreement on this point he was reluctant to commit himself to a war aim which might antagonize many Union supporters. Yet against this he had to balance the growing support for the belief that slavery was the root of all evil, while emancipation would probably confirm the sympathy given by European liberals to the Northern cause. And as portions of the Confederacy passed under military rule the treatment of the slaves and their possible enlistment as soldiers became important. On January 1, 1863 he moved at last with the celebrated Emancipation Proclamation, which freed no slaves, did not apply to the loyal slave states, exempted the areas under Federal military control, and was confined to those areas in rebellion against the United States. Yet with all its qualifications it meant that emancipation was now a war aim and that Federal troops would free slaves as they advanced. Whatever the appearances nothing could ever be quite the same again and slavery was doomed if the Union were saved.[1]

Men and money have been the perennial problems of modern war. At the outset the North had to contend with the problem of supplementing an insignificant regular army, which had lost many of the best officers, and with a fiscal system which had been carefully designed to keep central authority short of cash. The traditional military organization of the United States was based on the state militia, raised and trained by the states and led by state appointed officers (with junior officers elected by the men). The transference of these state troops to Federal command could, in theory at least, be accomplished only by the voluntary act of the men concerned. The first call was for a three months engagement, and a part of the rash urgency which led to the disaster of Bull

[1] 'It is by no means necessary that this measure should be suddenly marked by any signal results on the Negroes or on the Rebel masters. The force of this act is that it commits the country to this justice, — that it compels the innumerable officers, civil, military, naval, of the Republic to range themselves on the line of this equity. It draws the fashion to this side. It is not a measure that admits of being taken back. Done, it cannot be undone by a new administration. For slavery overpowers the disgust of the moral sentiment only through immemorial usage. It cannot be introduced as an improvement of the nineteenth century. This act makes that the lives of our heroes have not been sacrificed in vain.' (R. W. Emerson, *Address delivered in Boston in September 1862*.) (The passage refers to the preliminary proclamation which gave warning of the formal promulgation of Emancipation on Jan. 1, 1863.)

L

Run was explained by the imminent withdrawal from service of many state troops. An extension of the period to nine months did not greatly improve the stability of an army so raised. In 1863 this problem was met by the typically modern expedient of conscription, but the obligation to serve could be avoided by a payment of $300 or by finding a substitute; the resentment of the poor at a system, which virtually imposed upon them the sole responsibility of fighting, led to serious discontent, and at one of the supreme crises of the war, in the weeks after Gettysburg, troops had to be sent to New York to deal with anti-draft riots. Later conscription acts were more equitable, but their most important effect was in bolstering the morale of the volunteers who continued to supply the bulk of the fighting troops. In finance the United States were driven to the inevitable expedient of an irredeemable paper currency which combined with war demands on industry and agriculture to produce a great increase in prices. Wages lagged behind profits and prices, and a good deal of the financial burden of the war thus fell indirectly upon labour, while manufacturers and farmers reaped large rewards. Heavy government borrowing left wealthy men with a vested interest in victory, and in the restoration of money to its face value. Like later wars the Civil War helped to precipitate a social revolution, but the beneficiaries were not the wage labourers but the middle-class entrepreneurs. In a nation where the majority of the people were still small property owners, and where their political influence was even greater than their numerical predominance, it was they and not the working classes which the government was forced to conciliate as a part of the price for victory.

The difficulties experienced by the North were felt in exaggerated form by the South. To an even greater extent united effort was prejudiced by state autonomy, and Jefferson Davis proved himself too rigid, too unimaginative, and too preoccupied with trivialities to make a successful war leader. In Robert E. Lee the South had a general who will ever be honoured as a soldier and a man, but Davis, who had been a most successful administrator as Secretary of War, interfered too much and too often without being able to impose any grand strategic plan or to organize the home front efficiently. Though morale and the rate of voluntary enlistment ran very high at the opening of the war, the South was driven first to conscription in April 1862; as in the North the burden fell mainly upon the poorer classes, and though administered by the Confederate government its operation was riddled with fraud and evasion. Even so a higher proportion of Southern manpower was placed in the army, and foreign observers, perplexed by the apparent lack of discipline among the soldiers, were generally agreed upon their superb fighting qualities. Heavy recruitment and the use of an unusually large number of troops in the front line was made possible by the employment of slaves on the farms and in non-combatant military duties. The maintenance of an army in the field was however often beyond the resources of the country. Ragged, often without boots, and with their kit reduced to the minimum, the Confederate troops seemed a vagabond army sustained only by their morale. From the start the Confederacy was handicapped by lack of money. Paper currency was issued lavishly and depreciated rapidly. While the fortunes of Northern entrepreneurs were being established by the war, the old Southern ruling class put its accumulated savings into government loans which were to be entirely lost after defeat. Only a few speculators and blockade runners made money. In the first year much of the cotton crop was voluntarily withheld from the market in the vain hope of putting pressure upon foreign customers, and thereafter the Northern blockade clamped down on the cotton ports, while the price of imports rose far beyond the level to which any Federal tariff had ever raised them. Thus in the Confederacy the expedients of modern war impoverished the people and helped to ruin the old gentry without raising a new ruling class to take their place.

*　　*　　*　　*

Nothing in Southern errors seemed quite to justify the final tragedy of Confederate collapse. While Southern mythology continues to paint a picture of a heroic nation enduring the final agony of defeat with fortitude and with a glorious devotion to the cause which all now recognized to be lost, the reality saw a demoralization which was even more tragic. With its railway system in ruins, the supply system of the armies disrupted beyond repair, with food shortages growing daily more acute both among soldiers and in the towns, with a growing dissatisfaction with the central government and state particularism becoming more obstructive and less rational, and with desertions from the army rising to more than half the paper strength, Southerners could look forward only to humiliation. The refusal of Jefferson Davis to consider any terms which did not recognize Southern independence was magnificent but had lost touch with reality. Lee, with a dwindling and half-starved army hemmed in by vastly superior forces, felt the imminence of a disaster which could only inflict further suffering on the South. On April 9, 1865, he agreed to meet Grant to discuss terms for surrender at Appomattox Courthouse. The two men — Lee still splendid in full uniform, Grant in an untidy private's tunic — spoke as old friends rather than as enemies. Grant's terms were simple and generous: officers and men to go home on parole, those who claimed a horse to take it with them, arms to be surrendered except the swords of officers. Coming from the meeting the taciturn Grant delivered a short rebuke to cheering Union soldiers, which marks the zenith of his own career as a soldier and as a man: 'The war is over; the rebels are our countrymen again.'

A month earlier in his second inaugural Lincoln had spoken famous words in the same spirit: 'With malice toward none; with charity for all, with firmness in the right as God gives us to see the right, let us strive on to finish the work we are in, to bind up the nation's wounds, to care for him who shall have borne the battle and for his widow and his orphan, to do all which may achieve and cherish a just and lasting peace among ourselves and with all nations.' A few days before Appomattox Jefferson Davis was speaking in a different vein: 'I will never consent to abandon to the enemy one foot of the soil of any one of the states of the Confederacy.... If by stress of numbers we should ever be compelled to a temporary withdrawal from her limits ... again and again will we return, until the baffled and exhausted enemy shall abandon in despair his endless and impossible task of making slaves of a people resolved to be free.' The bitterness can be understood yet deplored; whatever the passions of war it was now certain that Southerners would have to acknowledge once more the same flag as the North, and it would have been better for the future of the Southern people to match in defeat the magnanimity of Lincoln and Grant; but the words of Davis underlined how far from solution was the fundamental problem of reconciling the people to an allegiance which they had repudiated and for which they could feel no affection. Five days after Appomattox Lincoln was dead, killed by a fanatical Southern sympathizer, within a month Jefferson Davis was a harmless prisoner. Could a new generation of leaders find a better cure for the sickness of the nation than the men who had chosen war?

*   *   *   *

Who had won the war? What had been lost? The radical Republicans had won: they had achieved emancipation, the overthrow of the Southern ruling class and an open door for business enterprise. New England had won: her ideals had triumphed over the rival system of the South and her sons had won the battle for the West. Northern capitalism had won: freed from the obstruction of a landed gentry and enormously stimulated by the war it looked forward to an age of unexampled prosperity. The small settler and migrant seemed to have won with the recognition, in the Homestead Act of 1862, of the citizen's right to free land in the West. The reformist urge had won and everywhere reformers — from temperance advocates to spokesmen of labour — looked forward to the realization of their aims. The Union had won and with it the sense of future greatness based on Union; the principle of majority rule had won; the idea that a republic could never defeat its internal enemies had been refuted.

An assessment of the losses is necessarily confused by the entanglement of myth with reality. The indefinable attraction of a lost cause, combined with the search for justification in the post-war South, casts upon the screen a picture which became ever more mellow, more attractive and more pure. The paradox of Southern society had lain in the combination of an inhuman labour system with a respect for human values. Between master and slave the certainty of status permitted the growth of real affection and a kindly give and take. Between great planter and small farmer the lack of incentive for economic exploitation had allowed a sense of equality which was none the less real because it seemed to contradict the class distinctions which everyone recognized. Southern society had had its sombre side: it had brutal masters, desperately unhappy slaves, wretched fugitives from the plantations, sadistic overseers, guilt-ridden sexual association between white and black, ignorant and petty-minded small farmers, degenerate poor whites; it had unnecessary duels, knifing, gouging, violence, degradation and disease. All this had delighted the abolitionists and filled the pages of their publications; what they missed was that, in practice, much was redeemed because the South judged men by their personality rather than by their use, by their leisure as much as by their work, by their human value more than by their material success. Southern chivalry had stood for something more potent than its absurdities and gracious living had meant something more than an advertiser's slogan. All this was however so tenuous — climatic rather than structural — that it could be explained only by myths which were patently unreal except to those who believed in them because they had no other means of restoring their dignity.

The war relieved the South of an incubus to which it would have clung with all tenacity. It has been argued that slavery was economically unsound and that it would have withered away without the drastic surgery of war. This view is difficult to accept. While the redundant slave was a problem in Virginia, and many masters had preferred to support unprofitable servants from the cradle to the grave rather than deal with the slave trader, the cotton plantations in the South had been insistent in their demands for labour, and it had been difficult to see how the hard and unpleasant work on the plantations could be obtained without coercion. Southern planters were well aware of what had happened in Jamaica where emancipation had been followed by a flight to the hills and a drift to the towns. Nor was it easy, in the Southern environment, to see where the free Negro could find a place. Yet slavery had, to an increasing extent, cut off the South from the rest of the civilized world. In retrospect the best and most intelligent of the Southerners realized this, and slavery passed away with far fewer regrets than might have been anticipated. What men had always feared became almost welcome once it had been forced upon them. Negro equality was however another and more fearful question which loomed in the future.

The United States had lost more than most Americans care to admit. With all their faults the Southern gentry had stood for integrity and principle in public life. It is hard to imagine the pre-war Southern leaders conniving at the scandals which disgraced Congress and Federal government in the late nineteenth century. If their concept of government had been negative it had also been as pure as one could expect in an imperfect world. The Northern and Mid-western concept of politics was liable to degenerate into a scramble for public favours which became orderly only through extensive log-rolling. There is a strong supposition that Southerners would have stood out against the politics of the tariff, of railway land grants, of the appropriations grab, and much as they had disliked the Homestead Bill they might have ensured that it worked equitably.

The departure of the Southerners from the centre of the national stage left a void which it was difficult to fill. They had provided the nucleus around which official life had revolved; in the government service, in successive cabinets, and in the judiciary, they had filled a majority of the positions and had imparted to national life an easy and gentlemanly standard which had offset crude self-seeking, rotation in office and the spoils system. The stability of the social system from which they emerged had fitted them admirably for public life; if they had not always been wise they had provided dignified leadership, and it was leadership which the nation now lacked. There were several competitors for the role of a new *élite*, but none spoke with the voice of accustomed authority or commanded general respect. The radical Republicans, emerging from the war with prestige and popular backing, lacked the momentum which would carry them beyond the achievement of their immediate objectives, represented no great economic interest, and their attempts to prolong the situation, which had earned them their power, eventually rebounded upon them. The professional politicians, soon to be known by the generic term of 'spoilsmen', were strong in their control of the Republican party machinery but lacked prestige and their attempt to capitalize radical idealism offended by its cynicism. The rising generation of businessmen were too preoccupied and too unaccustomed to the burden of public responsibility. It may be doubted whether even Lincoln could have mastered this situation and gathered around him men who would look forward from disaster to a constructive future. His untimely death accentuated the weaknesses which led to a political degeneration bringing public life to its lowest point in the national history. It is not that all men in public life were rogues; indeed a reading of political biography of the period leads one to believe that the majority were honest and served the nation according to their lights; but these lights were dim in an era of weak leadership which often relied upon the worst rather than the best. This crisis of leadership was at the heart of all the political troubles which followed and provoked a *malaise* from which the United States has not yet wholly recovered. Government without a ruling class is not necessarily bad government, but it does offer problems which cry for solution; these problems the United States were ready neither to solve nor even to face.

The Northern society which had won the war moved with all the tidal currents of the nineteenth century; it honoured and pursued ideals while writing avarice into the canon of Christian virtues, it paid equal deference to saints and to self-made men, it believed in universal improvement and in the survival of the fittest, it saw no contradiction between unlimited competition and the brotherhood of man. This jumble of beliefs and aspirations was well suited to the life of a diversified and expansive society but proved a poor guide for the reconstruction of the simpler and sadly stricken society of the South. It is useless to blame individuals; indeed those most usually blamed, the radical Republicans, formed the most high-minded group to control national affairs since the end of the eighteenth century. Their favourite aims — racial equality, representative democracy, and the overthrow of privilege — are today enshrined in the central canon of Western liberal civilization. The need for scapegoats may be satisfied by picturing them as malignant fools for having insisted that the fighting would have been in vain if it did not lead to a better society, but justice will not be served.

* * * *

The Civil War had had the characteristics of a war between nations and of a rebellion. The war had been fought to deny that there could be a separate government for the South and it was therefore impossible for the victor to follow the normal precedents for ending wars between nations by treating with a provisional government.[1] Neither was it possible to treat millions of people covering a vast area as though they were no more than rebellious subjects. Moreover, if the objectives of the war had been correctly stated the Southern states must now resume their normal places in the Union, they must send representatives to Washington, participate in Presidential elections, enjoy their share of Federal appointments, and resume their responsibilities for law, order and social regulation within their boundaries. It is unnecessary to impute to the North any special vindictiveness to understand why this prospect was viewed with alarm and bewilderment. Lincoln has been much praised for the moderation of his reconstruction policy but it depended upon a somewhat unrealistic appraisal of public opinion in the North. Lincoln believed that secession had been void, that the states had never

[1] Lincoln made this point in his last public address, April 11, 1865. 'Unlike a case of war between independent nations, there is no authorized organ for us to treat with — no one man has authority to give up the rebellion for any other man. We simply must begin with and mould from disorganized and discordant elements' (*Writings of Lincoln*, VII, 400).

been out of the Union, and that only individuals had rebelled. It followed that as soon as sufficient individuals had been found in a state ready to conduct a loyal government and accept emancipation of the slaves then that state ought to be readmitted to the Union. He fixed the sufficient number at 10 per cent, and under this plan states occupied by the Federal troops had provisional governments before the end of fighting and had sent to Washington representatives who claimed admission to Congress. Congress had already given notice that it would require a longer period of tutelage and some guarantee of freedmen's rights. Lincoln probably hoped that, by playing the game slowly, he could calm Northern fears and persuade Southerners to act reasonably towards the Negro; he did not believe that the Negro could be given civil or political equality, he believed that sooner or later the Southerners must settle the race question for themselves, and that it would be futile to hold up reunion because of the lack of formal guarantees. Lincoln had fought the war to preserve the Union, and he planned reconstruction to restore it in spirit as well as in the letter; but was Lincoln's political skill sufficient to convince those who thought that it was Southern society which required reconstruction? After his assassination responsibility fell upon his Vice-President and successor, Andrew Johnson, an ardent Unionist from a secessionist state and a fine example of the fighting Western Democrats who had modelled themselves on Jackson, but without the temperament or the skill to deal with the situation. He retained the outlook of the poor white class from which he had sprung and was equally hostile to Southern aristocrats and to Northern Negrophiles. The programme which he launched in the summer of 1865 allowed loyal Southerners — and most were now anxious to take oaths of allegiance — to form provisional state governments. Many have praised the justice of his policy but few have denied the ineptitude which not only permitted but also forced Congress to take the initiative.

It was clear that Republican opinion would display acute sensitivity on the Negro question, and to many it seemed that this was the only opportunity to prevent the occurrence of great wrongs. The possibility that the leaders of Southern secession would recover their former influence caused disquiet which was human though less humane. Their worst fears were realized when the provisional governments in the South set about the problem of making laws applicable to the freedmen; the so-called 'Black codes' contained provisions for labour discipline to replace that of the plantation, they attempted to deal with the problem of vagrancy, and they did give the Negro limited civil rights. What was questionable about the codes was their assumption that Negroes were inferior and their refusal to indicate any means by which Negroes could become full citizens.[1] Northern hostility might have been disarmed by proposals for Negro education or by the concession of political suffrage to Negroes of property and education. There were those in the South — and they included some of the most distinguished — who believed that these things must come and that they ought to be conceded with a good grace; but the provisional legislatures were dominated by second-rate men obsessed by fears of Negro equality. Johnson, inspired by a laudable desire to attach Southern leaders to the Union, accelerated the process by a lavish use of Presidential pardons to restore to them civil and political rights; but the re-emergence of Confederate leaders aggravated still further Northern anxieties. Faced by such policies and such men the Republicans could not abandon the Negro to whom so much had been promised.[2]

By December 1865 Johnson had completed his reconstruction; every Southern State had a government and was ready to resume normal relations within the Union. But when Congress met in

[1] A Southern lawyer in a semi-official publication described the situation of the Negroes in these words: 'They are placed equal before the law in the possession and enjoyment of all their rights of person — of liberty and property. To institute . . . between the Anglo-Saxon, the high-minded virtuous, intelligent, patriotic Southerner and the freedmen, a social or political approximation more intimate — to mingle the social or political existence of the two classes more closely, would surely be one of the highest exhibitions of treason to the race. These two great classes, then, are distinctly marked by the impress of nature. They are races separate and distinct: the one the highest and noblest type of humanity, the other the lowest and most degraded.' (From the editor's preface to H. Melville Myers, *Stay Laws . . . and Freedman's Code* (*Charleston 1866*), quoted L. M. Hacker, *Making of the American Tradition*, 629.)

[2] 'It is essential to complete Emancipation . . . . Slavery must be abolished not in form only, but in substance, so that there shall be no Black Code; but all shall be equal before the law.' (From a speech by Sumner, *Congressional Globe*, 39th Congress, 1st Session, 91.)

that month, for the first time since the end of the war, Radical dismay at the lack of guarantees for Negro rights or for Southern good behaviour had communicated itself to the Republican party at large. These honest doubts joined with a fear that a restored South would resume its former dominance in the nation.[1] Economic motives, especially the wish to retain the protective tariff enacted during the war, which have been stressed by some historians, played a comparatively small part in determining Republican policy. This policy, the work of moderates as well as of radicals, was summed up in the fourteenth amendment to the Constitution which made civil rights a national responsibility. The amendment did not enact universal suffrage but it provided that non-voters should not be counted when making the apportionment of congressional representation. Johnson's hostility, Southern intransigeance, and the inclusion of a clause disqualifying Southern leaders from public office, caused its rejection in every Southern State save Tennessee. Republicans now concluded that if the Southerners would not accept these terms, a more drastic policy was necessary, and that Negro suffrage was the only possible safeguard for civil rights and for the safety of the Union.

While the amendment was intended to effect a permanent change, the Reconstruction Acts of 1867 looked to the immediate problem of creating a new order in the South. The military governors were to call for the election of conventions by all adult males except those whom it was intended to disqualify under the XIVth Amendment; if these conventions drew up constitutions which were ratified by all qualified voters, included a provision for adult male suffrage, and were otherwise acceptable to Congress, and if the legislature chosen under this constitution ratified the fourteenth amendment, then the state could be readmitted to the

---

[1] Samuel Shellabarger of Ohio put the radical position briefly and forcefully. 'Let the revolted States base their republican State governments upon a general and sincere loyalty of the people and come to us under the guarantees of this renewed Union, and we hail their coming and the hour that brings them. If you ask again, "Suppose such general loyalty should never reappear, shall they be dependencies for ever?" Sir, convince me that the case is supposable, then with deepest sorrow I answer — FOREVER!' (*Congressional Globe*, 39th Congress, 1st Session, 145).

Union, but only when sufficient states had ratified the fourteenth amendment to pass it into law.[1] These ingenious measures ensured that Negro suffrage was the only road to reunion and the end of military government, and that the former confederates could resume their rights as states only when those rights had been drastically curtailed by the new amendment. The fourteenth amendment introduced a fundamental change in the character of American Politics; a central assumption of the old Constitution — that States would protect their citizens against the abuse of Federal power — was replaced by the thesis that the prevention of State injustice was a duty imposed upon Federal government.

Technically this policy was a complete success: in June 1868 seven states were restored to the Union and by 1870 all the former confederate states were readmitted. In Georgia an attempt after restoration to defy the spirit of the fourteenth amendment by expelling Negro members of the legislature was sternly checked and the state was forced into submission by the restoration of military rule. To prevent the abrogation of Negro voting rights the fifteenth amendment declared that the right to vote should not 'be denied or abridged . . . on account of race, color, or previous condition of servitude'. The new order had been imposed upon the South, it remained to see whether it could take root amongst a people who were opposed to its fundamental principles.

If the South had erred in failing to offer any hope of advancement for the Negroes, the Northern radicals were led astray by the hatred which many of them felt for the old leaders of Southern society. It was their intention, which received constitutional expression in a clause of the fourteenth amendment, to drive the old ruling class from public life; all those whose duties had required an oath of allegiance to the United States and had subsequently joined the Confederacy, could hold no public office unless

---

[1] The reader may like to be reminded of the procedure for enacting amendments. An Amendment must be passed by two-thirds of each house and then ratified in three-fourths of the states, either by the legislatures or by conventions as decided by Congress. Though some argued that ratification by three-fourths of the loyal states should be sufficient the legal basis of the new amendments would clearly be stronger if the former rebel states were forced to ratify.

pardoned by a vote of two-thirds of both houses of Congress. Yet it was vitally important to the success of the new order that it should gain the support of some at least among those who still enjoyed great social prestige, and the policy of disqualification ensured that the void in leadership must be filled by men of little repute. The Reconstruction state governments never lacked candidates for official responsibility but their nicknames — 'Scalawags' for Southern men who linked their fortunes with the new governments, and 'Carpetbaggers' for the Northern new-comers — did not promise respect for their new rulers among the Southern people.

Reconstruction did not hand the South over to an illiterate and ignorant Negro majority. Negroes were in a majority in only two states and there the margin was narrow; they were in a majority in the 'Black belt' (the plantation areas) but except in South Carolina and Mississippi these were outweighed by the white counties.[1] The Negroes were often ignorant and bewildered, but there is no evidence that they were more irresponsible than the voters in any democratic state; indeed their very lack of political training and the simplicity of their demands made them more likely to support conservative than radical régimes. A few of their leaders were ignorant and coarse, but most of them belonged to the semi-educated class of former free Negroes or to those who had been superior slave artisans. They enjoyed the vote at a time when it was still denied to the English agricultural labourer and to all women, but the case against their enfranchisement was the same as that against enfranchising the poor in any country. To rest the responsibility for the failure of Reconstruction upon Negro incapacity is too easy and too prejudiced an explanation for the failure of the nineteenth century's boldest experiment in democratic government.

What was now forced upon the South was a social and political revolution comparable to those which had shaken the *ancien*

---

[1] In South Carolina, which contemporaries regarded as the extreme example of 'black' reconstruction, Negroes were never a majority in the Senate; in 1872-3 they reached their peak in the House with 80 to 42 whites, after that date they were in a minority with just under half the representatives (W. E. B. Du Bois, *Black Reconstruction*, 404).

régimes in older European countries. Like other revolutions it combined a genuine care for the aspirations of the humble with demagogy, opportunism, charlatanry, and individual ambition. Its strongest point lay in its appeal to that common stock of ideas welded together by the reformist movements of the nineteenth century — to liberty, equality and humanitarianism — its weakest point lay in the absence of a dedicated and indigenous minority ready to guide the storm. And the counter-revolution when it came was not merely the conservative reaction of an upper middle class but also spontaneous and popular.

On paper the record of revolutionary democracy was good. The constitutions, modelled upon those of Northern states, were sound enough to last in several states for years after the counter-revolution. The attempt in every reconstructed state to create systems of free public elementary education were praiseworthy. Economic recovery went forward at a remarkable pace stimulated by the privileges offered to capitalist entrepreneurs and by state backing for railway building. Carpetbaggers representing small business of the North were able to tackle a problem which has plagued all revolutions, that of attracting capital to a disordered society. Many of the criticisms levelled at the governments — that they taxed heavily, spent lavishly and increased debts — arose because they were behaving more like modern governments in social and economic activity than anything which the South had known before. The accusations of fraud, corruption and scandal were the accusations which the white Southerners wanted to believe, while the story of improvement and honest endeavour was the one which they did not wish to hear. Yet the leadership was weak or unprincipled. If the corruption did not approach in scale the magnificent robbery of the Tweed ring in New York or in extent the network of bribery which enmeshed several quiet Northern legislatures, there was nevertheless a good deal of it and some which failed to observe the decencies of pretence.[1] There

[1] Sir George Campbell, an English M.P., made these comments. 'Before I went South, I certainly expected to find that the Southern states had been for a time a sort of Pandemonium in which a white man could hardly live, yet it was certainly not so.... "Well, then," I had gone on to ask, "did the black Legislatures make bad laws?" My informants

was also a fatal weakness in the political structure of reconstruction: faced with the urgent need for money the legislatures had to tax property, but Congress, whether from a reverence for property or from a sense of justice to the defeated, prevented the wholesale confiscation of land which would have made the Revolution economically viable.[1] So long as the Negro remained without property the economic basis of reconstruction was unsound, so long as the old ruling class remained with property which was taxed by and for those who had none there was a nucleus of discontented power ready for employment against the governments.

The political story of reconstruction obscures some struggles which were taking place in the South. There was a struggle for control of the new economic opportunities between small carpetbag business and the impoverished older families, there was a struggle between the poorer whites and the Negro freedmen for land and status, there was a struggle between certain white and certain Negro elements to fill the middle-class positions created by a more varied economy, and behind these local conflicts there was the force, both blind and calculating, of Northern capital seeking to control markets, production and investment. In the event the old ruling class combined with the poor whites, and once this alliance showed promise of permanent success it was able to effect an unwritten alliance with Northern capital. The drive for a Negro middle class was checked or narrowly confined. Negro suffrage became a dead letter save in the few areas where it was to the advantage of the whites.

The upper-class counter-revolution was not led by the old

could not say that they did . . . . "What then is the practical evil of which complaint is made?" The answer is summed up in the one word "corruption". . . . I believe that there can be no doubt at all that a great deal of corruption did prevail — much more than the ordinary measure of American corruption. It was inevitable that it should be so under the circumstances: but to what degree it was so, it was very difficult to tell' (*White and Black in the United States*, 176–8, quoted Du Bois, *op. cit.*, 419).

[1] 'A practical difficulty is this: Can emancipation be carried without using the lands of the slave-masters? We must see that the freedmen are established on the soil, and that they may become proprietors. From the beginning I have regarded confiscation only as ancillary to emancipation.' (Charles Sumner to John Bright. March 13, 1865, *Memoirs and Letters of C.S.*, ed. Pierce, IV, 229.)

secessionist fire-eaters (whose post-war influence was negligible) but by old Whigs whose interests were primarily commercial. They owned land and collected rent (often in the form of a share in the crops) from tenant occupiers, but the plantation had become a source of revenue rather than the social nucleus of a governing class. Their real interests lay in railways, cotton mills, banks, iron mines, and distributive trades. This new Southern capitalism was the result of desperate need; the alternative was poverty and the exchange of former authority for the hard life of a working farmer. Some of them were prepared to deal with the carpetbaggers (the scalawags included a number of dignified old Southerners who took this road), the majority judged that ultimate success lay in disassociation from the political masters of reconstruction.[1] White supremacy would make a surer foundation for a business régime and this meant alliance with the white farmers; thus what emerges is not old Whiggery but new Democracy as the vehicle for white supremacy and business conservatism.

Concurrently with the emergence of a white capitalist leadership ran the spontaneous struggle of the poorer whites against racial equality. Appearing first in a number of secret terrorist organizations, of which the Ku Klux Klan was the most famous, the vengeance of the whites was directed against Negroes who did not know their place, against those who associated with them, and against carpetbaggers. Locally the Republican party organization, strong in Federal patronage, backed by Federal troops, and with the law on its side, was locked in deadly struggle with the revived Democratic party which had nothing save the enthusiasm and purpose of the white majority. At election time (and in the United States elections must be very frequent) the normal bitterness broke out into violence and coercion. The better class

[1] The Louisville and Nashville Railroad became a great economic and political power in the South. 'It was characteristic of the times that in its battles to achieve monopoly, which differed in no essential from similar struggles the nation over, the L and N managed to identify its cause with that of the downtrodden South. This is the more curious in view of the road's service to the Union army during the war, the passage of control and ownership to Northern and European capital, and the appearance in the lists of its directors of the names of Jay Gould, Thomas Fortune Ryan, Jacob Schiff, and August Belmont' (C. Vann Woodward, *Origins of the New South*, Louisiana State University Press, 7).

M

whites drew back from the extremes of terrorism but co-operated with what came to be known as the 'Mississippi plan' under which social pressure, economic coercion and a show of white strength were used either to keep the Negro from the polls or to compel him to vote the Democratic ticket. These methods ensured that the history of radical reconstruction would be short. In 1876 Democratic presidential electors were chosen in all but three Southern states, and in these three the results were contested.

These three states proved to be of great importance for upon them hung the fate of the election. In each a Republican returning board had thrown out sufficient Democratic votes to secure a Republican majority, but in each the Democratic vote had been secured by means which might not bear full investigation. An electoral commission set up by Congress gave each of the contests to the Republicans and made Rutherford B. Hayes President by the narrowest margin in American history. Would the Southerners in Congress join the Northern Democrats in a filibuster against accepting the electoral count? The Southerners took time to consider and named their price to the Republicans: the withdrawal of Federal troops from the South and Federal aid for Southern projects such as the Texas and Pacific Railway and the Mississippi navigation; the price was accepted, the Southerners refused to support a filibuster, and Hayes was peacefully inaugurated as President.

This incident had more significance than a piece of political intrigue; it marked the consummation of a conservative alliance between Southern Democrats and Northern Republican businessmen which was to play a dominant part in American life. The Southerners did not forgo their Democracy, which enabled them to hold together a solid alliance at home and to play a leading rather than a subordinate role in one of the major parties, but they did accept the thesis that Northern and Southern business shared a community of interest. This had far-reaching implications for the relationship between the Northern industrial society and the South, for co-operation made it certain that the stronger element would prevail.[1] By 1900 the railways of the South had been consolidated into three great systems and behind each of them stood the financial power of John Pierpont Morgan. In 1907 the iron and steel industry of Birmingham, Alabama, long under Northern control, became a part of Morgan's gigantic steel combine. The masters of the Northern economy were more interested in control than in exploitation; as the custodians of the great vested interests and high material standards of the North they had to see that these were not endangered by the virgin resources and cheap labour of the South. The South at this period has been described as a 'colonial' economy;[2] but just as the eighteenth-century colonies were able to develop some activities which escaped the net of imperial control, so the economy of the 'New South' escaped complete subordination to Northern interests. In the manufacture of cotton textiles there was a tremendous advance in the late years of the nineteenth century; cheap and docile labour offset some of the technical disadvantages of spinning cotton in a hot dry climate, and the New England cotton industry lost ground while the South gained.

A curious feature of the industrial revolution of the South in the late nineteenth century was its popularity amongst all classes. Whereas other industrial revolutions had been deprecated by the upper classes and resented by the lower, the Southern entrepreneurs were regarded as benefactors by all. Industrial advance would help to regain what had been lost on the battlefield, and the cotton mills provided a safety valve for the redundant farm population. The factory labour force was white and this gave it a social prestige which had been lacking elsewhere. It was well

[1] C. Vann Woodward, the most perceptive historian of the 'New South' writes, 'As the old century drew to a close and the new century progressed through the first decade, the penetration of the South by North-eastern capital continued at an accelerated pace. The Morgans, Mellons, and Rockefellers sent their agents to take charge of the region's railroads, mines, furnaces, and financial corporations, and eventually to many of its distributive institutions. Southern counterparts of the North-eastern masters, however, failed to appear. The number of Southern businessmen increased steadily and some of them waxed in fortune. But the new men, as well as many of the old, acted as agents, retainers, and executives — rarely as principals. The economy over which they presided was increasingly coming to be one of branch plants, branch banks, captive mines, and chain stores.' *Origins of the New South*, 291–2.
[2] By C. Vann Woodward.

known that low wages were one of the South's principal weapons in the competitive struggle and nowhere was there more hostility to trade union activity which might reduce this advantage. In time the contrast between the highly paid and highly organized labour of the North and the low-paid labour of the South would provide another example of the way in which an industrial society prospered at the expense of its colonial dependencies.

The real losers from the concordat between Southern leaders and Northern business were the Negroes. With the abandonment of the political revolution by the North the Negro was allowed to slip back into the place for which the Southern white majority had designed him. Yet his losses were not immediately apparent; Negroes disappeared from the legislatures and from office, but in many areas they continued to vote in large numbers. Booker T. Washington, the most distinguished of Negro leaders, advised his people to abandon the vain search for political power and to concentrate upon education, technical training, and the winning of economic independence. He held out a promise inspired less by the dogma of human equality than by the belief that a Negro middle class would be accepted by the whites as responsible citizens. But this modest degree of Negro self-improvement helped to promote a wave of anti-Negro feeling which was linked with agrarian radicalism and with a revolt of white farmers against business leadership. The poor Negro share cropper was little threat to the white farmer, but a Negro middle class affronted his very being and caused the racial lines to be drawn more tightly. Voting tests were imposed which could be administered mainly against the Negroes, and the patterns of segregation in schools, transport, and public places were laid down. The Supreme Court obligingly interpreted the civil rights' guarantees of the fourteenth amendment to mean that the races could be separated provided that the facilities were equal.[1] 'Separate but equal' became in

---

[1] A favourite project of Sumner was a Civil Rights Bill which would have made illegal 'all laws or customs in such States establishing any oligarchical privileges and any distinction of rights on account of color or race', and would have given exclusive jurisdiction to the Federal Courts 'of all offences committed by persons not of African descent upon persons of African descent; also of all offences committed by persons of African descent;

practice a sham by which white superiority could be maintained. Yet something remained of the reconstruction revolution. After a generation of freedom few could seriously maintain that the Negro had been better off under slavery (and this had been often regarded as a commonplace immediately after emancipation). Whatever the Supreme Court might say, the plain words of the fourteenth amendment were still in the Constitution. And it was impossible to forget that the rulers of the nation had once insisted that all men were created equal.

and also of all causes, suits, and demands to which any person of African descent shall be a party'. In 1875, after his death, a weaker Civil Rights Act was passed, but this was voided by the Supreme Court in 1883.

[7]

The Evolution of a Liberal Capitalist Civilization

The Civil War marked a decisive stage in the evolution of a society unlike any which the world had known. The defeat of the rural society of the South left the masters of the North in undisputed control of the nation, meant the acceptance of the Northern ideology as the national ideology, and placed the businessman firmly in the centre of the American stage. It is easier to generalize about this triumphant civilization than to understand it. It placed a high value upon material success, but it believed itself to be thoroughly idealistic. It admired business efficiency but accepted government which was usually inefficient and often corrupt. It tolerated the flamboyance of wealth but retained a strict moral code. It achieved much in the realm of popular and higher education but accorded little prestige to the intellectual. Its thriving new cities could show some of the worst slums and its prosperous business and residential areas some of the ugliest architecture in the world. Sensitive Americans joined with upper-class Englishmen to attack the manners and the hypocrisy of the age; agrarian radicals piled up a vocabulary of abuse against the masters of capital which was to be appropriated by modern Marxists; conflicts between capital and labour sometimes attained a savagery beyond anything which Europe could show. Yet between the very rich and the very poor ran a broad stratum in which life seemed very good, and millions of humble Europeans still saw in America their promised land. Almost every year the migrant tide flowed more strongly, and though the booster and the trickster may be blamed for delusions which affected a few, millions were not enticed across the Atlantic by mirage or fraud.

It may be that 'Liberal Capitalist' is the best label to attach to this extraordinary civilization. Capitalist it certainly was, and the entrepreneurs sat almost unchallenged in the seats of the mighty, but it also embodies most of the liberal aspirations in an age of liberal revolt. Indeed it is largely to American economic success that these aspirations owe their survival into the present age. America was democratic; every adult male was legally entitled to vote and her complex governmental institutions had as their principle objective the prevention of the abuse of power. Elementary education was, in many states, compulsory and free, and in all public schools it was non-sectarian. Secondary education was provided for a higher proportion of the people than in any other country, and the objective of providing higher education for all who could benefit from it was already clearly defined. There were no established Churches, no tithes, and anti-clericalism (which was an obsession and a handicap to so many European liberals) was quite without meaning in America. If there were great differences in wealth social customs maintained the appearance of equality, and this was no small thing for the European peasant trained in obsequiousness. If the opportunities were not quite so great as the new immigrants imagined, they were still considerable; nearly all the new rich were self-made, no career was closed to talents, and though alien language was a heavy handicap no upper-class accent distinguished the *élite* from the mass.

Americans not only experienced these things; they also believed in them. The American's conviction that his country had achieved its revolutionary promise was sincere and well-founded; nor did he find much difficulty in reconciling a humane respect for the individual with economic individualism. Indeed he did not know how the two could be separated and regarded them as complementary to each other. The old Puritan blessing upon work fortified him in his anxiety for material self-improvement and idleness was the greatest of social sins. The theories which attempted to come to his aid by placing the sanction of nature behind the economic system — dogmatic *laissez-faire* and evolution — really complicated and obscured the spontaneous realization that communities could not grow unless individuals were encouraged to take both the risks and the rewards of economic enterprise.

The social utility of individual success was apparent when it meant prosperity and expansion to whole communities. The businessman inherited the accumulated respect for the pioneer and half-consciously assumed the mantle of the self-reliant farmer. Nor if one turned from the individual and the community to the people and the nation was the case for liberal capitalism any weaker. With the population rising from 31·4 million in 1860 to 76·0 million in 1900 the *per capita* income was doubled, and even though this increased wealth was unevenly distributed, the greatest happiness for the greatest number was closer to realization than anywhere else in the world. This society was also robust. Europeans might criticize Americans for measuring a man by his dollars; the reply might be that dollars were a symbol of energy and enterprise while a respect for birth and breeding was often an excuse for deferring to the effete and the spineless. Though the businessman was not normally respectful to the intellectuals he did in fact derive much comfort from his identification with what was fashionable and progressive in Western thought. The economists praised his social role, and Darwinians his adaptation to his environment. And if he did not pay honour to the prophets in his own country, he recognized the greatness of Herbert Spencer, the new Aristotle, who had anticipated Darwin as a theorist of evolution and who had enlarged it into a universal principle. The businessman also derived strength from the conformist pressures in American society. Once the amalgam of inherited traditions and current theory had set the bounds, social pressure tended to keep argument within them, and those who appeared to attack its fundamentals were branded as criminals, madmen or worse. The school, the pulpit and the political platform all joined in the conspiracy of affirmation.

Yet though liberal capitalism had great internal strength it had also its weaknesses. Though the economic trends were upward over the whole period, they were interrupted sharply in 1873 and 1893; in the 1870's the *per capita* income actually fell, and in 1877 America experienced violent and nation-wide labour troubles. After 1877 the old confidence in the American solution to social problems was never quite restored, and tension between capital and labour became endemic in many occupations. The failure of capitalism to avert economic crises was paralleled by its failure to solve poverty. In 1879, in an epoch-making book, Henry George, hitherto an obscure Californian journalist, demonstrated that poverty had increased hand in hand with material progress and that conventional economics were quite incapable of solving this problem. At the other end of the social scale surviving cliques of the older gentry — such as the Boston 'brahmins' and the renaissant Southern upper class — did not disguise their distaste for the new rich, and though their criticism had little influence alone, it joined with others and percolated through academic and literary channels.

There were also more immediate causes for weakness. While capitalism aimed at a national market it was largely concentrated in the Northeast and Mid-west; here were most of the large towns, most of the manufacturing plants, the great banking and financial interests, the railway magnates, and the controlling interests in marketing, distribution, and insurance. It was inevitable that, to less developed regions which stood outside this great complex of economic forces, industrial and finance capitalism appeared as alien and oppressive. In the United States the 'colonial' regions were however politically a part of the 'mother country' and their political institutions were the same as those of the older states. In consequence the protests of the dependent agrarian societies could become vocal and politically significant; though the businessman was trying to appropriate certain features of agrarian individualism he was liable to violent attacks from the agrarians themselves.

Business leadership is always liable to internal dissensions. Men engaged in a fiercely competitive activity may find it difficult to feel the same solidarity as members of the professions, of the landed gentry or of the working class. The largest rift in the ranks

of business came between large and small business but the division
was often obscured. In the post-war years America was moving
from the golden age of the small entrepreneur into the age of
consolidation and organization. The rise of monopoly capitalism
did not however precipitate a general conflict between small and
large because the forces were widely deployed and some were not
engaged at all. With the rapid expansion of the economy there
was still scope for a wide diversity of economic activities, and
while some small businesses were being forced to the wall by the
rise of the giants others were hopefully embarking upon a multitude of enterprises where individualism was still the rule. This
generally prevented liberal capitalism from recognizing the
collectivist enemy in its midst.[1] It might be difficult to reconcile a
belief in the benefits of unlimited competition with the survival of
the fittest, but most middle-class Americans believed that these
two aspects of the truth must be reconciled. To protest against
the success of others was to class oneself amongst the unfit, but to
connive at monopoly meant the sacrifice of competition, the
father of progress. There was therefore an uncertainty at the heart
of the liberal capitalist system which seriously handicapped it as a
social philosophy.[2]

There was one more weakness in liberal capitalism. The
businessmen were not a ruling but dominant class, for the one
thing which the businessmen did not do was to govern. In a
competitive world success depended upon unremitting activity
and the businessmen could never afford the time to achieve that
union of economic, social and political power which the English

---

[1] But see the quotation from Henry Adams, *supra* page 23.

[2] Senator Orville Platt of Connecticut had something to say about this in the debate
on the Sherman Anti-Trust Act (which sought to outlaw monopoly and restore competition). 'This bill proceeds upon the false assumption that all competition is beneficent to
the country, and that every advance in price is an injury to the country .... There never
was a greater fallacy in the world .... Unrestricted competition is brutal warfare, and
injurious to the whole country. The great corporations of this country, the great mono-
polies of this country are every one of them built upon the graves of weaker competitors
that have been forced to their death by remorseless competition. The true theory of this
matter is that prices, no matter who is the producer or what the article, should be such as
will render a fair return ...' (*Congressional Record*, 51st Congress, 1st Session, 2729,
March 27, 1890). The last sentence seems to contain a curious resurrection of the medieval
'just price'; but how to ensure a 'just reasonable and fair' price without invoking government price control was a problem seldom analysed and never solved.

ruling class had won in the eighteenth century. Politics remained the business of professional politicians and their hold was strengthened by the amount of political work which had to be done. The English businessman, though lacking the prestige of his American counterpart, could afford to fight an election once in six or seven years and to spend the necessary time in the House of Commons, leaving political management to a local agent and a central party office. The American politician was hardly ever free of elections and, since national party organization was so weak, had to give constant attention to his personal hold upon his constituency. The real politics of the period were local politics and here it was necessary to fight for survival not only against the opposing party but also against rival factions within one's own party. The direct participation of businessmen in politics was therefore unusual. Toward the end of the century the magnates of the economy often found it useful to fight for a seat in the Senate (if these seats were not filled by railway senators, steel senators, banking senators and so on they might be filled by agrarian senators with unsound views). At the other end of the political scale the outrageous behaviour of city bosses sometimes forced businessmen into politics at the head of reform movements; but these usually died away when the immediate objectives had been attained.

Business had, however, a great deal of indirect contact with politics. From the tariff at the national level to local privileges at the state and municipal level there were a great many things which businessmen wanted and which only the politicians could give. And the politician could not afford to ignore the support of businessmen and might not wish to reject the pecuniary inducements which they offered. The eighteenth-century English aristocrat had used corruption to maintain his power; the American businessman used it to pay for political irresponsibility. In the long run this was to do as much as anything to damage the prestige of the businessman and to weaken the appeal of liberal capitalism.

*　　*　　*　　*

The political history of the late nineteenth century has been bedevilled by over-simplification and by the belief that politics were of minor importance in this age. Grant, Hayes, Garfield, Arthur, Cleveland, Harrison and McKinley (to name only the Presidents) were not men likely to arouse the interest of posterity, and the most important things in the American future were being settled by the men who built railways, managed banks, expanded industry and opened the great West. If one compares these epic achievements with the drab and wasting political activities of the period, there seems to be little doubt which was the more important.[1] Yet politics offered a challenge to contemporaries and ought to have a greater share of the historian's attention. With the passage of the fourteenth and fifteenth amendments the United States became the most complete form of democracy the world had ever known, and upon the foundation of adult male suffrage was raised a structure through which flowed the popular will. The results were not encouraging; on the one side power seemed to pass into the hands of an oligarchy of wealthy monopolists, and on the other into the hands of political bosses. But if democracy is not intended to create a government wiser than the people whom it serves, then there is no cause for surprise when it displays a good many human failings; and there is no more reason to believe that the people will always choose well, than to believe that others can make a better choice for them.

The Republican Party emerged from the Civil War as something very similar to the contemporary Gladstonian Liberal Party; it ended the century as something not unlike the British Conservative Party over which Lord Salisbury presided. In 1865 it had its business element and its intelligentsia, it was radical yet eminently respectable, it was respectful to power won by individual enter-

---

[1] Henry Adams, who sensed a sharp break with the past in 1896 wrote, 'For the old world of public men and measures since 1870, Adams wept no tears. Within or without, during or after it, he never saw anything to admire in it, or anything he wanted to save; and in this respect he reflected only the public mind which balanced itself so exactly between the unpopularity of both parties as to express no sympathy with either. Even among the most powerful men of that generation he knew none who had a good word to say for it. No period so thoroughly ordinary had been known in American politics since Christopher Columbus first disturbed the balance of American society....' (*The Education of Henry Adams*, Massachusetts Historical Society, Ch. XXIII.)

prise and hostile to hereditary privilege. It united the austerity of the New England upper classes with the ebullience of Mid-western self-made men and the equalitarian principles of farm settlers. Its significant achievements included the Homestead Act (the charter of agrarian idealism), the protective tariff, Negro emancipation, the struggle for civil rights, and the approval of land grants to finance both Pacific Railways and higher education. The Republican mind found little difficulty in imagining these various measures as different aspects of a single political drive for the betterment of American man.[1]

By 1900 the Republican Party was in essence a defensive alliance for the business civilization; it retained all its respectability, was still the party of the Eastern intelligentsia, and continued to command the loyalty of a majority of the electorate in all classes, but many of its original radical precepts were honoured rather than observed. The party's move towards conservatism was the result of an alliance between groups which might have diverged: small business and large business, Eastern capitalism and Western capitalism, manufacturers and bankers, spoilsmen and middle-class reformers. The terms of the alliance were adherence to the gold standard (the particular objective of the financial interests), a high tariff (dear to the manufacturers), a token recognition of the limits to which business consolidation might be pressed, and a tacit understanding that professional politicians would use their arts with discretion to underpin and not to undermine the established power structure.

The radical Republicans emerged from the war as the dominant group in Congress and in the party. Their hero was Charles Sumner, senator from Massachusetts, whose learning and ardent devotion to reform scorned compromise; the architect of their Congressional policy was Thaddeus Stevens, an extraordinary man whose vices are apparent but whose virtues have perhaps

---

[1] 'I hope nothing is to be uttered here in the name of "conservatism", the worst word in the English language. If there is a word in the English language that means treachery, servility and cowardice, it is that word "conservative". It ought never to be on the lips of an American statesman. For twenty years it has stood in America as the synonym of meanness and baseness' (Senator Henry Wilson (a leading radical Republican), Dec. 21, 1866, *Congressional Globe*, 39th Congress, 1st Session, 112).

received less than their just reward. Their great weakness was that they became identified with a reconstruction policy which was heading for failure and which could only be sustained by an ever greater use of Federal authority which the majority of Americans still regarded with suspicion. Their great strength lay in the response which their policies evoked among Northern and Western people. They were strong also amongst small business-men, to whom their belief in free competition appealed, and amongst professional politicians, who realized that it was their interest to go with the tide.

The first stage in the transition came during the Presidency of General Grant, who had little sympathy with radical ideas and leant heavily for advice upon political magnates whose main concern was with the preservation of the Republican Party and their own place within it. The Grant era saw the heyday of the spoilsmen, though Grant himself has had to bear too much blame for the demoralization of public life. Grant also shifted Repub-licanism a stage nearer to big business and banking. The test problem was that of the currency. The war had been financed by inflation, and bankers who were acutely aware of American dependence upon foreign investment, and foreign confidence in American currency, strongly favoured a return to the gold standard. Some were not perhaps unmoved by the increased value which deflation would give to government securities. The resumption policy was opposed by some influential eastern Radicals, representing small business and labour; farmers and expansive Western business had been helped by easy money and paper currency, were unmoved by arguments which turned on international finance, and extremely hostile to the use of Federal taxes for the service of an appreciated debt. After some hesitation Grant threw his influence behind the sound money movement; he recommended the resumption of specie payment in 1869 and 1874; in April 1874 he vetoed a bill to increase the issues of paper cur-rency (passed as a measure of relief after the panic of 1873); in January 1875 he backed the specie resumption act which put America back on the gold standard in January 1879.

Grant's Presidency saw the emergence of a middle-class group — the liberal Republicans — in reaction against the radical Southern policy, against high tariffs, and above all against corruption. The liberal Republicans sadly mismanaged their break-away campaign in 1872 and the movement petered out, but there remained a demand for clean government at municipal, state and national levels. Liberal Republicanism failed to attract great popular support but it included some men of influence and high standing. In national politics their favourite measure was civil service reform which would substitute an examination system and promotion on merit for political appointment. For the professional politician this last was dangerous hypocrisy; ideas might change and enthusiasm must evaporate but the future of the nation depended upon the continuity of party organization, and this would fail if it could not be nourished by promises and rewards.

This ancient political dilemma — the reconciliation of political decency with the need for political management — dogged the Republican Presidents of the later nineteenth century. Two of them, Hayes 1877–81 and Harrison 1889–93, were men of monumental respectability who owed their elections to a very considerable exercise of political arts by their supporters, who subsequently broke with the spoilsmen magnates, and who had to endure the paralysis of their administrations as a result. Garfield was in office for too short a time (he was assassinated soon after becoming President in 1881), but his early efforts at mediation between the needs of the party and of the public were not encouraging. Chester Arthur, who succeeded Garfield, was a political realist trained in the hard school of the New York spoils system (Hayes had dismissed him from the Collectorship of the Customs), and proved himself the most effective of the four by providing enough reform to conciliate the liberals without alienating the professionals. By bringing business conservatism and professional politics into line, without offending the high-minded, Arthur presided over a significant stage in the evolution of the Republican party.

If the Republicans can be misunderstood by over-simplification, no one is likely to make the same error over the Democrats. Most American parties have thrived as parties of 'antis', but the peculiar complexity of the post-war Democratic Party arose because it was against so many different things. Defeated and disorganized after the war the party survived as a loose alliance of local parties rather than as a national movement. Its choice of presidential candidates illustrates the many faced character of the party: Horatio Seymour, a former Governor of New York and a wealthy advocate of sound money; Horace Greeley, nominee of the liberal Republicans, an ardent protectionist, formerly a bitter enemy of all Democrats and editor of the *New York Tribune* which claimed to hold the conscience of the Republican Party; Samuel J. Tilden, an extremely wealthy New York lawyer and leader of the reform movement against Boss Tweed; Winfield Hancock, a good general with no political qualifications; Grover Cleveland, a sturdy and unimaginative representative of small business; and William Jennings Bryan, spokesman of the agrarian West. To be complete this gallery should also include a conservative Southerner, rebuilding the shattered party on a basis of white supremacy, a city boss (perhaps William Marcy Tweed himself), and a foreign born Roman Catholic. Yet the Democratic Party had certain elements of strength amidst this diversity which facilitated its recovery as a great national party. In the reaction against Grant and the spoilsmen it inevitably picked up some votes among the respectable professional classes. As the cities grew, more voters were found among the depressed and outcast lower classes. Recent immigrants were naturally attracted to the party by its name and by its claim to represent the common man. In the South the break-down of radical reconstruction left the Democrats unchallenged masters of the region's politics. Yet as Republicanism moved towards conservatism, the Democrats made only tentative gestures towards radicalism. Both parties were struggling for the middle-class business vote upon which, in the long run, political destinies would depend. This and the Southern anchor often made the Democrats appear as conservative as their rivals without their identification with the dynamic of liberal capitalism. Nor did the Democrats make much impression upon the intellectual life of the nation; the best writers, editors and academics remained Republican though sometimes with misgivings.

* * * *

Beneath the surface of politics there was much which was shocking. That men seized the opportunity for gain which politics presented is not surprising nor particularly reprehensible; it is the toleration of corruption which is disturbing. There were few years during the late nineteenth century during which someone was not somewhere conducting a reform campaign, yet it was only when corruption became outrageous that reform became popular. Generally men required a clear demonstration that their taxes were being misused before rallying to the standard of reform. Apathy or a genial tolerance of corrupt practices were more common.

When the legal rewards of office were so meagre, few blamed the politician for using official responsibilities for personal gain. With so many favours required by business which only governments could grant, the elected official became the target for innumerable pressures; trading his control of votes and his legal responsibilities for cash or other considerations he acquired, with each deal, more allies deep in the heart of respectable business. The elected legislator was subject to the same pressure and was also expected to serve his constituents (or the more influential groups among them). The separation of powers and the large number of elected officials tended to diffuse responsibility; protected by constitutional safeguards against normal bureaucratic discipline and pleading responsibility to 'the people' (in fact to the machine which controlled the vote), the state or municipal official could not be brought to account. The real control was exercised, often behind the scenes, by the boss who managed the local party machine (occasionally both party machines) and through this the votes of the people together with the administrators, legislators or judges whom they elected. Yet no one

N

doubted that the business of politics was arduous. It required unremitting attention and depended ultimately not upon force or fraud, but upon the human relations between party workers and the poorest and most numerous of the voters.[1]

Barely acknowledged by the respectable elements in society the machine politicians performed for them important services. They facilitated the tremendous expansion in the economy. They gave cohesion and stability to a system which might have produced anarchy. They enabled the business *élite* to obtain what it wanted from a society with strong equalitation traditions. They kept control over an electorate which might otherwise have erupted into radicalism. They played an important part in the assimilation of immigrant hordes whose initial bewilderment might easily have turned to rebellious discontent. They provided rudimentary social services where no one else thought of doing so. And being so often without principle, they would cheerfully sell these services to the highest bidder or to the interest which could generate enough electoral pressure. Whichever way one looks at him the professional politician, coarse and corrupt, amoral and self-seeking, was not an excrescence upon American society but an important part of its mechanism. Few of his contemporary critics realized this and wasted much effort in trying to reform the system by overturning a machine or by ousting a few bad men. Bosses were beaten, municipal governments were reformed, new provisions were written into state constitutions, yet new bosses arose silently from the ruins of their predecessors' machines, and a new generation of reformers would reveal the same old shocking practices, while the mirage of Republican purity seemed as elusive as ever.

There were two more hidden factors which went to explain this

[1] From a twentieth-century source comes a good description of these personal relationships. 'Pendergast (the boss of Kansas city) built his organization on the proved principle of personal favors.... People go to the two-story brick building at 1908 Main Street for a load of coal, an order for groceries or clothes. They go to get jobs, to get streets repaired, or to keep them from being repaired. They go with a complaint about taxes or a policeman. They go to have domestic troubles straightened out. They are never turned away without the satisfaction of an answer, and, whenever possible, of a promise that will be kept' (Irving Dillard in *Nation*, Dec. 19, 1936, quoted Peter H. Odegard and E. Allen Helms, *American Politics*, Harpers, 479).

situation. Where social distinction depended largely upon wealth there were few privileges which wealth could not buy. Unrestrained by an aristocratic code no stigma attached to the use of any means for self-defence or self-advancement in the political jungle, and the businessman who corrupted officials, influenced legislators, and made deals with bosses suffered very slight social penalties if discovered. The amorality of unregulated competition could erode public spirit as it eroded everything else. But this disruptive factor operated only because there was an underlying cohesion in the system. The most favourable climate for political corruption is one in which men are agreed upon fundamentals; the dishonest politician becomes a menace when he threatens the established order, he can be tolerated when his misdeeds are limited to petty pilfering, and when there is assurance that, in the face of a real threat, the corrupt and the incorruptible will close ranks to resist the attacker. It was such a threat, presented by agrarian radicalism in the West, which helped to cement the conservative alliance.

* * * *

In the states of the Mississippi valley agriculture had been stimulated by the war, and rising prices had fostered expansion on credit; prices remained high until 1869 but thereafter a steady fall left the farmers carrying a burden of debt. The familiar experience of agricultural depression was given an unusual twist by the settlement of the great plains. By giving to every citizen the right to 160 acres of the public domain the Homestead Act of 1862 seemed to fulfil the dream, dear to Jeffersonian hearts, of peopling the West with a race of hardy and independent freeholders. Unfortunately the right was exercised on a treeless plain subject to recurrent drought, where only large farming could pay, where cattle ranchers had every incentive to defeat its objects by monopolizing large tracts of land, and where large land grants deprived the homesteaders of access to the most valuable land. Moreover Western farming could not carry on without the services of Eastern capitalism and some submission to exploitation was necessary for survival. Without railways crops could not be marketed, without banks the homesteader could seldom start and certainly could not survive bad seasons, without elaborate processing and distributive services the Western farmer would be condemned to extinction. Inevitable as this was it did not commend itself to a people bred in the traditions of local autonomy and taught to expect economic independence. Nor did it excuse the abuses of power to which the great capitalist interests, in particular the railways, often resorted. The Western farmer saw himself threatened with economic slavery; the high hopes of freehold land in the West might dwindle away into farm tenancy, hired labour, or an ignominious flight to the towns. This was the frontier of discontent which existed throughout the late nineteenth century and which was to have a profound effect upon American political history.

Agrarian radicalism was the product of this situation and it advanced upon two fronts: in an attack upon the business civilization at its periphery and in an attack upon its heart. The first was directed mainly against the railways — the most obvious examples of exploitive monopoly — and led through a succession of state battles, to laws for the regulation of rates, for the prohibition of discriminatory practices and for checking monopoly,[1] and to the enactment, in 1887, of the Interstate Commerce Act which established the principle (inadequately implemented in the early years) that an independent Federal commission should supervise the railways. The second was a battle for control over the central financial institutions of the country; it aimed to substitute for the gold standard and the authority of the great Eastern bankers a flexible currency and a decentralized banking system. In the early

---

[1] These state laws were upheld by the Supreme Court. In *Munn v. Illinois*, 94 U.S. 113, Chief Justice Waite made the historic observation that 'Property does become clothed with public interest when used in a manner to make it of public consequence, and affect the community at large. When, therefore, one devotes his property to a use in which the public has an interest, he, in effect, grants to the public an interest in that use, and must submit to be controlled by the public for the common good, to the extent of the interest he has thus created.' This was in 1876, but a new generation of lawyers and jurists coming to the fore in the later years of the nineteenth century were more impressed both with the dogma of *laissez-faire* and with the benevolence of business.

years this programme in its various forms was wholly defeated; the United States were back on gold by 1879 and the arguments for a managed paper currency had made few genuine converts. But in the 1880's the greatly increased production of silver raised new possibilities.

Pre-war America had been on a bi-metallic standard but this had had little effect because the official ratio between gold and silver undervalued the latter and little was sold to the Mint. In 1873 a recoinage act dropped the older provisions for a silver coinage, so that when specie payments were resumed in 1879 only gold was purchased by the government. Increases in silver production soon lowered the value of silver and it would then have been very profitable to sell silver to the Mint at the old ratio; the possibility had a strong appeal to silver miners and propaganda soon convinced many Western farmers that this was the solution to their monetary difficulties. The coinage of silver would greatly increase the money in circulation, it would emancipate banking from the control of London, it would avert the depressing effects of deflation, but it was not open to the reproach of being irredeemable paper currency. The prospect raised great alarm in the East. It was quite clear that bi-metallism was regarded as heresy in London, and that its institution might cause a serious reduction in American investment, perhaps even the wholesale withdrawal of foreign funds. No one could blame the foreign investor if he became frightened of depreciation, though the advocates of silver may have been right in feeling that, in the long run, the attraction of an expansive economy showing large profits from virgin resources would overcome monetary scruples. The argument can be put most fairly by saying that the opponents of silver were probably right in predicting an immediate crisis if silver were adopted but too pessimistic about later recuperation; the advocates of silver were right about its immediate benefit to the Western farmer, wrong in discounting its immediate effect upon investment, and right about the long term need for adjusting the supply of money to the needs of the economy. But the silver question was not merely an argument about money; it asked where the focal

point of the American economy ought to lie, who should exercise
control, and upon what principles.

The comparative success of the drive to regulate railways had
not absorbed radical discontent. Indeed the assumption of
Federal responsibility had been preceded by a denial to the states
of the right to regulate interstate commerce, and as the Supreme
Court was hostile to the new regulatory commission, the railways
might well continue their exploitive practices with immunity.[1]
Other agrarian discontents accumulated with the coming in 1887
of a succession of dry years in the West. The farmer might now
even count himself lucky if he could persuade anyone to foreclose
on his mortgage; it was more likely that he would find himself a
tenant on the land he had owned, burdened with debt, and reduced
to extreme poverty. This situation precipitated the greatest and
most far-reaching movement of agrarian radicalism, Populism or
the People's Party.

The Populists, uniting the convergent movements known as
Farmer's Alliances, opened their attack with a great convention at
Omaha in 1890. The preamble to their programme was a scathing
attack upon American civilization of the late nineteenth century.[2]
They demanded public ownership of the railways, the restoration
to the public domain of unused land grants, a Federal income tax,

[1] In the *Wabash, St. Louis and Pacific Railroad Company* v. *Illinois*, 118 U.S. 557, 1886,
Justice Miller of the Supreme Court announced that 'It cannot be too strongly insisted
upon that the right of continuous transportation, from one end of the country to the other
is essential, in modern times, to that freedom of commerce from the restraints which the
States might choose to impose upon it, that the commerce clause was intended to secure.'
There was, of course, considerable force in this argument, but it rendered very few
activities of the great corporations immune from state regulation. The decision in this
case was the immediate cause of the Interstate Commerce Act, but in *Cincinnati, New
Orleans and Texas Pacific Railway Co* v. *Interstate Commerce Commission*, 162 U.S. 196,
the Court could find no provision in that act which empowered the Interstate Commerce
Commission to fix railroad rates.

[2] 'The conditions which surround us best justify our co-operation: we meet in the
midst of a nation brought to the verge of moral, political and material ruin. Corruption
dominates the ballot-box, the legislatures, the Congress, and touches even the ermine of
the bench. The people are demoralized .... The newspapers are largely subsidized or
muzzled, public opinion silenced, business prostrated, homes covered with mortgages,
labor impoverished, and the land concentrating in the hands of capitalists .... The fruits
of the toil of millions are boldly stolen to build up colossal fortunes for the few, unprecedented in the history of mankind; and the possessors of these, in turn, despise the
Republic and endanger liberty. From the same prolific womb of governmental injustice
we breed the two great classes — tramps and millionaires.'

and the secret ballot. They suggested the use of the initiative and referendum, the direct election of senators, and a single term for the President. The greatest prominence was given to the proposal for a national paper currency (treasury notes not bankers' notes) and for the 'free' coinage of silver. This was the most radical programme to gain any widespread support since that of the Loco Focos. The Populists gained a million votes in 1892 and men began to think of analogies with the early days of the Republican Party and wondered whether the Populists were embarking upon a similar career. The comparison was more superficial than real: the Populists were provincial rather than national in their outlook, their basis was too narrow, their appeal too limited. The rank and file of the party were angry and ignorant farmers, and however much their principles might be enshrined in American history it was now too late in the day for them to change the course of events. Despite the radical proposals for public ownership and political reform the party was backward looking; it did not understand and attempted to repudiate the international economic society in which they lived, and it was incapable of discovering a philosophy which would maintain its momentum when prosperity returned to the farms. Though the Populists sought an alliance with industrial labour, and with small business alarmed by the growth of monopoly, they had little to offer these groups.

These weaknesses were less apparent in the 1890's than they are today and the party's appeal challenged the older parties. As the country moved into a severe economic crisis in 1893 Cleveland, the first Democratic President since the Civil War now serving his second term, responded with a dose of gold standard orthodoxy — suspending the small amount of silver purchases which had been legalized — and by making a deal with J. P. Morgan. Cleveland acted honestly according to his lights at a time when the gold reserves had sunk dangerously low, but an endorsement of his policy by his party would ruin their position in the West. Instead the party swung violently against Cleveland and nominated the Nebraska radical, W. J. Bryan. Bryan was young and vigorous, and his oratory moved even the hard-bitten professionals; his great speech of the 1896 convention was strewn with the allusions which all good Democrats love, with a passionate reassertion of the agricultural foundations of the country, and ended with a magnificent sentence: 'We will answer their demand for a gold standard by saying to them: You shall not press down upon the brow of labor this crown of thorns, you shall not crucify mankind upon a cross of gold.' Bryan was a big, generous, and simple man. He typifies much which has prevented America from becoming the sordid technocracy which her enemies believe her to be. He was sincere, hated mean things, and had an attractive streak of humility. But he would not have made a good President; his intellectual equipment was too meagre, his notions too simplified, and his methods too devoid of finesse. Many Populists looked askance at him, for while emphasizing silver he had done so to the exclusion of everything else, and apart from silver the Democrats were committed to none of the Populist demands. Yet the country was not large enough to hold two Western agrarian candidates and the Populists were forced into a position in which they had to endorse Bryan, seal the doom of their party, and sell out its more radical aspects.

The ensuing election was a struggle between classes, between occupations and between regions; and the last was the most significant. Every state carried by Bryan was in the West or the South; in the North and the Mid-west he received less votes than Cleveland had done in 1892 (despite the increasing population) and in some states less than Cleveland in 1888. Business had seen the Bryan candidature as a challenge and for the first time all the high powered propaganda which it could command was used on one side. Yet it would be wrong to accept the implication that Bryan's defeat was caused only by economic pressure upon the voters; propaganda and influence succeeded because they reinforced the conviction that Bryan, silver and Populism had nothing to offer the industrial society and might endanger its living standards.

Though decent men in the East rallied to the defence of what they believed to be civilization, the election of 1896 — the most important since that of 1860 — left an awkward question un-answered. Had America come to the point where she must choose between the rural demagogue and the plutocrat? Refined men saw not only the heresies of the essentially likeable Bryan but also the rise of squat, coarse, intolerant Ben Tilman, first a Governor of South Carolina and then Senator. 'Pitchfork' Ben relied upon what was perhaps the most ignorant white electorate in the world; alternately he bullied and aided business interests, and the heart of his policy lay in a series of repressive anti-Negro laws. McKinley, the successful Republican President, was respectable and able, of the type which might now become the executive head of one of the great corporations. He seemed to incarnate business con-servatism, and to this he added aggressive imperialism in the Spanish-American War. Demagogue, big businessman, imperial-ist: the trinity formed an alarming prospect for those who still believed that America was the best hope of the world and this was the point of departure for a more significant movement than Populism, for Progressivism which was to change the course of American politics.

In contrast to the Populists the Progressives were middle class, urban, educated and young. They moved in a different stratum of society and it is probable that most of them voted for McKinley in 1896. It has been argued that Progressivism was a late stage in the 'status revolution'.[1] In the mid-century America had had an upper class consisting of lawyers, ministers, teachers and mer-chants who were linked with and shared the prestige of old-

---

[1] Richard Hofstadter, *The Age of Reform*, New York, 1956, Ch. IV.

William Allen White, whose letters contain a most illuminating commentary upon the mid-western progressivism in which he played a leading part, had a most interesting analysis of Progressive support at a late stage in its development: 'Our vote was a town vote, an upper middle class vote, so far as Kansas can be said to have any upper middle class vote. By this I mean the professional man, the college professor — who is of the legion family in Kansas, as the state is full of little colleges — the young doctor, the lawyer, the railway engineer, the conductor [that is the engine driver and the guard — an illumin-ating inclusion in this list] the banker and successful merchant. . . . The average farmer was not with us. He was getting splendid prices for a big crop. It wasn't the belly issue with him. It was partly tradition. . . . What is true of the farmer is equally true of labor . . . . The men with whom we conferred were sincerely for us. They were engineers and con-ductors, and plutocracy of labor. But they couldn't interest the man at the forge or in the switch shanty' (White to Theodore Roosevelt, Dec. 15, 1914, *Selected Letters of William Allen White*, ed. Walter Johnson, Henry Holt).

established families. The rise of plutocracy on the one hand and of mass democracy on the other, of monopolist and boss, isolated this class and steadily reduced its importance; Progressivism is seen as a struggle between the old and the new *élites*. This analysis is important and interesting, but it does not give a complete explanation for Progressivism, which was not merely the reaction of a challenged group but also looked forward to the middle class, managerial, urbanized, self-conscious world of the mid-twentieth century.

The roots of Progressivism may be briefly summarized as anti-boss, anti-trust, and anti-slum. The variable but persistent influence of the 'good government' men has already been noticed — liberal Republican in 1872, Mugwump in 1884 — holding the conscience of the old upper middle class, and nourishing numerous local reform movements in the late nineteenth century.[1] Anti-trust drew upon a wider field; it embraced small producers and farmers, and it appealed to hallowed American traditions.[2] While diffuse and unco-ordinated it could arouse ready responses and was a thing to be respected in practical politics. The greatest triumph of anti-trust was the Sherman Act of 1890 which declared flatly that 'Every contract, combination in the form of trust or otherwise, or conspiracy in restraint of trade or commerce among the several states, or with foreign nations, is hereby declared to be illegal'. It need hardly be said that the simplicity of this

---

[1] The 'Mugwumps' were a group of independent Republicans who backed Cleveland rather than Blaine in the election of 1884. The name is supposedly derived from Indian word for great chief and indicates by its sound as much as by its sense the professional politicians contempt for the 'high-minded' reformer.

[2] The word 'trust' as the symbol for capitalist monopoly enshrines a comparatively brief phase in the history of business consolidation. An obstacle to the concentration of control was the provision, in the charters issued by most states, that a corporation could not hold stock in another corporation. In 1879 the Standard Oil combination of J. D. Rockefeller found a way of evading this by using the well-established legal device of a trust. Stockholders in the various corporations which it was desired to control surrendered their holdings to a body of trustees and received in return shares in the Standard Oil Company. A trustee is empowered to exercise power of attorney in administering the property which has been placed under his care, and consequently the Trust was able to exercise voting rights in numerous corporations and to exercise control when a majority of the stock had been relinquished by the stockholders. After 1897 the Holding Company became the favourite device for exercising control; this took advantage of the laws of a few states such as New Jersey which permitted the state chartered corporations to hold stock in other corporations. The Trust remained however in popular parlance the descriptive name of a great industrial combination.

language proved a challenge to the lawyers and that within the next few years the consolidation of business went forward at an accelerated rate; yet the early ineffectiveness of the Anti-Trust Act should not conceal its real importance. In the relations between government and business it was to fulfil a role similar to that of the fourteenth amendment in racial relations. The forces of anti-trust would now be asking for an enforcement of the law and not for a theorist's dream.

Many people in the late nineteenth century were becoming alarmed at the sad state of the poor in a land of plenty, but the most decisive single influence was Henry George. *Progress and Poverty* had a tremendous influence, not so much because of the remedies it proposed as because of the problem which it posed: 'Where the conditions to which material progress everywhere tends are most fully realized — that is to say, where population is densest, wealth greatest, and the machinery of production and exchange most highly developed — we find the deepest poverty, and sharpest struggle for existence, and the most enforced idleness.' George shook the easy belief in a materialist millennium and he had a most telling criticism of the orthodox economists who acted as the intellectual publicity agents for the established system. He also attacked the fatalistic belief — older than capitalism — that poverty and suffering could not be dispensed with.

It would be possible to trace the separate histories of anti-boss, anti-trust and anti-slum in the later years of the nineteenth century, but the most important question is why they combined about the turn of the century to create a ferment unparalleled in American history. The causes are various. The economic crisis of 1893–7 shook confidence in business leadership, and the better times which followed gave the middle classes sufficient confidence to turn to reform. An upward turn in prices seemed to draw attention to the trust-tariff conspiracy. There was a sudden awareness that political corruption had not been eradicated but forced to become more skilful (the career of Mark Hanna, McKinley's political manager and a man of great intelligence, did something to demonstrate this). The questions asked by the

Populists remained unanswered. There was an inflow of destructive and constructive criticism from England where the Fabians, radicals and iconoclasts were beating upon the assumptions of nineteenth-century civilization. The most powerful immediate influence was 'muck-raking' by journalists who specialized in the exposure of corrupt politics and business. It was characteristic of the middle-class mind that it could be moved to action by abuses on his doorstep; it was the function of the muck-rakers to bring them to his doorstep and to present them in such a way that they could not be ignored.

For Lincoln Steffens, best of the muck-rakers, the diagnosis of the situation was finally reduced to the proposition that 'It is privilege that causes wickedness in the world, not wickedness; and not men'.[1] This was a restatement of the old American thesis that men were naturally good and that the corrupting force was the special power which bad law gave to certain men. It could combine a concentrated attack upon the power claimed by privileged individuals with a belief that this could be rectified through democratic processes which transferred authority to those who were aggrieved or disinterested. Progressivism was a state of mind rather than a movement, but it did lead men along two distinct roads; to an acceptance of business collectivism combined with control exercised by the collective force of the people operating through their governments, or to a belief that bigness itself was dangerous and ought to be outlawed. In practice the gap between the two might narrow because both wanted government to act and both could combine against the more obvious examples of corruption.

---

[1] Steffens was much impressed by some words of Tom Johnson, the reform mayor of Cleveland: 'Oh, I could see that you did not know what it was that corrupted politics. First you thought it was bad politicians, who turned out to be pretty good fellows. Then you blamed the bad businessmen who bribed the good fellows, till you discovered that not all businessmen bribed and that those who did were pretty good businessmen. The little business didn't bribe; so you settled upon, you invented, the phrase 'big business', and that's as far as you have got: that it is big business that does all the harm. Hell! Can't you see that it is privileged business that does it? Whether it is a big steam railroad that wants a franchise or a little gambling-house that wants not to be raided, a temperance society that wants a law passed, a poor little prostitute, or a big merchant occupying an alley for storage — it's those who seek privileges who corrupt, it's those who possess privileges that defend our corrupt politics' (Lincoln Steffens, *Autobiography*, Harcourt Brace, 479).

Robert La Follette of Wisconsin was the first prophet of Progressivism. Starting almost from scratch in a state largely settled by conservative Germans and Scandinavians, and dominated by railways and other large corporations, he built up a reform organization which controlled the state for a quarter of a century and imposed an iron discipline on capitalist enterprise. He captured the state Republican organization and made Wisconsin a laboratory for social and economic reform. Not the least important was the way in which he co-opted the intellectuals; the campus of the state university at Madison became the focal point of the reform movement.

La Follette was an inspiration to reformers throughout the Western states, but far more important on the national stage was Theodore Roosevelt, whom the assassination of McKinley brought to the White House in 1901. Roosevelt had been a successful reform governor of New York, though there, as in later life, what he said he was doing was often more important than what he actually did. He had been physically weak as a boy and this had an important psychological effect of which the external symptom was the fetish of physical fitness and a domineering manner. He thoroughly enjoyed the Spanish-American War in which he played a small but active and much publicized part. Coming from a patrician family he never felt the kind of inferiority complex which other politicians experienced when dealing with men of great wealth.

Roosevelt put teeth into the Anti-Trust Law and the Interstate Commerce Commission. He took an active personal interest in 'conservation' (the preservation of the resources of the public domain against private exploitation). He showed his readiness to appeal to the people as their special representative against the interests. He made Progressivism respectable by demonstrating that its object was not to override or alter but to enforce the law. He revived the idea that government had a moral responsibility for the welfare of the people.[1] But he was also conservative; he

---

[1] In 1905 one of his supporters summed up the impression created by Roosevelt in these words: 'The election of Theodore Roosevelt means that no power in this Republic,

never had any intention of sponsoring radical reform, he never broke off the lines of communication with big business, and he welcomed the concentration of energy represented by the great capitalist enterprises. He insisted that government must be detached, must mediate and guide, and ought to look to results rather than to forms. Trusts could be good or bad, according to whether they helped or harmed the people, and in a well-run state the gentle pressure of the law would ensure that all behaved well.[1]

In 1912, when Roosevelt believed that his chosen successor, Taft, had betrayed Progressivism he tried to return as leader of the Republican Party; thwarted by the Old Guard, which had control of the party machinery, he accepted nomination as candidate of the new Progressive Party which was mainly composed of dissatisfied Republicans. As Progressive leader he had to formulate a programme which would satisfy the most enthusiastic body of reformers who had ever banded together in a political party. The Progressive Party of 1912 had a revivalist tone about it, but it also looked to the future with a wide programme of public responsibility in the industrial age. Following the influential Progressive writer, Herbert Croly, Roosevelt preached that Hamiltonian means must be used to attain Jeffersonian ends; the positive power of government must be used to protect and

---

however strong or rich, no organization, however numerous or determined, is too great for the sovereignty of the law; no citizen however poor or humble, no interest however small or weak, is too insignificant for the law's protection. And this was the largest issue of the campaign — that common equality before the law which Theodore Roosevelt's public personality represents' (Albert J. Beveridge, quoted Claude G. Bowers, *Beveridge and the Progressive Era*, Houghton Mifflin, 213).

[1] The real test came when law had to be enacted against the pressures exerted by short-sighted business. It is difficult to realize the extravagance of such opposition. In 1906 a bill to provide for the inspection of meat was proposed by Senator Beveridge with the full support of the President. The shocking condition of the Chicago slaughterhouses had been exposed by Upton Sinclair in *The Jungle*, by articles in the British *Lancet*, by an investigation conducted by the Department of Agriculture, and by special commissioners personally appointed by Roosevelt. Nevertheless the packers and cattlemen brought terrific pressure against the bill, and the comparatively small expense which they would incur blinded them to the advantages which they might expect from established standards. Beveridge's bill passed the Senate, but crippling amendments were added in the House. The full influence of the President, combined with considerable public agitation, could not save the bill in its entirety and only publication of the report of the President's commissioners saved its substance. Even so the cost of inspection was placed on the public and not on the packers, and the latter were relieved of the obligation to stamp the date on canned meat (Claude G. Bowers, *Beveridge and the Progressive Era*, 226–33).

promote democracy, but it was to be power in partnership with the beneficent forces of large-scale capitalism. All the enthusiasm generated by the Progressive Party could not wean Democrats from their party allegiance and though Roosevelt ran far ahead of Taft he was far behind Woodrow Wilson, the Democratic nominee. No two men could have been more unlike or have disliked each other more, but it now fell to Woodrow Wilson to take up the Progressive mantle of Theodore Roosevelt.[1]

Wilson had been President of Princeton and Governor of New Jersey. He was austere and high principled; human and likeable in his family circle, and occasionally able to move a crowd with superb oratory, he was at his worst in dealing with his immediate subordinates. His cabinet meetings were formal and unhappy, and at one time or another he bitterly offended most of those who had stood closest to him. Though an intellectual he was often surprisingly ill-informed and one gets the impression that he had read very little since his early academic days. On the other hand he was a man of ideas; he liked to play with them, to hear what others had to say, then to clarify, 'and in a few minutes time has stripped the whole situation to the bare bones of its fundamental aspects, and has rested his conclusions and decisions upon a few simple and elemental principles.'[2] But the bare bones were often a little too bare and the resounding phrases lacked contact with reality. Wilson imagined that the aim of his 'New Freedom' was nothing less than the restoration of popular government. 'Bring the government back to the people. I do not mean anything demagogic: I do not mean to talk as if we wanted a great mass of men to rush in and destroy something. That is not the idea. I want the people to come in and take possession of their own

[1] From 1916 comes this gem from the pen of Theodore Roosevelt. 'Wilson, with his adroit, unscrupulous cunning, his readiness to about face, his timidity about any manly assertion of our rights, his pandering to the feelings of those who love ease and the chance of material profit, and his lack of all convictions and willingness to follow every gust of popular opinion, will be supported by the mass of our fellow citizens' (*Correspondence of Theodore Roosevelt and Henry Cabot Lodge*, II, 478). This was written in criticism of Wilson's foreign and defence policy, but it is typical of Roosevelt's feelings about Wilson.

[2] A. S. Link, *Wilson. The New Freedom*, 64, quoting R. S. Baker in *Collier's*, Oct. 7, 1916. Professor Link, whose biography is likely to become a classic, quotes with approval a remark of Senator John Sharp Williams: 'He was the best judge of measures and the poorest of men I ever knew' (*ibid.*, 70).

premises; for I hold that government belongs to the people, and that they have a right to that intimate access to it which will determine every turn of its policy.' It was not Wilson's way to translate this into constitutional or administrative proposals; one feels that it was not campaign tactics which prevented him from doing so but a genuine reluctance to get beyond what he believed to be first principles. He could work with arduous precision at detailed measures when necessary, but it was the generality unsupported by practical application which was to ruin his international policy as it clouded some of his domestic measures.

At the outset any energetic Democrat had certain lines of policy laid down for him. He must preside over a lowering of the tariff, favour a decentralization of banking which would preserve the public interest in national credit, and he must enforce the anti-trust laws. Wilson believed that free competition must be restored and protected against the threat of monopoly. He believed that in economic and social affairs government ought to be an umpire rather than a player. He thought that government could advance the welfare of the people while leaving the direction of the economy in private hands. As his first term drew towards its close he found himself moving nearer to Roosevelt's New Nationalism though without acknowledging that he was doing so. There was a political reason for this: Wilson had won in 1912 on a minority vote, he could not be re-elected in a straight fight without attracting a fair proportion of the Progressive vote. *Laissez-faire* and states' rights must be jettisoned and positive legislation enacted, and under this pressure Wilson personally sponsored bids for labour support in a workmen's compensation bill for federal employees, for humanitarian Progressivism in a child labour bill, and for enlightened business in a tariff commission and other measures which offered government co-operation to business. This abrupt break with the Democratic past helped Wilson to win in 1916 by a narrow margin; it also forced the Democratic Party along the road which would make it the main vehicle for twentieth-century reform.

At the national level one is often compelled to describe

Progressivism in generalities — it saw the injection of a new spirit into government rather than far-reaching changes — but at the state level it left a record of detailed change with the common purpose of strengthening the democratic basis of the political system. The Progressives thought more democracy the remedy for bad democracy and their reforms were of great significance for the American future: at a time when the democratic drive was weakening in Europe, the United States saw a proliferation of experiments which invigorated and intensified the popular pressures in society. The Progressives erred in believing that democratic government would always be good government, but their work ensured that the Americans would not sacrifice democratic processes on the altar of efficiency. The most important of their reforms — and one which was generally adopted — was the Direct Primary by which each party holds a preliminary election to decide which candidates it shall nominate for office. Like any other piece of machinery this can be rigged, but it can also act as an open door through which reforming amateurs can attack, and in areas where there is virtually one party rule it is the only occasion on which the voters can express their choice between rival policies. The secret ballot was also generally adopted and its utility can hardly be questioned. The direct election of United States Senators became the general law under the Seventeenth Amendment. The founders of the Republic had believed that upper houses ought to differ in character from the directly elected lower houses; now both houses of Congress were directly elected and the different function of the two houses became less clear, but the prestige of the Senate, already high, rose still higher with the popular mandate of its members.

The Western states, where Progressivism was strong, added to their constitutions provisions for the initiative, for the referendum, and for the dismissal by popular vote (recall) of officials and judges. In consequence the voter in these states is now faced not only with a bewildering list of offices on the ballot sheet but also with a long list of initiative proposals and of measures which must be referred to the people. It need hardly be said that bewilderment

o

is more common than intelligent appraisal, and that pressure groups have found ways of turning things to their advantage, but it is impossible to resist the conclusion that, for good or ill, this is more like real democracy than the sham democracy which prevails in some other countries.

The defeat of 1912 sealed the fate of Progressivism as a separate political party. Save in a few states the Republican Party organization had not been captured and the Progressives had no corps of professionals who could carry the party through lean years. Progressives might admire Wilson but they disliked most other Democrats and could not contemplate a course which would give them prolonged tenure of the White House. By 1916 Theodore Roosevelt was converted to Republican reunion and refused the Progressive nomination; he also knew that the twilight of Progressivism had already set in.[1] The movement tended to divide between those who were satisfied and those who were disillusioned with what had been done, between those who were becoming conservative and those who expected a new departure, between those who would become the intellectual allies of big business and those who would feel the magnetism of the Russian Revolution. The European war introduced new distractions, with Theodore Roosevelt becoming aggressively militant and La Follette bitterly isolationist. Nor was it easy to keep the Progressive ferment alive while civilization was on trial in Europe.[2]

Progressivism passed as a movement, even as a state of mind, but it remains the great fount from which have flowed the ideas and experiments which condition modern America. If Progressives

[1] 'For two or three, and in some cases for four years — since 1910 — we have been living upon our emotions. We have been putting spirit into others. We have been spurring literally thousands at first hand, and holding ten thousands almost at first hand, in fighting trim. And the thing I saw was that we went through the motions — all the motions of real crusading soldiers — but the whole thing was automatic. The spiritual well from which we dipped was physically low. We need emotional rest' (William Allen White to Roosevelt, Dec. 15, 1914, *Selected Letters of W.A.W.*, ed. Walter Johnson, 157).

[2] 'The whole trouble with our humanitarian platform, as I see it at the moment, is that it hit the war. Kaiser Bill blew it up. You cannot get humanitarian progress on the face page when humanitarian retrogression is occupying the headlines. You cannot get people interested in minimum wages and laws for service and equitable railroad rates in the face of the news from Verdun' (*Selected Letters of W. A. W.*, ed. Walter Johnson, Henry Holt, 169, White to Rodney Elward, Jan. 24, 1916).

had not overturned the established order this was something which they had never intended to do. Progressivism was not, like Populism, an external attack upon the liberal capitalist system, but an internal revolt which sought to make it more liberal. Identified with Presidents, Senators, Governors and men of unchallengeable respectability it had influenced even those who professed to dislike it. Though a short period was to ensue during which Progressivism seemed to be utterly defeated, the argument, when it recommenced, started lower down the stream. The implications of anti-trust, anti-boss and anti-slum were then accepted even by the most conservative, and in consequence American capitalism had a resilience which enabled it to meet new threats. In criticizing the abuses of American capitalism the Progressives had strengthened rather than weakened it; they had helped to rid the system of crude and imprecise notions, of some of its more barbarous practices, and had restored confidence in the political system. In an era when European intellectuals and working-class movements were repudiating capitalism, the Progressives had committed themselves to a gallant and influential attempt to make it work better.

[8]

The United States in a World of Conflict and Revolt

In the nineteenth century Atlantic civilization had a frontier of expansion in the Mississippi valley; by 1950 it maintained, under American leadership, a defensive frontier in Germany. In the nineteenth century the stabilizing factor was British naval power, in the twentieth it has become the power of the United States. As late as 1870 America was feared in Europe as the symbol of radical democracy and the 'pro-Americans' were to be found in the lower and middle classes; by the middle of the twentieth century America had become the symbol of capitalist conservatism and anti-Americanism was one of the hall-marks of left wing opinion. In the nineteenth century the flow of capital and culture was to the West; in the twentieth vast sums have been lent or permanently donated by Americans to the countries of Europe and their former colonies, the great American Universities have taken their places at the forefront of learning and an indigenous literary culture is now among the most lively in the world.

All these changes have occurred so quickly and with such profound consequences that it is no surprise that the citizens of the world's most powerful country often present a curious blend of anxiety to please and desire to project their own aims upon the rest of the world, of great generosity and of bitter recrimination, of self confidence and self criticism. A rich country necessarily gives hostages to fortune; her interests overseas accumulate, her own living standards are raised to an artificially high level, and her own internal structure becomes less stable as the access of wealth fosters conflict over its use and distribution. Economic 'imperialism' has played a less significant part in American policy than her critics imagine: it is a virtue of competitive free enterprise that losses must be accepted as well as gains, and the American public has not usually wasted much sympathy upon businessmen whose interests have been prejudiced by events overseas. The kind of impulsion which led to the conquest of South Asia, the partition of Africa and the assault upon the independence of China has not played much part in American policy, save perhaps in South America where the extension of American business has often coincided with the needs of hemispheral defence. However the American economy has become ever more closely integrated with that of the rest of the world, and the problem shifts from the defence of a few capitalists overseas to the protection of domestic interests and living standards against the pressures exerted by unstable foreign economies. The traditional method of doing this through tariff policy is no longer adequate, for it tends to increase the weakness which it ought to cure; and it has become increasingly clear that the United States must either import goods or export capital (and may sometimes have to do both) in order to sustain foreign economies. The problem is also entwined with that of subversion; depressed or undeveloped economies breed communism which is regarded as a threat to American civilization, and Americans and Russians were led into fierce competition for the privilege of helping those who could not help themselves.

If the development of the arts of peace have brought the United States into an entirely new relationship with the rest of the world, wars and the weapons of war have accelerated the changes and given them a sinister twist. If one date stands out more than another as marking an epochal stage in American history it is April 6, 1917, when the United States declared war on Germany. Behind lay the old isolationist nation, confident in its own institutions, convinced of moral superiority to the rest of the world, yet still receiving from that world so many contributions to its

civilization; before lay alliances and entanglements, troops overseas, capital exported, and the defence of a bastion against heresy
and military threats. The industrial and scientific revolution
brought with it military changes which destroyed the old foundations of American security. The change was first observed in
America when the rise of modern navies made possible an attack
from the sea. The vast improvement in aircraft during the Second
World War, and the increase in the destructive power of bombs,
raised the spectre of direct attack upon American soil. The
development of atomic explosives and rocket missiles of enormous
range made it certain that a powerful enemy could damage at long
range and devastate at close quarters. Thus military developments
forced the United States into association with foreign powers in
an effort to build up a distant defence perimeter.

*   *   *   *

In the latter part of the nineteenth century the United States
attempted to conduct three distinct foreign policies: a policy for
the Atlantic, for the American continent, and for the Pacific. The
first concentrated upon freedom from European entanglement,
the freedom of the seas, and a moralistic approach to foreign
countries which was ultimately to develop into ambitious and
altruistic plans for international organization. It was not apparent
to most Americans that this policy was possible because of the
European balance of power in which an essential factor was
British naval superiority in the Atlantic. The second started with
the Monroe doctrine — that no European power can enlarge or
acquire territory in the American continents — and goes on to
the position that the United States has a vital interest in the
stability of other American countries. Again success owed much
to Great Britain whose interest ran on parallel lines and whose
navy relieved the United States of the responsibility of policing
the Atlantic. The third or Pacific policy was never so closely
defined, though some approach to definition was made in the last
years of the century with the 'open door' policy which maintained
the right of all nations to develop trade with China while respect-

ing the territorial integrity of that country.[1] The 'open door' was never very successful for it tried to impose restraint upon other powers without providing the means to enforce it; after the rise of Japan as a first class power with very definite designs upon the Chinese mainland it became impossible. Yet the United States adhered to the 'open door' long after it had become unrealistic to do so because there was no other definition of American policy in a region where the interests of the United States became ever more intimately involved. It was inevitable that a great nation should seek to control events in the Western ocean; it is surprising that the United States did so with so much hesitation.

An unnoticed landmark in American history was the defeat of France by Prussia in 1871. The European balance of power began to disintegrate and a new, vigorous and unified Germany — with nothing to lose from an overthrow of the established system — was brought within range of the Atlantic. The threat was emphasized by the Anglo-German naval rivalry which developed after 1900 and by the writings of Captain Mahan and other apostles of naval power. By 1914 the advocates of a big navy had succeeded in turning the United States from a minor into a major naval power, though the effect was somewhat diminished by British and German advances in naval construction which had already rendered obsolete a large number of the American ships. The final dissolution of the European balance of power in general war found the United States divided; a large majority felt an emotional commitment to England and France but an equally strong determination that America should not be involved, a large minority (mainly of German descent) were sympathetic to the central powers, and a vociferous minority (of whom the most eminent was Theodore Roosevelt) wanted early intervention on the Allied side. Wilson won re-election in 1916 as the man who had kept America out of war; six weeks after his second inauguration the United States declared war on Germany.

The explanation for this abrupt change lies in belligerent inter-

---

[1] The American attitude to China was much influenced by the missionaries, who built up a network of churches in China.

ference with American ships in the Atlantic, which meant that the United States must either play a tame role of acquiescence or fight to defend the lives and property of her citizens at sea. The United States had cause for quarrel with both groups of belligerents on this score, for both were desperately anxious to prevent American shipping and supplies serving the cause of their enemies, but because the British blockade of German ports was effective the major part of American war-time trade had developed with Great Britain and France, and the demands of these powers for food and munitions had led them to place huge orders with United States suppliers. At the same time British naval superiority in European waters and the stalemate on the western front caused the German strategists to see in the paralysis of the Atlantic commerce their main hope of winning the war. Early in 1917 the Germans announced a campaign of unrestricted submarine warfare and it was this which brought the United States into the war on the side of the Allies on April 6, 1917. It was necessary to stress the role of a vital American interest — the freedom of the seas — in bringing on war; yet for many Americans, perhaps even for Wilson himself, it was a rationalization of a growing and purely emotional conviction that America's mission was to save the civilization from which she had sprung.

It was a matter of enormous significance for the future of the United States that at their head was a man who was able to take this vague and subjective feeling and turn it into a declaration of purpose. In doing so he transformed the old repudiation of Europe into a programme of salvation and reform. 'We are glad,' he told Congress, 'now that we see the facts with no veil of false pretense about them, to fight thus for the ultimate peace of the world and for the liberation of its peoples, the German people included: for the rights of nations everywhere to choose their own way of life and of obedience. The world must be made safe for democracy. Its peace must be planted upon the tested foundations of political liberty. We have no selfish ends to serve. We desire no conquest, no dominion. We seek no indemnities for ourselves, no material compensation for the sacrifices we shall freely make.

We are but one of the champions of the rights of mankind. We shall be satisfied when those rights have been made as secure as the faith and the freedom of nations can make them.' Despite the post-war defeat of Wilson, and despite attacks by both the cynics and the so-called realists, these historic sentences charted the course of American policy and radically changed the American self-portrait.

Wilson's idealism united his people and had a tonic effect upon a war-weary world. Beyond the seas he appeared as an almost superhuman figure; not merely as the leader of a powerful nation whose troops would turn the scales of war, but also as the eloquent spokesman for the quiet and decent life which all men wished to enjoy. At the same time a war begun to protect national interests but accompanied by the discovery that 'the present German submarine warfare against commerce is a warfare against mankind', bequeathed to the nation's foreign policy a dichotomy which has never been fully resolved. Is it the function of American foreign policy to protect national interests or to conduct a crusade, or is there a wider analysis in which both can be reconciled?[1]

Wilson was able to effect such a reconciliation to the satisfaction of himself but not ultimately to that of the majority of his countrymen. 'What we demand in this war', he said, 'is nothing peculiar to ourselves. It is that the world be made fit and safe for every peace-loving nation which, like our own, wishes to live its

---

[1] 'I see the most serious fault of our past foreign policy formulation to lie in something that I might call the legalistic-moralistic approach to international problems.... It is the belief that it should be possible to suppress the chaotic and dangerous aspirations of governments in the international field by the acceptance of some system of legal rules and restraints.... It is the essence of this belief that, instead of taking the awkward conflicts of national interest and dealing with them on their merits with a view to finding the solutions least unsettling to the instability of international life, it would be better to find some formal criteria of a juridical nature by which the permissible behavior of states could be defined' (George F. Kennan, *American Diplomacy*, Chicago University Press, 1951, 95–6).

'The American commitment to the ideal of the juridical equality and moral integrity of states explains our participation in two world wars.... To some these American notions seem impractical and foolish. Influential scholars and counselors would have us abandon them. They suggest that we should cease being childish and idealistic and recognize that the national interest requires us to become disciples of Machiavelli, take our lessons from Richelieu, Bismarck or Clemenceau. The fact that Germany and Japan have committed national suicide by consistent adhesion to these doctrines seems not to dampen the eloquence of those who would persuade us to abandon the beliefs and practices by which we have lived and prospered from the beginning' (Frank Tannenbaum in *Foreign Affairs*, Oct. 1951).

The debate continues.

own life, determine its own institutions, be assured of justice and fair dealing by the other peoples of the world as against force and selfish aggression. All peoples of the world are in effect partners in this interest, and for our own part we see very clearly that unless justice be done to others it will not be done to us.' From this issued the Fourteen Points, the programme for a just peace which included the proposal for a League of Nations. It is a paradox which is perhaps too obvious today that Wilson combined his supra-national authority with 'the freest opportunity for autonomous development' for national groups. It was also paradoxical that a nation which had fought a great civil war to determine that a section should not be independent should now sponsor a kind of international Federal authority while blessing the disruptive force of nationalist self-determination. Wilson bequeathed to the world the problem of reconciling vigorous local loyalties with a vaguer allegiance to Union, which his own nation had solved only after the total victory of those who had captured the Federal government.

To posterity and to many American contemporaries an attractive feature of Wilson's policy was his advocacy of humane treatment of the defeated German people. He had always insisted that this was a war by peoples against bad governments, and with the latter overthrown reconciliation should prevail. It was precisely at this point that Wilson was forced to yield to the mature wisdom of European statesmen who demanded reparations, guarantees, and humiliation of the vanquished. Forced to choose between breaking with his allies and salvaging the League of Nations Wilson chose the latter as productive of the greater good; the choice was understandable but it was probably wrong. He had abandoned something which many Americans would have counted an immediate gain for an untried experiment which would commit the United States to that continuous participation in international responsibilities for which their people were yet unprepared. Within a few months of his return from Versailles Wilson was a sick and beaten man with his policy in ruins: the United States did not ratify the treaties, did not join the League, and sought isolation once more; not in ignorance of their associations with the rest of the world but as a conscious attempt to reduce the consequences of that association.

* * * *

The years which followed 1918 were crowded with symbols of America's changed relationship to the world. The war left the United States, which had normally had a debit balance, as the world's greatest creditor nation.[1] America was already the greatest steel producer and the experience of war stimulated her industrial economy while it weakened that of Europe. The census of 1920 revealed that for the first time urban exceeded rural population; the resilience of a nation of small farmers was being succeeded by the vulnerability of a city-based culture dependent upon so many outside factors for its well-being. With a new series of immigration laws the door was closed against most of those who wished to come — that is against the Italians and Slavs — and thus tore down for ever the self-portrait of America as the asylum for the oppressed and poor.[2] And for the first time, in the great 'Red Scare', Federal and state authorities conducted a calculated war upon opinion.

Yet many Americans failed to recognize the portents which were so abundantly displayed. They ought not to be blamed excessively for the common failure to recognize that the past was dead, but they may perhaps be blamed for making their failure so

[1] It is estimated that in 1897 foreign long-term investments in the United States were $3,400,000,000 and U.S. long-term investments overseas $690,000,000; with small short-term investments on both sides the net indebtedness was $2,710,000,000. In 1919 the figures were respectively, $2,500,000,000, $6,500,000,000, and $3,700,000,000 net credit.

[2] The immigration law of 1924 fixed the total of permitted immigrants at 150,000, but this total was apportioned amongst the countries of the world in proportion to their contribution to the total American population in 1920, with a minimum quota of 100. The calculations on which the quotas are based are extremely complicated and statistically unreliable but their effect is, of course, to favour the countries which contributed to the 'old' American stock at the expense of those from which came the more recent immigrants. Thus Great Britain and Northern Ireland had 43% of the total quota in 1935 while the quota for Italy was 3·8%; a very large part of the British quota was left unfilled but thousands of Italians who wished to go to America were unable to do so. The quota system does not however apply to other countries of the New World and there are no restrictions upon the immigration from United States possessions; the exclusion of the poor and restless from Mediterranean and Eastern Europe has left more room for those of Mexico, French Canada, and Puerto Rico.

strident. An imperceptive isolationism was accepted as political wisdom in foreign affairs. The businessmen were singularly ill-informed about the nature of the world's business, and led their country into a disastrous depression which was, in turn, to contribute to the weakening of former allies and the rise of dictatorships and anti-capitalist movements. And though the American economy was clearly based upon the home market, preoccupation with this alone caused a myopia which helped to raise once more the intellectual barriers between the United States and the rest of the world. The great lack was inspired leadership; Theodore Roosevelt would have rejoiced in the opportunities of power and imposed an American will upon the world, Woodrow Wilson would have sensed the responsibilities of the age and translated them into phrases which would have lingered in men's minds; but Roosevelt and Wilson were both dead and of their successors Harding was a fool, Coolidge limited, and Hoover able but with a personality which did not impress itself upon the people at large. American influence might have meant much to the world, but America did less than nothing to prevent the drift of Western civilization towards social failure and renewed war.

The 1920's which are sometimes seen as a period of reaction back to the age of McKinley actually witness a decisive stage in the rise of the modern system. If Americans were aware of the plight of Europe, the knowledge served to emphasize their own happy destiny; to them the age seemed buoyant and challenging. Historians who have been preoccupied only with liberal criticism and with the evolution of regulated capitalism, and who see these years as the last of the 'old order', have missed the essential character of this decade in which the economic revolution engineered by mass production produced its first and most profound effects. Led by Henry Ford, manufacturers realized the enormous potentialities of the great consumer market (with millions of well-paid men buying cheap standardized goods) and there was a significant shift in emphasis from work done to wages spent. This was the era of the cheap motor car, of rapid agricultural mechanization, and of a revolution in the kitchen which made the labour-saving device synonymous with Americanism. It was also the period in which the propaganda of business assumed its modern form, and in which the great charitable foundations began to have a significant effect upon the world of learning and of the arts. The expressions with which business-men described, justified and applauded their new role as leaders of American civilization appear, in retrospect, to have been crude and narrow minded, but they were not insincere and they were not essentially different from the more polished phrases with which modern businessmen celebrate their mission.

There were however two aspects which appeared profoundly disturbing: the first — which was obvious to all — was the phenomenal increase of organized crime, the second, of which few were conscious, was the alienation of the intelligentsia from the established order. Big crime may have arrived later on the field than big business but its growth was equally striking. It arose from a convergence of causes. The total prohibition of the manufacture and sale of alcohol, which became a part of the Constitution with the eighteenth amendment, created a law which the thirsty but otherwise law-abiding citizens would not observe. A principal argument for prohibition had been to promote the moral and material condition of the poor — of slum dwellers, of industrial workers and of Southern Negroes — but evasion of prohibition became mainly a crime of the upper and middle classes. And because the middle-class law breaker would not extend his criminal activities beyond the purchase of an illicit bottle, a great organization sprang into life to supply him with the bottle. A second factor was the emergence of pre-war Italian immigrants from the obscurity of the slums; in an America in which opportunities were becoming more limited and almost closed to the sons of Italian peasants — among a race with strong traditions of illegal secret societies — crime was an outlet comparable to that of politics for the mid-nineteenth century Irishman. There were, of course, thousands of law-abiding and hard-working Italians, but the environment in which they found themselves gave the vicious their opportunity. The American system of politics made matters worse. Though prohibition was a national act passed by a heavy majority in Congress, that body demonstrated its normal suspicion of executive power by making provision for the Federal enforcement of the law so niggardly that it was farcical. The detection and punishment of crime, apart from that against the United States, was the function of the separate states; this left the burden of coping with the disastrous effects of prohibition with the authorities least likely to deal successfully with it. State police forces were notoriously weak or corrupt, and their inability or unwillingness to arrest criminals was increased as the criminals themselves moved into local politics. It was in fact easier to convict the gangster criminals for evasion of income tax (a Federal crime) than for murder. The situation was desperate; far more so than that resulting from political corruption in the nineteenth century. Crime had built up its own hierarchy, its own code, and its own system of punishment (almost invariably death). This organization was able to defy the normal law enforcement agencies and through its political influence to protect itself against interference. As the business of crime increased it spread from bootlegging (the illicit alcohol trade) to rackets under which small tradesmen were forced to pay for 'protection' or risk their businesses and lives. What was even more alarming than crime — which could be diagnosed — was the apparent paralysis of the American people. Men who were readily identifiable and well known as prominent criminals went unmolested, committed more crimes and amassed some of the largest fortunes in the country. A nation dedicated to the rights of life, liberty and the pursuit of happiness was manifestly failing to protect any of them.[1]

---

[1] The evils have not been eradicated. In 1951 a committee headed by Senator Kefauver came to the following conclusions, (1) A nationwide crime syndicate does exist in the United States, (2) Behind the local mobs which make up the crime syndicate is a shadowy international organization known as the Mafia, (3) Although dishonest politicians and office holders are a small minority political corruption in the United States seems to have sunk to a new low, (4) While law enforcement primarily is a local responsibility much of the responsibility for what is going on rests squarely upon Federal enforcement agencies, (5) Infiltration of legitimate business by known hoodlums has progressed to an alarming extent in the United States (Estes Kefauver, *Crime in America*, Ch. 1). Senator Kefauver made the following comment upon the evolution of organized crime: 'In the earlier and more violent days of rumrunning and hi-jacking the big city gangs thrived on murder and other crimes of violence. As the years went by and the mobsters grew suaver and more experienced they realized that killings were not only bad business but bad public

The nineteen-twenties were the springtime of the American intellectuals. Men of the Progressive era had been serious minded and given to politics and good works; the men of the next decade had a lighter touch, generally despised politics, and thought mainly about themselves. Their philosophy combined an intense individualism with a Freudian denial of individual responsibility. While there was much which was weak and frivolous there was also much to be gained from a mood which respected the intellect even when it appeared useless. The search for creative imagination produced bizarre results but also produced novels and poetry which may well come to occupy an honourable place in the literature of the world. In the South the new spirit combined with an intense awareness of tragedy to produce a literary movement of prolonged significance. The great majority of these intellectuals felt themselves alienated from the government of their country and from the dominant business class. They were rebels against convention rather than against political authority, but their contempt for the established order was likely to be more destructive than conscious revolt. A civilization can survive criticism but it may be corroded by the contempt of its most active minds.

Crime and the alienation of the intelligentsia were the greatest threats to American civilization, but other weaknesses were apparent to those who looked below the surface. Large segments of the population were not sharing in the general prosperity and very little was being done to help them. The distinction between a highly developed industrial society and a retarded rural economy was again apparent, and there was a constant accumulation of human waste in the lower strata of the growing cities. Agriculture as a whole passed from a war-time boom and expansion to a post-war slump and over-production. In some parts of the South, there seemed to be a complete retrogression in material and intellectual standards. Many American cities could show a diseased heart in

relations, that "in union there is strength...." Hoodlums — that is, the smart ones who lead the new-style gangs — started cleaning their finger-nails, polishing up their language, and apeing the manners and trappings of captains of industry. While "muscle" — the willingness to bomb and kill without scruple — still remains an indispensible business accessory of the mobs, "brain" has supplanted "muscle" as the dominant factor in mob leadership.' Illegal gambling seems to be the mainstay of these criminals.

which a depressed race of slum dwellers dragged out a miserable existence, making a precarious livelihood out of casual and sweated labour. Whilst the propagandists of capitalism were hailing the 'new era' in which poverty and class conflict would be abolished under the stimulus of enlightened self-interest, critics of the system could point to this evidence of its failure.

At the same time business itself was showing the most alarming signs of mental disease. On the one hand no project seemed too fantastic to attract the savings of the small businessman, on the other no deceit seemed too elaborate for the master minds engaged in building extraordinary hierarchies — corporation upon corporation, holding company upon holding company, share issue out of share issue — until it became increasingly difficult to fix the responsibility for anything. The great speculative boom gave a touch of unreality to everything it touched, to land in Florida, to films in Hollywood, and to the soaring prices of shares in the great corporations. An unprecedented number of Americans had mesmerized themselves into the belief that prosperity must go on for ever, and it was almost unpatriotic to throw doubt upon this astounding defiance of the business cycle.[1]

By 1929 the questions were not whether the 'new era' could go on, but how it would end and what would succeed it? Would the next stage be a revolution or accelerated evolution? The severe depression which began at the end of the year revealed the hollowness of business propaganda and added to the critics of American capitalism a ruined middle class; such a combination of disillusion with resentment might have provided the opportunity for a revolutionary minority. The missing element in the chemistry of this hypothetical revolution was the pre-existence of such a

---

[1] This had its human, its pathetic and almost its idealistic side. In a brilliant piece of journalistic history F. L. Allen wrote (*Only Yesterday*, Ch. XII), 'In the Big Bull Market there was compensation. Still the American could spin wonderful dreams — of a romantic day when he would sell his Westinghouse common [stock] at a fabulous price and live in a great house and have a fleet of shining cars and loll at ease on the sands of Palm Beach. And when he looked forward to the future of his country, he could envision an America set free — not from graft, nor from crime, nor from war, nor from control by Wall Street, nor from irreligion, nor from lust, for the utopias of an earlier day left him for the most part sceptical or indifferent; he visioned an America set free from poverty and toil. He saw a magical order built on the new science and the new prosperity.'

minority. There were neither Bolsheviks nor National Socialists ready to exploit the disasters of the time. Another check upon revolution was the very magnitude of the depression. In the four years 1929–33 the *per capita* income dropped 100 per cent, and unemployment rose from the unusually low level of under 500,000 in 1929 to nearly 12,000,000 in 1933. The most disturbing aspect of the depression was its continuance: the Wall Street crash which began it in 1929 could be dismissed as a normal though unusually severe economic crisis, but things were worse in 1930 and every prediction of a coming upswing was falsified. In 1931 conditions were worse again and by the opening of 1933 they were appalling. The catastrophe benumbed rather than infuriated, and created an atmosphere of gloomy frustration rather than of incipient insurrection; but its dangers were none the less real. The depression was more than an economic event, it was also a crisis in the American faith. The whole trend of American development came under severe criticism and desperate forces might assume the centre of the stage and force a new departure.

It was a tribute to the political traditions of America that what followed was not a revolution but an election and a legislative programme. The brunt of public displeasure fell upon the able and humane Herbert Hoover, elected to the Presidency in the halcyon days of 1928, who was unable to convince the people that he had either the skill or the will to deal effectively with economic catastrophe. As a result the Democrats swept the field in 1932 and carried their nominee, Franklin D. Roosevelt, to the White House. Roosevelt's inauguration in March 1933 was followed by a period of intensive legislative activity christened the 'New Deal'.

* * * *

The revolution did not take place. The New Deal accomplished many things, earned extravagant praise and bitter denunciation, but the result was to leave the existing system reinforced, underwritten, and remarkably resilient.[1] It accelerated certain changes

[1] The name 'New Deal' derives from a chance phrase in F. D. Roosevelt's acceptance speech to the Democratic Nominating Convention in 1932, in which he promised 'a new deal for the American people'.

P

which had been maturing since the Progressive Era, it effected a political upheaval, and it raised both government and organized labour to a new stature in American society; but it was not revolutionary, it was not anti-capitalist, and it plays a decisive part in the evolution of modern American capitalism as a system which is regulated, corporate and benevolent.

The New Deal never achieved a coherent philosophy and it utilized many different strands of criticism, which had tended to diverge, but which were drawn together by the depression. There were old Progressives of the Theodore Roosevelt brand; by 1932 some of these had become extremely conservative but others were more than ready to support a modernized version of the new nationalism. There were old Bryanite Democrats always critical of industrial capitalism, but thinking of restraint rather than of positive action. There were Wilsonian Democrats — forming the main body of the party — who were violently opposed to monopoly, friendly to small business, ready to see a measure of government intervention but suspicious of anything which smelt of socialism, and generally orthodox in their economic views. Then there were the City bosses increasingly anxious about their hold upon electorates driven desperate by poverty; the boss had thrived upon poor social services but he was now faced with a situation which he could no longer control by the dispensation of petty favours, and hoped for government funds which he could administer. Organized labour was weak in 1933 (they had not gained during prosperity and the depression was too rapid for them to stand against loss of wages and security) but it was a potential source of support for any government which would appear to fight the battle for the underdog. There were the intellectuals alienated from Republicanism by its low cultural temperature. Finally there were the Socialists and Communists — both of whom ran their own candidates with record polls in 1932 — but many of whom were ready to align themselves with any government which promised vigorous action in the hope of influencing its policy. Over and above the difficulty of uniting such diverse opinions lay the perennial problem of uniting a party which always tended to be sectional rather than national, which cherished states' rights and a suspicion of Federal authority among its traditions, and of bringing its anarchic forces together behind a government capable of dealing with both the economic and the psychological crisis. The performance of this task, rather than the precise measures which he initiated, is the true measure of the greatness of Franklin Delano Roosevelt.

Roosevelt in 1932 looked most unlike the hero to whom desperate peoples turn. He was a cripple from the waist downward. His manner was mild and genial. He was a patrician by birth and his conventional education at Groton and Harvard had brought out nothing which distinguished him from other rich young men of real but superficial ability. He was not a profound thinker, he was not an outstanding administrator, and he did not appear mentally tough. He had been a bright young man under Wilson and Vice-Presidential candidate in 1920 when the Democrats fell on evil times. Stricken with infantile paralysis he became more reflective, more human, and perhaps a more humble person; he learnt his dependence on others not only for physical aid but also for conversation and ideas. Intellectually he remained aloof and secretive, but this was now overshadowed by a willingness to hear advice, to discuss, to consult all manner of persons from college professors to old-time bosses. By 1928, when he re-entered politics as Governor of New York, he probably knew more about the way in which people thought about politics than most experienced politicians. He developed an uncanny sense of knowing how people felt, what their reactions would be, and of the way to approach so that they would feel good as well as grateful. He had also to a marked degree that wonderful politician's gift for seeing problems in the mass while treating persons as completely important individuals. Though his thought was never precise or profound its range was very wide, and he had a real gift for synthesis and exposition.

Roosevelt was the least doctrinaire of reformers. Sensing that the psychological need of the people was for 'action and action now', he had no rigid views about the form which this action should take. He required plans, proposals, suggestions, information and ideas and believed that differences could be reconciled if men were forced to work together. He liked administration to be active and purposeful rather than tidy, and the executive pattern of the New Deal became a mass of overlapping responsibilities, a frequently illogical assignment of duties, and the continuous use of unofficial advisers. For the solution of short-term problems the drive imparted by Roosevelt made this makeshift machine work quickly and effectively; for the creation of a permanent central administration, designed to carry out duties not previously performed by government, it was less successful. An important temporary innovation was the importation to Washington of the 'Brains Trust' which had advised him as Governor of New York. The brains trust was recruited largely from Columbia and Harvard Universities, and its use meant more than the search for expert advice by the President; for the first time since the earliest days of the Republic the intelligentsia could feel that it had a vested interest in government.

Under the Constitution as it then existed Roosevelt, elected by a great majority in November 1932, could not take office until March of 1933. For four months more the unfortunate President Hoover, whose inauguration had taken place in the full sun of the new era but whose administration had become identified with depression, continued in office. Hoover was a man of distinguished ability with a Progressive background who might, in happier times, have done much to humanize and reform the 'new era'. He was weak precisely where Roosevelt was strong: in his failure as a politician, in his misunderstanding of depression psychology, and in his rigid adherence to economic theories which had ceased to have much meaning with twelve million unemployed. On the day of Roosevelt's inauguration the banking system came to a standstill. The ordinary relief schemes dependent upon private charity had proved completely inadequate. Neither manufacturers nor farmers could see the small opening through which prosperity might return. From bankers to the unemployed, men were bewildered and demoralized. During the next few months massive action brought the guiding hand of government into every corner of the nation; for good or ill precedents were set which could never be reversed.

The first phase of the New Deal included measures intended to provide immediate relief and to 'prime the pump' of the exhausted economy. Consciously or unconsciously the New Dealers followed Keynes in diagnosing government expenditure and deficit financing as the remedy for depression. At the same time the old inhibitions about the use of Federal funds were swept away and the Government co-operated with the states in unemployment relief, underwrote mortgages to save middle-class homes, and set the able-bodied unemployed to work. These measures of relief were accompanied by others designed to reconstruct the economy upon new lines. The guiding principles were derived from the New Nationalism of Roosevelt and from the later phases of Wilson's policy.[1]

The Agricultural Adjustment Act aimed to restore farm income by restricting production under voluntary agreements presided over by government officials. It was successful in its immediate objective, it tied the farmers politically to the New Deal, it turned Jefferson's chosen people into foster children of the Federal Government, and it raised wider questions of the ethics of restricting production in a time of scarcity. The Tennessee Valley Act took in hand one of the most depressed rural regions in the South, set up a great government corporation to harness rivers, generate electricity, provide irrigation, and undertake agricultural education to enable people to use the new facilities. It was intended as a pilot scheme which would lead to similar

[1] Raymond Moley, one of original Brains Trust, explained the principles of the New Deal in this way: 'The early New Deal . . . was dominated by the theory of Concentration and Control — by the beliefs that competition is justified only in so far as it promotes social progress and efficiency; that government should encourage concerted action where that best serves the public and competition where that best serves the public; that business must, under strict supervision, be permitted to grow into units large enough to insure to the consumer the benefits of mass production; that organized labor must likewise be permitted to grow in size but, like business, be held to strict accountability; that government must cooperate with both business and labor to insure the stable and continuous operation of the machinery of production and distribution' (Raymond Moley, *After Seven Years*, Harpers, 372).

developments, but its very success created opposition from private business which has not yet been overcome.

The most characteristic and controversial feature of the New Deal was the National Industrial Recovery Act which invited industry to organize under government supervision. Pooling and price fixing — long anathema to the proponents of anti-trust — were now officially sanctioned, and once approved by the President the codes drawn up by businessmen had the force of law. For business the price was to be paid in the government's insistence that standards must be fixed as well as prices and that Trade Unions must be recognized as the collective bargaining agents. The act was welcomed with moderate enthusiasm by big business, with reserve by small business, with modified approval by the American Federation of Labour, and with unqualified enthusiasm by the industrial unions which rightly regarded it as a charter for the organization of unskilled labour. For many ordinary working people it meant a government guarantee for shorter hours, better pay, safer conditions of work, and increased employment through the shortening of individual shifts.

The New Deal operated within a Constitution which had been specifically designed to limit the powers exercised by national authority and it reopened the old argument between strict and loose construction. Some readings of the Constitution saw Federal authority as capable of indefinite expansion: though the limits were fixed the national government could move as far as it liked between them. Others argued that a barrier ought to be fixed beyond which government could not go, and among such were the majority on the Supreme Court which proceeded to strike down the AAA and the NRA and other lesser New Deal measures. The Court has been much abused for its stand and some of its arguments were unconvincing, even within the framework of their constitutional theory; but if men choose to live under a written constitution its provisions ought not to be whittled away as soon as a plausible argument commends itself. The Court was also fulfilling some of the functions of an upper house (which the Senate could no longer carry out since the seventeenth amendment), that is of calling for second thoughts when great changes are made by a popular majority which may be transient. It may be argued that it is not proper for a court of law to perform this function, but it is probably right that someone should do it.

It is often implied that the resistance of the Court was futile. Roosevelt's landslide re-election in 1936 tempted him to propose an unsuccessful reform of the Court and persuaded the Court itself to allow re-enacted features of the New Deal. The earlier decisions of the Court had however a permanent effect. The new measures were carefully framed so that they would not provide precedents for a general enlargement of Federal power and they provided *ad hoc* remedies for particular ills; what the Court had defeated was the idea of government as the central planning and executive authority in the economy.[1] The Federal Government would be a watch-dog and it would employ a staff to deal with casualties, but it would not become a managing director.

It is possible that this was in line with Roosevelt's own intentions. He was far removed from socialism, he never really believed in big government as a universal principle but only as a reserve of power which could be employed as society demanded, and his own instincts were to keep the balance between conflicting forces rather than to plan continuously. After 1936 the older anti-trust theme was heard audibly once more and the brief honeymoon between the New Deal and corporate capitalism was ended in divorce. At the same time there was a drive to provide 'security' for the working population, and the political centre of gravity in the Democratic Party shifted significantly in the direction of the urban masses. In a sense therefore the 'Second New Deal' was

[1] In *Schechter Poultry Corporation* v. *United States*, 295 U.S. 495, 1935 (the decision which destroyed the N.R.A.), Chief Justice Hughes said, 'It is not the province of the Court to consider the economic advantages or disadvantages of such a centralized system. It is sufficient to say that the Federal Constitution does not provide for it. Our growth and development have called for wide use of the commerce power of the federal government in its control over the expanded activities of interstate commerce, and in protecting that commerce from burdens, interferences, and conspiracies to restrain and monopolize it. But the authority of the federal government may not be pushed to such an extreme as to destroy the distinction, which the commerce clause itself establishes, between commerce "among the several States" and the internal concerns of a State.'

more radical than the first — it was at this period that Roosevelt became a hated symbol for respectable conservatives — but also radical in the traditional way with business conservatism developing the familiar reactions. There was also some disillusion amongst former supporters of the New Deal because the shock therapy of 1933, while successful in restoring the patient's self respect, did not seem to have eradicated the disease. Unemployment remained high and there was sharp business recession in 1937. New Dealers could argue that American recovery was held up by the instability of European economies and politics, but this was suspiciously like Hoover's argument that the depression was a European phenomenon and proved no weaknesses in American society. The outbreak of higher lunacy in Europe in September 1939 provided the real cure for American under-employment; war demand soon set the factories humming, while war anxieties were largely responsible for Roosevelt's renomination and re-election as the first President ever to serve three terms.

A belief that the New Deal helped rather than hindered the evolution of modern American capitalism must be reconciled with the fact that many Americans believe it to have been revolutionary. The main explanation for this is found in its political effects, which converted a normal Republican majority into a normal Democratic majority and made the latter party the main vehicle for American liberalism.[1] The majority of Americans had come to live in towns, and by 1932 the sons of the thirteen million immigrants who entered between 1900 and 1914 were of voting age. There had also been a great migration of Negroes into the Northern cities. The Republicans had relied upon the allegiance of industrial workers, Negroes and small urban property owners to the Grand Old Party; they had failed to understand or to calculate upon the character of a country in which the balance would be held by city masses who felt that they were outcasts in American society. In 1920 the twelve largest cities gave the Republicans a majority of 1,600,000; in 1932 this became a Democratic majority of 1,900,000

[1] The argument here follows Samuel Lubell, *The Future of American Politics,* New York 1951, Ch. 3.

which was enlarged to 3,600,000 in 1936. At the same time the Republican hold upon the Western prairies was weakened, and though Roosevelt did much to offend Southern conservatives the Democrats never lost a Southern state during his Presidency. Thus Roosevelt achieved that alliance between farm and factory which had been an elusive mirage for all earlier reform movements. He also won the intellectuals. Numerically insignificant but strong and increasing in influence, college and school teachers, writers, artists, and many journalists were attracted to the New Deal; ignored by the Republicans they became active in the Democratic Party. In spite of massive Southern conservatism on the right wing of the party, reformers and liberals looked to the new alliance of power for the fulfilment of their aspirations. The new character of the party was confirmed under Harry Truman, who succeeded to the Presidency after Roosevelt's sudden death early in 1945 and who won re-election in 1948.

It was of enormous significance for the American future that organized labour and the restless intelligentsia found their haven within one of the traditional parties. If they made the party more radical, the party, with its Southern anchor and its rural traditions, made them more conservative. Whilst a minority of the intellectuals and labour leaders drifted into communism, and some of these seem even to have attained high government office, anti-capitalism almost disappeared as a significant political factor. In 1932 the socialists and communists polled nearly 1,000,000 votes, in 1936 just over 200,000 and in 1940 under 150,000. An affirmation of belief in free enterprise became essential for any man who wished to make his way in politics, and many of the Unions gave only a bare tolerance to socialists. Thus the way was opened for a reappraisal of American capitalism which seemed on examination to be very unlike the model of the classical economists or of the Marxists; the conservatism of the mid-century is not a reaction against the New Deal but a direct consequence of it. The New Deal was not a revolution but it may have averted a revolution; and if it did this it was an event of major importance in the history of the world.

In 1939 history seemed to repeat itself. The outbreak of a European war found the United States undecided, unarmed, and committed to neutrality. From the start the case against Hitler looked much stronger than that against the Kaiser and a majority of Americans hoped for a benevolent neutrality in favour of the Allies. There were however counter currents: for many the new outbreak seemed the last disease of a rotten continent from which America should stand aside however much the tragedy was to be regretted. There was deep distrust of the French and British governments which entered the war. The poor record of the European nations as debtors after 1918 was remembered. At the same time there was always the desperate hope for a short war in which Hitler would be defeated or overthrown. After the collapse of France, Italy's entrance into the war, and the invasion threat against Britain, intervention might leave the United States to fight alone a war which they had not sought, and in spite of the growing sympathy for Great Britain this caused further hesitation. In the summer of 1941 the German attack on Russia once more raised the hope that the war would settle itself without America. By this time however the United States were already far gone in the experiment of trying to win a war without fighting, culminating on March 11, 1941, with the Lend-Lease Act by which America undertook to supply vast quantities of arms and other supplies to the Allies at the expense of the American taxpayer. On August 14, 1941, President Roosevelt met Mr Churchill in mid-Atlantic and drafted the Atlantic Charter which met the American demand for a definition of war aims. In October there was initiated the programme of co-operation between British and American scientists which was to lead to the Atom Bomb.

The United States had done everything to ensure an Allied victory short of committing American troops; could the Allies win with aid and without military support? It seemed very doubtful. At the best the Allies were doomed to a long defensive struggle, and the fateful year 1941 brought little news save that of continuing German success. The Balkan countries and Greece were overrun. The hopeful development of a British offensive against the Italians in North Africa was ruined by the arrival of German troops. The first German offensive against Russia reached the gates of Leningrad, Moscow, Sevastopol and Rostov. Allied shipping losses in the Atlantic continued to be very heavy. Time was running out and America must soon decide whether to fight or lose, whether to reinforce failure or to take the field herself. The decision was never taken. On December 7, 1941, the Japanese attacked the American fleet at Pearl Harbour in the Pacific; on the following day the United States declared war on Japan, and three days later, in pursuance of an agreement with Japan, Germany and Italy declared war on the United States.

*   *   *   *

To understand the sequence of events which brought Japan into the war against the United States it is necessary to go a long way back, to the year 1898 when the United States forced war upon a reluctant Spain in order to 'liberate' Cuba, which had been thrown into anarchy by revolts and Spanish reprisals. In a short and glorious Cuban campaign the United States lost 459 men on the field of battle, 5,063 from accident or disease, and woke from a fit of war fever to find themselves responsible for the Philippines as a result of action taken by naval men on the spot, with some connivance on the part of expansionists in the Navy Department.

Conservative business interests had been lukewarm or hostile to the war, but in the debate which followed over the future of the Philippines their influence was thrown heavily in favour of annexation. So handsome an outpost of American civilization, won so unexpectedly, ought to be treated as a gift from God rather than as a sacrifice to anti-imperialist sentiment. The Philippines and some small Pacific islands were annexed, though leaving a costly campaign against Philippine nationalists as the legacy of acquisition. War enthusiasm had also enabled the expansionists to force through the annexation of Hawaii, where American sugar planters had overthrown the native régime and set up a republic in 1897. Thus the United States had, within a few months, emerged as a colonial and Pacific power, and this had been achieved as a result of that characteristic mingling of aggression and self-justification, of power politics and a civilizing mission, which one had come to expect from other imperialist powers. Further pieces were added to the jig-saw of Pacific power when the Samoan Islands were divided with Germany in 1899, and again in 1903 when Panama was incited to rebel against Colombia and, as a price of independence, to cede to the United States a strip across the isthmus as the route of a future canal.

The rise of Japan posed new problems. Her war with Russia in 1904 won American sympathy but her unexpected success threatened to dissolve the Far Eastern balance of power and to place American interests at the mercy of the victor. With great skill President Theodore Roosevelt, who was invited to act as mediator, negotiated a settlement which gave Japan a free hand in Korea and a footing in South Manchuria but did not eliminate Russia's Far Eastern power. The aims of Japan were clear. With an expanding population and a rising industry she wished to model herself upon England as a sea-power with control over colonial markets, raw materials and food supplies. It was her misfortune that she could not move in any direction without meeting established European interests or attacking Asiatic nations whose development was retarded but whose civilization was somewhat older than her own. It was the error of Japanese rulers that they sought to meet this situation by the creation of a military state; Japan would become not the England but the Prussia of the Far East. In 1914 the Japanese joined the Allies and obtained former German colonies, the elimination of one European competitor, and extended opportunities in China as her reward.

It was in the Pacific rather than in the Atlantic that the United States paid the first instalment of the price for isolation. In 1931 the Japanese began a systematic aggression against China; the United States failed to get British diplomatic support against Japan because the British preferred to work through the League of Nations; but when the League proposed a stiff policy — which might have included economic sanctions against Japan — the

United States refused to incur the risk of a war in which they would have had to have borne the major burden. Under pressure the Japanese withdrew from the international port of Shanghai but retained control of Manchuria as a puppet state. While the balance of power in the Pacific had shifted against the United States, these events also contributed to the collapse of the peace system in Europe, and to the paralysis of those powers whose interest lay in the avoidance of war.

Faced with the rise of Japan the United States might have offered co-operation, asking concessions won from China or the European powers as their price. They might have recognized danger from the start, declared the integrity of China to be a vital American interest, and attempted the containment of Japan by force. Neither policy would have found ready acceptance from the American people, and the strong pressure groups concerned with China — the missionaries and traders — both favoured peace and conciliation rather than policies which might bring disturbance and war to Asia. In the event the United States clung to the 'open door' policy, long after it had ceased to have any reality, until its formal denunciation by Japan in 1938. Refusing either to condone or to combat Japanese policy, adhering to the 'open door' while failing to obtain that support from European powers without which it was meaningless, opposing force with words while drifting into a position of unmistakable hostility, the American Pacific policy had come to include most of the text-book errors of weak diplomacy. The war of 1939 seemed to provide Japan with an opportunity which could not be missed; the French colonies were an easy target, the British might soon follow. American aid to the Allies made it comparatively easy to obtain from Germany and Italy promise of support if the United States declared war. The United States, still trying by remote control to check Japanese expansion, declared that intervention in French Indo-China would be regarded unfavourably; this led Japan to the conclusion that if the United States would not cut their losses in Asia by voluntary withdrawal they must be forced out by war. When the Americans refused to withdraw, the attack upon Pearl Harbour followed. It was symbolic of the paralysis of American Pacific policy that the forces at Pearl Harbour were not alert, and that the attack by Japanese carrier-borne aircraft sank or disabled nineteen naval vessels including eight battleships.

Partly by the pressure of events, partly by the dramatic intervention of Japan, the United States had been drawn into a position in which they were the mainstay of the Allied cause. This was emphasized by the decision (taken in conjunction with the British staffs and before the Japanese attack) to concentrate upon Europe first if America was drawn into the war. In the Pacific America fought a defensive war and a naval war; in Europe an offensive war to crush Germany and Italy was planned from the start. The fullest co-operation with Great Britain was a military necessity, and so was a rather more restrained understanding with Russia. Thus the Americans found themselves defenders of the British Empire (though with lingering suspicions of British colonialism), and (with even greater reservations) of Russian communism. The old and the new phobias had both to be sublimated. It also became clear that American responsibilities could not end with victory, and in 1944 the decisive steps were taken which pledged the United States both to a large share in economic reconstruction and to participation in a new international organization to succeed the defunct League.

Within a short space of time Americans were therefore forced to make further changes in their world view. Acquiescence was not always given readily. From the start there were those who argued for major concentration upon the Pacific, who continued to distrust Great Britain and to fear Russia, and who hoped that with the end of war the United States could withdraw into diplomatic isolation. To some extent this policy was caught in its own inconsistencies: concentration in the Pacific must help to restore the crumbling Asian Empire of Great Britain; Great Britain was the only remaining European power with the prestige and strength to counter Russia; Europe might be despised but it must be held either by friend or foe and it seemed that only American aid could ensure the former. The isolationists lost the debate but their resentment was to lead to much trouble in the post-war world.

The Second World War gave an entirely new aspect to American defence and diplomacy. In effect the Monroe doctrine was extended to Europe and the United States came to regard the integrity of the west European states as an American interest. Such a policy could not be carried through without troops on the spot and economic aid. When American troops landed in England in 1942 few anticipated that they would become a familiar sight in post-war Europe, but this was already implicit in the logic of events. Lend-Lease came to an abrupt end in August 1945, but in June 1947 the Marshall Plan of economic aid to Europe was launched.[1] 'Its purpose', explained Marshall, 'should be the revival of a working economy in the world so as to permit the emergence of political and social conditions in which free institutions can exist.' The Marshall Plan was generously conceived and generously executed, but its necessity lay in the needs of the United States. These needs were now so different, and so differently explained, from those of the recent past that one can forgive the man on Main Street for some bewilderment and for a failure to understand whether he was a benefactor of mankind or an imperialist ogre.

[1] General George C. Marshall, Chief of Staff throughout the war, was appointed Secretary of State by President Truman in January 1946.

[9]

Conservatism and Liberalism

The years since 1945 have seen the combination of unprecedented prosperity with unprecedented anxieties. The implications of America's new position in the world have not been easy to understand or to accept. Peacetime conscription, military bases overseas, enormous defence budgets, economic aid to foreign countries, membership of the United Nations and the difficult task of living with allies are some of the things which middle-aged Americans find it difficult to accept even while they may recognize their necessity. Through the North Atlantic Treaty Organization (something more than a military alliance and something less than an international authority) the idea of an Atlantic community begins to receive substance. The old political habits of lengthy debate, obstruction, and the rough treatment of public men become embarrassments in the conduct of foreign policy in a swiftly moving world. The constitutional division of authority over foreign affairs hampers quick decision. The emotional implications of living in a challenged civilization also perplex the Americans; in the past they have always assumed that their occasional enemies were knowingly sinning against the light, and the notion of an enormously powerful nation regarded by millions as the hope of the future and committed to the ultimate destruction of the American system, is not one which is easy to accept. This and the counter effort to project a favourable image of America upon the world has led to a mood in which Americans seek to define their own qualities and elucidate the characteristics of their civilization, and this combines with a fear of the un-

American activity which may erode that civilization from within. The Federal Bureau of Investigation, a secret police originally formed to fight organized crime, is employed mainly upon the detection and prevention of subversion. The right accuses the left of being 'soft' on Communism, the left accuses the right of betraying American liberties. Old problems, long regarded as purely domestic (the tariff, the treatment of Negroes, and the restrictions on immigration) assume international significance.

The war in Korea occupies a pivotal point in the development of modern American attitudes. It was fought under international auspices; it was, for so small a fighting front, enormously expensive in men and money. It demonstrated the aggressiveness of Communism and the comparative weakness of the non-Communist nations who had gone ahead with their disarmament programmes. And it was the first war in which the Americans suffered a major defeat in the field and only a limited success in the final peace settlement. It showed that the destruction of Japanese military power had opened the door for a Chinese Communist state with enormous manpower, able to draw upon the industrial production of Russia, and completely intransigent in negotiation. When the expectation of early victory dimmed, the war became almost as unpopular amongst certain sections of opinion as the war of 1812 or the war against Mexico. When President Truman dismissed General MacArthur not for military failure (which might have been excusable after his disastrous miscalculation of Chinese intentions on the Yalu River), but for political insubordination, the critics of the war tried to make a hero of the General. But the legacy of the Korean War was not the triumph of the isolationists, of opponents of the United Nations and of foreign military aid, or of the politicians who attempted to sweep the country against the Democratic Party and its 'twenty years of treason'. In 1952, at the height of the Korean War, both parties chose candidates committed to the widest degree of international co-operation, the great N.A.T.O. alliance became a political expedient for continuous consultation and a formidable military power, foreign aid increased, and though Eisenhower, the Republican, won a land-

Q

slide victory his party won Congress only by the narrowest of margins. Thus the shock of Korea turned America definitely towards building a permanent structure of world-wide defence against Communism and Russia.

The nineteenth-century American was an introvert so far as the rest of the world was concerned and an uncritical extrovert so far as his own civilization was concerned; the modern American tries to present to foreigners a picture of confident extroversion, while becoming increasingly introspective about the character of his own country. What is the experience of being an American? The official information services abroad pour out pamphlets and import lecturers to give the answer; supported by government funds, or by the great philanthropic foundations, the travelling scholars, scientists, and technical experts are found in every non-Communist country trying unofficially to explain America by precept and example. Yet at home the answer seems far from clear; Americans are often their own most severe critics, and though the field of debate may sometimes seem narrow the acrimony and passion is great. The truth is that concurrently with the great change in her external relationships America has been passing through a crucial phase in her own internal development. The outward picture of the conservative bastion is wholly misleading when one examines the ferment of ideas, the ceaseless debate, the healthy uncertainties, and the less healthy aberrations which constitute the true picture of recent American history. The internal conflict, arising from these foreign and domestic tensions, can be described as that between conservatism and liberalism.

Neither conservatism nor liberalism are terms indigenous to American political history; neither is in common use until the period of the Civil War and then with restricted meanings. It was not until the early years of this century that the struggle of Progressives against Old Guard taught Americans to distinguish sharply between those who defend and those who would modify the existing power structure. The words remain ill-defined; descriptions of attitudes not of organizations. The struggle between conservatism and liberalism is not coincident with the party struggle; there are liberal Republicans and liberal Democrats, and each party contains a strong conservative element (though trying to conserve slightly different things). The future of America is determined not so much by the outcome of party battles, but by battles within the parties and by the degree to which conservatives or liberals dominate them.

Conservatism in America suffers under one peculiar disadvantage and one special advantage. The disadvantage is that the basic slogans and beliefs of American life are hostile to the concentration of authority in any hands, and it is difficult — though by no means beyond the wit of astute public relations officers — to twist these beliefs into a defence of the accumulation of power in the hands of great corporations. The advantage is that the thing defended is dynamic, successful and forward looking. American conservatism does not carry with it the stigma of retarding progress, and its popular appeal rests on the claim that it welcomes movement and encourages the rising standards of the mass consumer market upon which the prosperity of business depends.

The disadvantage of conservatism has led to a movement of 'new' conservatism which rejects entirely the radical and revolutionary heritage, which takes as its heroes Burke, John Adams and Calhoun, and which affects to despise the raw culture and philosophy of business conservatism. They have sacrificed the assets of American conservatism and look backward as resolutely as the Jeffersonians whom they regard as their particular enemies. It may be that some future conservative thinkers will be able to weld together the thought of Alexander Hamilton — the true father of dynamic American conservatism — and Calhoun, and to discover that the points on which John Adams and Jefferson disagreed were more important than those upon which they were agreed, but at present it does not seem that such a synthesis would be either useful or true. In a world of rapid change 'conservatism' can have a less rational appeal. People are likely to be hurt, in their interests or in their traditional beliefs, and react by repudiating recent tendencies and by reaffirming virtues which are supposed to have existed in the past. Groups which have lost status or influence, men who cannot accustom themselves to the increase of governmental power, men with qualms about expensive commitments overseas, and opponents of racial integration feel the appeal of this vaguely defined 'conservatism'. On the extreme right vocal and sometimes violent men attract more attention than their numbers deserve, but the great bulk of conservatives are decent-minded people who are honestly perplexed by the problems of the world in which they live.

Less self-conscious than the new conservatives and more intellectual than the reactionaries are the various streams which converge to create a new theory of capitalist society to supercede the old *laissez-faire* model. The mainspring is Theodore Roosevelt's distinction between good and bad trusts with its ruling idea that big business misused is a danger but that a country without big business will stagnate. This constructive conservatism must find a way to counteract both the ingrained suspicion of all in authority and the still prevalent belief that the right to the pursuit of happiness enshrines free competition.[1] 'Competition,' writes an influential exponent of the new economics, 'which, at least since the time of Adam Smith, has been viewed as the autonomous regulator of economic activity and as the only available regulatory mechanism apart from the state, has, in fact, been superseded.' The new regulator is defined in the proposition that 'Private economic power is held in check by the countervailing power of those who are subject to it'.[2] Organization begets organization, bigness begets bigness, and though there may be an initial stage in the development of capitalism during which exploitation is possible and the

[1] David Lilienthal, himself the former head of the giant government-controlled Tennessee Valley Authority, writes, 'If we are to understand the United States today, if we are to develop a conviction about her future, we must fully comprehend that Big Business is basic to the very life of this country; and yet many — perhaps the most — Americans have a deep seated fear and an emotional repugnance to it. Here is a monumental contradiction' (*Big Business: A new Era*, Harpers, 1952, 1).

[2] J. K. Galbraith, *American Capitalism*, Houghton Mifflin, 1952, 118–19. The theory of countervailing power is presented with more subtlety and more qualifications than might be imagined from these two statements (Professor Galbraith describes the second as 'a broad and somewhat too dogmatically stated proposition') and an important limitation is that it does not operate during inflation. But the purpose here is not to discuss the theory but to estimate its effect upon non-professional opinion.

concentration of economic power is harmful, these dangers set in motion defence mechanisms which are bound to place restraint upon monopoly and regulate the economy in the interests of all. Thus big business has produced big labour, big production big distribution, while the ordinary consumer-voter is the force behind big government. This theory helps to emancipate men from bondage to dead ideas, and it accepts the dynamism of the economy which is America's greatest asset, but its political implications are profoundly conservative. It defends the existing power structure, it seeks to reassure critics, and stresses the beneficient operation of a new style Providence which will deliver men from the consequences of their own greed and folly.

For a second source of modern conservatism one must go back to Andrew Carnegie. In 1889 this engaging steel magnate sought to reconcile his Calvinist upbringing with the enormous power which he exercised in an extraordinary amalgam of realism and idealism which he called 'The Gospel of Wealth'. The realism lay in the acceptance of the facts of capitalist life. There were two basic 'laws' — the law of competition and the law of the accumulation of wealth. Competition may be questioned by the moralist but 'It is here; we cannot evade it; and while the law may be hard on the individual, it is best for the race, because it ensures the survival of the fittest in every department. We accept and welcome, therefore, as conditions to which we must accommodate ourselves, great inequality of environment; the concentration of business, industrial and commercial, in the hands of the few; and the law of competition between these, as being not only beneficial, but essential to the future progress of the race.' For this a great price has to be paid in the separation of man from man; this can be remedied only if the 'man of Wealth' considers 'all surplus revenues which come to him simply as trust funds, which he is called upon to administer in the manner which, in his judgment, is best calculated to produce the most beneficial results for the community — the man of wealth thus becoming the mere agent and trustee for his poorer brethren, bringing to their service his superior wisdom, experience, and ability to administer, doing for them better than they could or would do for themselves.'[1] The modern European is apt to treat such altruism with cynical disbelief, but no one can travel far today in the world of learning, medicine or social welfare without realizing that the names of Carnegie, Rockefeller, Ford and of other magnates bear witness to the Gospel of Wealth. Has any other plutocracy endowed culture and welfare so munificently or so intelligently? The critic of American capitalist society may well ponder the answer to this question, and he is likely to find it not only in Carnegie's passing expression of the Gospel of Wealth but also in the ingrained habits of a society which once revolted against privilege based on status. It is, however, undeniable that the wholly admirable work of the great 'foundations' acts as a protective barrier for the established order. The combination of good works with producing the goods is irresistible as an argument for conservatism.

The political problem of conservatism remains severe, for there is no escaping the facts of life in a democracy with an equalitarian tradition. Sooner or later every argument must come down to stump speeches, television interviews, and press conferences. Popularization has usually an unfortunate effect upon conservative arguments, and in America it has perhaps a worse effect than in those countries where the traditions of an *élite* are still strong. To defend the established order, which can really best be defended by subtle and historical arguments, the American conservative is driven to exploitation of crude emotions and fears; in European democracies the sound, fury and demagogy is found mainly on the left, in America it comes from the right. The right wing has built up a whole vocabulary of symbols designed to exploit the fears of the people. A great many Americans find it difficult to believe that the prosperity they enjoy is permanent, and even more potent is the fear of their standing in the community. This anxiety is summed up in the fear of 'un-American' activities. What is feared is the individual or idea which seeks to change the environment in which men are accepted and feel secure, and they are all the more fearful because it is so difficult to define American-

[1] These passages are from an article in *North American Review*, June 1889, CXLVIII.

ism. The ideas of conservatives are thus degraded by contact with democracy, and democracy in turn is degraded by them; it does not necessarily follow that either the ideas or the system are at fault.

Liberals trace their immediate ancestry to Theodore Roosevelt and Wilson. In time this liberalism belongs not to the era of Gladstone in his prime but to that of the glorious revolution of 1906, and it is associated not with *laissez-faire* but with government activity. While conservatives appropriate individualism and states' rights which were once the hall-marks of Jeffersonian radicalism, liberals have taken up (usually without acknowledgement) Hamilton's idea of creative government. Like the conservatives they have one great strength and one great weakness. Their strength lies in their appeal to the broad humanitarian sentiments which find a ready response in the American mind. No American has ever accommodated himself to the belief that suffering is a necessary part of human existence, and most Americans will feel uneasy when told that there are 'under-privileged', persecuted minorities, or abuses of power. The liberal position has, on the whole, been strengthened by the recent extension of these sentiments to the rest of the world. The liberal is quite ready to take upon his own shoulders the suffering of under-developed countries, the aspirations of colonial nationalists, or the need for American economic aid, and so profits by the modern mood of altruistic sympathy. The great weakness of the liberals is that they are always arguing special cases; always pleading for justice to this minority or that region, and losing their force by dispersion among sectional objectives which may be mutually inconsistent. While conservatives have something which is both coherent and national to defend (however badly it may be explained), the liberal gives his central allegiance only to a body of aspirations which conservatives have already appropriated with some success. The liberal is also at a permanent disadvantage so long as the American political system remains in its present form. Nearly all liberal causes demand that something shall be done, yet so many features of the American system are designed to stop things from being done; yet here the liberal is caught in a dilemma because he is not a radical aiming at widespread political change.

The Liberals have consciously avoided commitment to any doctrinaire programme; this has weakened them when a driving force was necessary but facilitated their penetration of established institutions and modes of thought. Their philosophic descent is in the direct line from John Locke to Jefferson, Emerson, William James and John Dewey. This family of philosophers has dealt with principles rather than systems; it does not attempt to explain the whole world but only that part of it which the individual can know. With Emerson and the Transcendentalists this had a mystical twist but it was still the individual mind which was illuminated by the divine light and the individual's world which was explained by it. While the individual could know only certain things, what he did know taught him to be active and altruistic in his dealings with others; whether it was the urging of conscience or a deduction from experience, the responsibility of the individual for making a better world was clear. The link between the unknowable compulsion to do good and the knowable experience of the world around us has been the main difficulty for these philosophers, but Americans of the late nineteenth century evaded the problem by concentrating upon philosophic behaviour rather than philosophic knowledge. William James, who gave the name Pragmatism to this brand of philosophy,[1] was acutely interested in religious experience and rejected the rationalist assumption that man is master of his world, but he also believed that men have responsibilities which they ought to accept and that the pragmatic or experimental method can tell them how to act. The inner compulsion to act may be spiritual, the modes of action can be discovered by observation of results. 'The truth of an idea is not a stagnant property inherent in it. Truth happens to an idea. It becomes true, is made true by events . . . . The true is the name of whatever proves itself to be good in the way of

---

[1] Both the name and methods of Pragmatism take their origin with Charles Pierce who was the most considerable philosopher of the school; but his more important works were not published until long after his death and his ideas influenced only a small group of disciples, of whom James was one.

belief, and good, too, for definite assignable reasons.' John Dewey, the only philosopher in American history to have an immediate influence upon affairs, became the oracle for all movements of liberal reform; nothing was blessed at the liberal altar until he had approved its principles and he took an active part in formulating progressive aims over a wide field. With Dewey the task of philosophy ceases to be concerned with the spiritual problem of the individual and becomes the clarification of men's ideas about the environment and its improvement. Society becomes a laboratory with the philosopher directing the experiments and evaluating the results. An experience is true if it works, but like other objective philosophies the subjective element remains; a process works because the individual thinks it works and what is universally valid is that which is believed by the greatest number of people. Thus the philosopher makes no claim for authority and provides no justification for those who act with authority, and Pragmatism becomes another way of explaining the democratic life of America. But if what is plausible to large numbers is also good, there may be little room for the nonconformist; if the Pragmatists provide the liberals with critical tools for an attack upon right-wing obscurantism, it also tends to create a new orthodoxy slightly further to the left.

Liberal criticism of the business civilization occupies much space in the history books; it almost seems that since 1890 there has been a continual war of attrition against the central citadel. Yet the citadel remains and is today perhaps stronger than at any previous time; each major concession has been converted into a major defence and each victory of the attackers has been followed by their disarmament. Capitalism has succeeded not only by performing its function well but also by adapting itself to its environment. American capitalism has its evolutionary history; if one is able to look back from the sixth decade of the century, and to forget the impact of the depression, the evolutionary picture becomes clear.

The development of the idea of regulated capitalism, from vague assertions to a complex code of rules for business, has been a principle feature of this evolution. The rules are ultimately set by public opinion but immediately by the Department of Justice and the courts. Government has become a kind of watch-dog which welcomes friends with a wag of the tail, growls if they touch something which does not belong to them, and raises a furious clamour when an enemy draws near. Though businessmen have frequent occasions to curse the Anti-Trust Acts their existence convinces the public that businessmen normally obey the rules, observe professional ethics, and suffer if they fail to do either. Regulated capitalism has thus helped to substitute for the image of the 'robber baron' that of the private servant of the public. A second great service performed by the government for the capitalist civilization has been to place a safety net under the economy to help break the fall in bad times and to deal with the normal casualties of the system. A good deal of this social service is performed in co-operation with the states and it has also stimulated many employers to supplement public relief with private welfare schemes. The system of social security is less thorough-going than in England, there are a good many holes in the net, and Americans feel more reluctant than their European counterparts to throw themselves upon public charity; but it has removed American society far from the world of *laissez-faire* fancy in which some Americans still live. While these welfare services were won gradually against the bitter hostility of business conservatism, their value to the latter day defenders of capitalism is enormous; they are thereby relieved from the duty of explaining away Henry George's awkward question about progress and poverty. The third great function performed by the government is of more recent growth and has been more readily accepted: this is the use of budgetary policy and public works as regulators of the economy. The doctrine preached by Lord Keynes — that depression could be met if governments would borrow, spend and reduce taxes when private individuals were cutting down on productive investment and expenditure — has been more thoroughly adopted in the United States than in any other non-Communist country. The world may owe much to the English economist, for a major American depression after 1945 would have been a disaster of incredible magnitude; American capitalism certainly owes him a great deal, for the abandonment of the old 'automatic' regulators has meant that business behaviour is no longer held responsible for the business cycle. If the worst comes to the worst, and a depression should occur, the responsibility now lies firmly upon the shoulders of the Federal Government.

A further great feature in the evolution of modern American capitalism has been the rise of the corporation; indeed if nineteenth-century capitalism can be christened Liberal Capitalism, Corporate Capitalism might be appropriate for that of the mid-twentieth century. Business has become collectivized and its collectivized form is the corporation, a vast organization with world-wide interests run by salaried officials. The corporation has its own hierarchy, its own customs, its own social order, its own way of life. Under the leading executives there is a vast army of salaried officials ranging from salesmen to research scientists. All these people are indoctrinated with loyalty to the corporation and are expected to conform to the standards set by it. The ultimate object of the corporation is to make profits but its 'owners', the holders of its stock, are so remote that they exercise no influence upon ordinary management; dividends become, for the manager, one factor in a highly complex operation and no corporation today would make a 'kill' at the risk of future sales. Continuous expansion is the ideal for all corporation managers, and this means an acute sensitivity to popular opinion.

'Our program', remarked a leading official of General Motors, 'is finding out what people like and doing more of it; finding out what people don't like and doing less of it.' What the public likes about a corporation is not only its product but also its reputation for good labour relations, its generosity to deserving charities, the architecture which it commissions, and the character of its advertisements. A hundred years ago Commodore Vanderbilt could epitomize the spirit of predatory capitalism by saying 'The public be damned'; today the public relations officer is a power in the world of the corporation, and 'service' is a word to conjure with in the board room. When President Eisenhower's first Secretary for Defence, Mr Charles Wilson, dropped a notable brick with the statement that 'What is good for General Motors is good for the United States', he did not mean that the United States should serve the interests of the great corporation, of which he had been head, but that the interests of General Motors could not be disassociated from those of the public.[1]

These aspects of corporate capitalism merge into the concept of benevolent capitalism. Public relations may often be guided by calculation of immediate consequences, but there is also a tradition of communal service which the modern businessman carries on. Though businessmen have not participated to any great extent in the formal responsibilities of local government, they have often been extremely active in other aspects of communal leadership. Hospitals, many colleges and charitable organizations could not carry on at all without their unpaid services, and their voluntary work still plays a far more important part in the life of the community than government activity. It has been a natural development for this individual responsibility to be transferred to the great corporations. Individual businessmen still play a very large part in the administration of voluntary associations but the great corporations provide much of the money with which they are carried on. This provision of funds by active businesses supplements the massive and institutionalized charity of the great foundations, and with them helps to create the picture of capital accumulation as the great mainspring from which flows the vitality of American life. The picture of benevolent capitalism is not one which is neglected by the propagandists of corporate

---

[1] The modern spokesmen of the great corporations are likely to echo with approval the words of one whom their predecessors hated with particular ferocity. Louis B. Brandeis was the lawyer who successfully intruded into the courts of law the consideration of social needs in determining the constitutionality of economic regulations. A prolonged fight occurred in the Senate before his nomination, by Wilson in 1917, as a Justice of the Supreme Court was confirmed. In 1914 he wrote, ' "Big business" will lose its sinister meaning, and will take on a new significance. "Big business" will then mean business big not in bulk or power, but great in service and grand in manner. "Big business" will mean professionalized business, as distinguished from the occupation of petty trafficking or mere money making. And as the profession of business develops, the great industrial and social problems expressed in the present social unrest will one by one find solution' (*Business — a profession*, 1st ed., 1914, 12).

business, and if their self-satisfaction is sometimes nauseating it is none the less real.

* * * *

As the United States grew closer to the rest of the world they became conscious that these other countries were very unlike their conventional pictures and even more unlike America. The world was filled with people who were not struggling to be Americans but to prevent themselves from being anything of the kind. The shock of discovery was profound. The great social democratic revolutions, accelerated by two world wars, had weakened or destroyed the *anciens régimes* and, even in western Europe, half or more of the population voted against capitalism. Organized labour, both in unions and in political parties, was enormously strong, and even European conservatism looked suspiciously pink. Some great social reforms the Americans could approve: the introduction of egalitarian education in Great Britain, for instance, followed a road which the socialized public education of the United States had taken in the nineteenth century — but the nationalization of industry, the national health service, and cradle to grave welfare services seemed to sap at the foundation of what the American had been taught to regard as freedom. One could perhaps tolerate measures such as the nationalization of essential but run-down concerns such as the British railways and coal mines, but what galled was the assumption of socialists that this somehow gave them a moral superiority over Americans. At a time when even liberal thought in America was moving towards an appreciative acceptance of American capitalism, Europeans seemed about to throw free enterprise out of the window and to congratulate themselves upon the loss.

An observer in the 1880's might have predicted a very different future. In 1886 an organization called the Knights of Labor had over 700,000 members and had been increasing fast. At a time when British trade unionism was unambitious, non-political and confined to skilled men, the Knights included large numbers of unskilled men, pressed for the eight-hour day, organized consumers' and producers' co-operatives, and sponsored a number of political reforms. Might this not be the beginning of a movement which would do for the wage earner what Jacksonian democracy had done for the small property owner? And with many socialists among the immigrants from Europe would not the American working men soon repudiate American capitalism? These questions were answered in the negative. Sixty years later Union membership was large but its most striking period of growth had been in the very recent past. Unskilled labour had had little organization until after 1935. Even with a membership of 14,000,000 in 1947 the Unions commanded only 22·4 per cent of the labour force and in that year Congress passed the Taft–Hartley Act which imposed restrictions upon Trade Union practices which would have been unthinkable in any European democracy. There was no Labour Party and under the Taft–Hartley Act the Unions were forbidden to make contributions to political campaigns. American labour had not gone socialist and a declaration of faith in free enterprise was a part of the conventional armoury of the labour leaders.

Most of the explanations for this divergence between American and European social evolution are capable of two interpretations. The 'safety valve' of the frontier is sometimes supposed to have drawn off the potential leaders of working-class organization; but men who have become accustomed to urban and industrial life are seldom attracted to the ardours of pioneer farming, there was little about the frontier to attract ambitious men in the late nineteenth century (the towns were more likely to act as safety valves for the frontier), and so far as it did attract industrial workers it created a scarcity of labour in the East which ought to have been an advantage for labour organizers. Opportunities in an expanding industrial system did provide an outlet for the ablest working men; but the success stories of the self-made men were more likely to create restlessness than acquiescence. Immigration constantly added to the labour force men who were alien in language, religion and customs; but their very differences might have provided an incentive for self-assertion as ethnic minorities through labour unions. The free political institutions of the United States were more likely to stimulate than to thwart the development of working-class political movements. Each of these explanations might in fact have been used to explain the growth of a labour movement as readily as they have been adduced to explain its failure.

The first explanation for the lack of able labour leaders is to be found in the educational system rather than in the frontier or in business opportunities; the real drain took place when the potential leaders were infants, not when they had already formed adult habits of mind. Already in 1870 57 per cent of the children between five and seventeen attended school, and of those who did not a high proportion were in the backward districts of the South. The educational ladder, though less broad and more subject to regional variations than it is today, already ran from the public elementary school to the free high school and to the state universities. The American tradition of working one's way through college even made it possible for relatively poor men to attend the private universities. Immigrant parents who were themselves ready to accept a humble situation in life were often desperately anxious to see their children climb the educational ladder to business or professional positions of middle-class status. In the late nineteenth century America was already familiar with the fact, which did not become apparent in Great Britain until after 1945, that it was becoming difficult to find real ability at the workbench; and one explanation of America's abortive social democratic revolution is that an equalitarian educational system was already on the way to achievement by the end of the nineteenth century.

More immediately organized labour had to contend with the overwhelming strength of the employers. In every industrial civilization the battle was fought, but nowhere else did the employers start with so many advantages or survive with so few concessions. In all Western countries organized labour had to make its way against law and institutions based upon the sanctity of property, and no other country had gone so far as the United

States in identifying liberty with economic freedom.[1] The preservation of property was not only the primary function of government but also its only domestic function which was likely to be exercised without influential disapproval. Despite states' rights a majority could approve the use of Federal troops to break a strike against the express opposition of the Governor of the state concerned.[2] Though normally suspicious of judicial interference in political affairs Americans approved the issuance of injunctions against strikers which seriously curtailed constitutional rights. It is difficult to imagine any other circumstances which would have excused the use of private mercenary armies against citizens of the United States, yet the Pinkerton detectives could be employed not only to provide immediate protection but even to defeat imagined threats from unionization. Though employers displayed a savagery unmatched in other civilized countries, public opinion did less to condemn them. In a nation still dominated by small property owners and a rural vote these things

[1] In the most famous of all dissenting opinions (*Lochner* v. *New York*, 198 U.S. 45, 1905), Mr Justice Holmes criticized the tendency of his fellow jurists to write *laissez-faire* into the Constitution, and in particular their use of the Fourteenth Amendment as a means of restraining state regulation of free enterprise. 'The Fourteenth Amendment does not enact Mr Herbert Spencer's Social Statics. . . . A constitution is not meant to embody a particular economic theory, whether of paternalism and the organic relation of the citizen to the state or of *laissez-faire*. It is made for people of fundamentally differing views, and the accident of our finding certain opinions natural and familiar, or novel, or even shocking, ought not to conclude our judgment upon the question whether statutes embodying them conflict with the Constitution of the United States.'

[2] The reference is to President Cleveland's action in sending Federal troops to Chicago in 1894, ostensibly to prevent interference with the U.S. mails but in fact to break a great strike of railroad employees. He did so without consulting, and over the protest of, Governor Altgeld of Illinois. But the responsibility of the Federal Government for public order during labour disputes is not easy to limit or define; Justice Brewer of the Supreme Court observed (*In re Debs.* 158 U.S., 564) that 'The national government, given by the Constitution power to regulate interstate commerce, has by express statute assumed jurisdiction over such commerce when carried upon railroads. It is charged therefore with the duty of keeping those highways of interstate commerce free from obstruction.' In other words Cleveland need not have justified himself by adducing protection of the mails as ground for intervention; the Supreme Court held that the Federal Government had unlimited authority to keep the railways 'free from obstruction'. This argument would leave real authority in the hands of the Federal judges who could decide whether the local situation amounted to 'obstruction'. The controversy is complicated by the fact that those who instinctively condemn Cleveland's strike breaking and the reasoning of Brewer are likely to approve the action of President Eisenhower in sending Federal Troops to Little Rock in 1957 to force the admission of Negro children to the High School, following a ruling of the local Federal judge, and against the express wishes of the Governor of Arkansas.

passed at the best as instruments of justice and at the worst as evil necessities.

Partly because of this unfavourable climate, partly because of the presence of real revolutionaries cast by the migrant tide upon the coasts of America, violence and conspiracy gave substance to the fears of the property owners. In a few instances this was to anticipate the racketeering of the twentieth century, and from 1877 to 1896 there were few years which passed without tragedies which bewildered and discredited the ordinary working men as much as they gave moral strength to their employers. A bomb outrage in Chicago in 1886 (the Haymarket Affair) was partly responsible for the ruin of the Knights of Labor, who had seemed on the way to becoming a colossus of labour. Big employers naturally profited most and the timidity of some small employers in the face of violence was a contributory factor in the rise of monopoly capitalism.

It was this position of strength which enabled the employers to exploit the various elements in the American situation to their advantage, and to engage public opinion on their side, against attacks which appeared to be subversive of the American system. The intellectuals gave ready assent to this view, and even amongst working men themselves it was widely accepted. This helps to explain the rejection of socialism. There was nothing in the American tradition which forbade the idea of supplementing public by private enterprise, but socialism, by positing a total abandonment of private property, generated a faith in the entire competence of individual enterprise to fulfil the needs of man. Many Americans were perplexed by the abuse of power by some capitalists, but they defended restraints as necessary deviations from the normal, as reactions to the abuse of right not as repudiations of the right itself. The farmers and small businessmen who led the fight against big business were as anxious to avoid the stigma of socialism as their opponents were to label them with it. There was also an instinctive distrust of public authority which ran deep in the American system. While European socialists were able to talk hopefully of a people's government, the United States

R

had experienced popular government for over a century. It was a country grown old in the ways of democracy, which had put its faith in representative institutions while preserving a cynical distrust of representatives, and which believed that any authority would be misused if unchecked. Socialism would place overriding authority exactly where it ought not to reside, with the professional politician. The economic and political bosses already knew how to rig democracy; why put more power into their hands? In a capitalist system the employer might be strong but he was not invulnerable, and organized labour was to win more by exploiting the competitive system than by fighting it; but the men who could do so were not the unskilled but the skilled, not the rank and file of labour but its aristocracy which had a technique to sell provided that this could be protected.

From the ruins of nation-wide and industry-wide unionism arose the American Federation of Labor under its first and perennial president, Samuel Gompers. Gompers was sometimes clearer about what labour could not do than about what it could do. He knew that it could not attack the competitive system. He knew that it could not achieve a disciplined national organization. He knew that it could not create a third political party and that adherence to one of the existing parties would bind it to a master by whom it would soon be smothered. He knew that the unskilled could not be organized and that if they were they would be as great a danger to the skilled as to the employers. He distrusted the intellectuals who professed friendship for labour. To these negative propositions he added a shrewd mind and a domineering personality. The A.F.L. was a federation of craft unions; the autonomy of its member unions would be carefully preserved; the central organization would be directed to settling jurisdictional disputes between member unions; there would be no industrial unionism and non-members would be treated with as much hostility as bad employers. So far as they had any political programme it was to reward friends and punish enemies; a Republican vote was as good as a Democratic vote so long as both helped the A.F.L. (an eminently sane decision when both parties were as anxious to avoid commitments to organized labour as they were to win labour votes). Broadly the aim of the A.F.L. was to raise the status of labour, to win middle-class standards while creating an impression of middle-class reliability, and to offer employers stability in return for satisfactory agreements. The system tended to create two types of labour leader: the majority looked and often spoke like moderately successful businessmen, the minority were the labour bosses who stepped in to exploit a situation in which employers would pay for labour discipline.

The new direction given to Trade Unionism was of great importance for the future of American civilization. Organized labour, unlike that of Europe, began to take its place among the supporters of an established order which it would seek to ameliorate but not to change. In 1880 the United States seemed to be heading for a gigantic class struggle which would dwarf those of Europe because the forces of wage labour and capitalism would be more starkly opposed. By 1900 this crisis had passed without the theory of the class struggle winning acceptance. Socialism was left high and dry as the fad of a small group of middle-class intellectuals and would raise its head again as a popular force only in the exceptional years such as 1912 and 1932. The mould of union thought was so firmly set that when unskilled labour was at last successfully organized it too accepted the assumptions of the capitalist system. There were, of course, many hectic struggles to come between employers and the unions, violence was not to be banished, and there remained conservative Americans who could not distinguish between the A.F.L. (or the equally conservative Railway Brotherhoods) and the red peril; but the way was being prepared for the acceptance of conservative unionism as a permanent feature of American life. A new force had entered the field, but the price of recognition was the abandonment of ideas of working-class politics and of radical economic reform which inspired the labour movements of all other industrial countries.

For European socialists this necessarily appears as the refusal of a challenge and the betrayal of an historic mission. The American might reply (though he seldom does so) that European labour politics have simply taken over the same concepts and much of the language used by the middle classes in their struggle against privileged aristocracies, and that they have had little appeal in the United States because there is no feudal past; that unencumbered by this heavy luggage the Americans look at their problems pragmatically, and are evolving a way of life in an industrial society which recognizes increased productivity as the first ingredient of social welfare. If European critics point to the under-nourished and underpaid lower fifth, and at the harsh treatment meted out to the casualties of the economic system, the American points to the high living standards of the productive part of the labour force. If socialists can deprecate the enormous profits of American capitalists, it is arguable that profits are only an insignificant part of the wealth produced by capitalist enterprise. The argument will not be easily resolved but evolution of American labour has contributed greatly to the gulf fixed between the United States and their would-be allies in the mid-twentieth century. The ideological battle against Communism is constantly hampered by the fact that almost as wide a gap separates the Americans from the British Labour Party or from the west European socialist parties. The emotional uplift of 'hands across the ocean' oratory cannot conceal the deep undercurrents of pained disapproval, and it is a grand paradox of the modern situation that the United States are forced to aid and protect men who would be regarded as subversive on American soil.

* * * *

The new world situation of the United States brings Americans into association with Asian, Arabian, and African peoples, and here again a domestic problem creates unexpected difficulties. For many the acid test of America's goodwill is the treatment of her own Negroes, and racial tension in some obscure Southern town will make headlines round the world and destroy months of patient work by diplomats and information officers. On paper the record of the United States on this question could hardly be better; amendments to the Federal Constitution assert that Negroes are entitled to exactly the same civil rights as the whites, the foundation document of the American nation declares in unequivocal terms that all men are created equal, and throughout the United States more continuous thought is given to the problem of race relations than in any other country. Nor does the reality depart so far from the ideal enshrined in law and tradition; in a majority of the forty-eight states Negroes encounter few barriers in education, in business or in the professions; Negroes are employed in the Federal service and in the armed forces in positions which generally correspond to their talents; some social discrimination exists everywhere, but in many regions it is of the mildest kind and the public authorities are actively engaged to prevent its extension. There are many wealthy Negroes, and even where the standards are admittedly low — as in the cotton districts of the South and certain Northern slums — the Negroes are better fed, better paid and better educated than the peasant masses of Africa and the East. Nowhere does one encounter the kind of swarming poverty which is of ordinary occurrence in the countries of the Middle and Far East in which criticism of American racial discrimination is likely to be most vociferous.

Yet there are shortcomings which cannot be circumvented by pretending that racial differences do not exist (as some Northern liberals are inclined to do) or by following Southern extremists in holding that these differences are the first premise of social life. Wherever the Negro lives, and wherever he migrates in large numbers, he is likely to arouse white hostility; some of the worst racial disorders of recent years have been in Northern cities to which Negroes have moved in large numbers during the past generation and where the law and established customs are all colour blind. It is not bad law which makes racial hatred, but the savage and primitive fear of the man who is different. Englishmen who adopt a pharisaical attitude may care to be reminded that the South, against which most of their criticism is directed, is the most purely Anglo-Saxon part of America. The dominant fears are those of mixed marriage, mixed education, and Negro political influence, and in a sense all these fears are rational provided that one accepts certain premises about the differences between the races; these premises are accepted, as a part of the inherited intellectual armoury, amongst the vast majority of Southern people, and tend to be adopted by Northern whites wherever the two races are thrown into social and economic competition.

To say that the differences at present are real does not however imply acceptance of any of false racial theories, assert the inherent superiority of one race over the other, or deny that a great many white genes enter into the biological composition of most American Negroes and that (through the 'passing' of near whites) there are Negro genes in a great many more white American people than most of them care to admit. It does imply that racial antagonism arises spontaneously and cannot be easily eradicated. There are two possible solutions and only two: segregation or integration. Segregation is the choice of most Southerners and in the early years of this century the Supreme Court conceded that the races might be separated, by a series of discriminatory laws, provided that the facilities offered were equal. Thus Southern education was allowed to develop two completely separate systems of Negro and white schools; legal provisions kept the races separate in their homes, their recreations and their use of public transport; and Southern Negroes were usually prevented from exercising their voting rights.[1] No one would deny that under this system some

---

[1] The fifteenth Amendment prevents disenfranchisement on grounds of race, creed or colour; it leaves the franchise where the Constitution placed it, with the states. The qualification for voting in Federal elections must be the same as that required for the most numerous house of the state legislature. States can therefore legally impose voting qualifications which apply to all its citizens and the puzzle of Southern segregationists has been to devise qualifications which, though nominally the same for all, disenfranchise more blacks than whites. The favourite devices have been the poll-tax and the exclusion of Negroes from primaries. Many states impose a voluntary poll tax and make its payment a necessary qualification for being entered on the rolls of electors; as so many Negroes are poor and ill-informed they are likely to neglect this while a registration officer can ensure that whites do so at the proper time. Exclusion from the primary — where the real political struggles take place in a one party State — was secured by regarding the primary as a purely private election conducted by the party. Educational tests imposed by some states can always be manipulated to the disadvantage of Negroes. But the most potent weapon against Negro voting has always been social pressure reinforced with terrorism if necessary. All methods are gradually yielding before adverse legal judgments, but the last is the most difficult to eradicate.

Negroes advanced rapidly, that the majority made some progress, and that, where Negroes kept strictly to the rules, racial relations might not be too bad. But for the Southerners 'equality' was always a legal fiction; the real object was to maintain white supremacy, and this was reflected in the greatly inferior facilities which were normally provided for Negroes. At the same time the limited advances, which the Federal Courts were able to ensure for the Negro people, raised an educated generation of Negro leaders who constantly resented the inferior position to which they were condemned; and these aspiring coloured men could appeal to the established orthodoxy of the American law and tradition. From another aspect segregation tends to break down: it is impossible to separate the races geographically or economically, and as Negroes and whites tend to mingle in place and in occupation the laws enforcing segregation must become fiercer and more irrational. Quite apart from the racial considerations the American conscience dislikes laws which are severe, difficult to enforce without constant supervision, and commit palpable injustice upon individuals; and even in the South liberal-minded men become increasingly uneasy about those laws which can alone keep segregation in being.[1]

Integration cannot be easy, but Americans can point with pride to the way in which other racial minorities have been assimilated and many will ask why the Negroes, who have been American longer than a majority of the white people, cannot be assimilated in the same way.[2] The argument receives powerful support from the evident desire of the Negroes themselves to be American; revolutionary creeds have made little headway among a people who might have been particularly susceptible to them, and Negro

[1] 'The South has been, and is, changing rapidly, and Southern liberalism has been coming to be a force though it was practically nowhere in political power and today is fearfully timid on the Negro issue. Even the ordinary conservative white Southerner has a deeply split personality. In the short run this can be suppressed, and the tension can lead to violent reactions. But in the long run it means that the conservative white Southerner himself can be won over to equalitarian reforms in line with the American creed' (Gunnar Myrdal, *An American Dilemma*, Harpers, 1944, 1015).

[2] There is one aspect which most integrationists avoid. 'And the old man in north Tennessee, a burly, full-blooded, raucous old man, says: "Hell, son, its easy to solve. Just blend 'em. Fifteen years and they'll all be blended in. And by God, I'm doing my part" (Robert Penn Warren, *Segregation*, Random House; Eyre & Spottiswoode, 1957, 68).

leaders appeal not to Communism but to the American traditions. Exponents of integration readily admit that time must be allowed for old hatreds to be damped down, but they do insist that this cannot happen without the pressure of the law. As in other aspects of American thought one encounters here a dichotomy which is difficult to resolve: the men who believe in integration are often those who also believe in individual freedom, yet to secure integration they are forced to demand an authoritarian execution of the law. Facts seem however often to be on their side. Young children seem to have no instinctive racial antipathies until they are taught them by their parents, and integrated primary education seems the surest way of breaking down ancient racial barriers. Negro participation in politics, on an equal footing with the whites, seems to bring almost immediate returns. In fact the success of the present drive against segregation seems to be directly related to the strategic position of Negroes in several Northern cities where their votes can decide an election and even make a President of the United States. The gradual break-down of the various devices by which Southerners kept Negroes from the polls seems also to have an immediate effect upon the treatment of Negroes in the states where they vote in numbers. Nor, once a break with the past has been forced, may Southern resistance to integration be so marked as has been expected.[1]

A Swedish sociologist, Gunnar Myrdal, concluded his massive study of the Negro problem with a section entitled 'America's Opportunity'. In it he remarked that 'The Negro problem is not only America's greatest failure but also America's incomparably

[1] 'Within the individual there are, or may be, many lines of fracture. It may be between his own social idealism and his anger at Yankee Phariseeism. . . . It may be between his social views and his fear of the power state. It may be between his social views and his clan sense. It may be between his allegiance to organized labour and his racism — for status or blood purity. It may be between his Christianity and his social prejudice. It may be between his sense of democracy and his ingrained attitude towards the Negro. It may be between his own local views and his concern for the figure America cuts in the international picture. It may be between his practical concern at the money lost to society caused by the Negro's depressed condition and his personal gain or personal prejudice. It may be, and disastrously, between his sense of the inevitable and his emotional need to act against the inevitable. There are almost an infinite number of permutations and combinations, but they all amount to the same thing, a deep intellectual rub, a moral rub, anger at the irremediable self-division, a deep exacerbation at some failure to find identity. That is the reality' (Robert Penn Warren, *Segregation*, 72).

great opportunity for the future. If America should follow its own deepest convictions, its well-being at home would be increased directly. At the same time America's prestige and power abroad would rise immensely. The century-old dream of American patriots, that America should give to the entire world its own freedom and its faith, would come true. America can demonstrate that justice, equality and cooperation are possible between white and coloured people.' Since 1942, when these words were written, the Federal Courts have sustained almost every application by Negroes for a recognition of their civil rights,[1] and this culminated in the epoch-making decision in 1954 of a unanimous Supreme Court that segregation in public education was unconstitutional.

Education was crucial to the whole problem of racial integration; children who learned to accept each other might have a better chance of doing so when mature, but nothing was more likely to arouse the hostility of white parents. Little difficulty was encountered where Negroes were few and of comparatively high status (and in many such areas schools had already been integrated for many years), but the problem was acute where they were numerous and poor. In the 'border' states gallant and largely successful efforts were made to comply with the Supreme Court ruling, but ten years after the decision of 1954 there were hardly any Negroes in predominantly white schools in most Southern states. Meanwhile Northern cities, which had accepted somewhat smugly the principle of integration, were brought to realize, by Negro protests, that *de facto* segregation existed when Negroes were confined to single districts. Should integration be sought for its own sake by moving children to schools outside their own

---

[1] Thus in *Smith* v. *Allwright*, 321 U.S. 649, the Supreme Court suppressed the 'white primary'. Justice Reed said, 'The United States is a constitutional democracy. Its organic law grants to all citizens a right to participate in the choice of elected officials without restriction by any state because of race. This grant to the people of the opportunity for choice is not to be nullified by a state through casting its electoral process in a form which permits a private organization to practice racial discrimination in the election. Constitutional rights would be of little value if they could be thus indirectly denied.' The Supreme Court has also held that a Negro had been denied a fair trial because it was shown that in his county no Negro had ever been placed on a jury. The National Association for the Advancement of Colored Peoples is constantly on the watch for favourable test cases with which to chip away at the segregation pattern.

districts in order to enjoy the benefit of being educated with people of a different race? Or should the exclusion of Negroes from white residential districts be prevented by law? The questions moved Northern whites to protest against forms of integration which they had never expected, while Northern Negroes began noisy demonstrations against poor housing, lack of economic opportunities, and discrimination in employment. Against this background of anger Congress acted in 1957 and again in 1964 to pass the first Civil Rights Acts since the abortive Act of 1875: the 1957 Act dealt mainly with voting rights but was not strong enough to ensure widespread Negro voting where local opinion was hostile; the 1964 Act strengthened the safeguards for Negro voting and outlawed many forms of social discrimination. No one familiar with modern America would deny that the problems are still severe, but the slow majesty of the law and the inexorable force of the American conscience force the nation along the road to integration.

In several ways the Second World War confirmed and strengthened the patterns imposed upon natural life by the New Deal. In the first place war demand ended the nagging disease of unemployment which the New Deal had failed to cure, and made a strong, centralized and regulatory government one of the necessities of survival. With France fallen and Great Britain in mortal danger, isolationism withered, and the New Dealers — never very clear in earlier years on foreign relations — acquired a new sense of purpose, linking American liberalism with international commitments. The immediate result of war was to strengthen Roosevelt's personal prestige. In 1940 German successes convinced Democrats that they could not risk putting an untried man in the White House, and their National Convention compelled a publicly reluctant but privately willing President to run again. He defeated his Republican opponent, Wendell Willkie, easily. Significantly the Republicans had not tried to run a representative of their old guard, but had chosen a man who only recently changed his party allegiance, supported most New Deal measures though attacking their administration, and favoured aid to Britain. By 1944 Roosevelt, with victory in the air, had all the prestige of a great war leader and was nominated and elected for the fourth time. Five months later he was dead.[1]

The stirrings and tensions of modern American life have been reflected in politics. The sudden death of Roosevelt in 1944 brought to the White House Vice-President Harry S. Truman, who had made a useful record in the Senate, but had no executive experience and very little public stature. In office Truman proved himself resourceful, courageous, and worthy of his great responsibilities; in domestic politics he was less subtle but in several ways more radical than Roosevelt, combining old Populist traditions with a real understanding of the meaning of power in the modern world. In 1948 he won a victory against a strong Republican opponent, which no one but himself had predicted, largely by campaigning against the negative record of a Republican-dominated Congress. The old political commentators, still accustomed to the idea that the best government was that which governed least, had failed to realize how a generation of new voters, accustomed to active government, would regard a 'do-nothing' Congress. Though Truman was now President in his own right his second administration was less successful than his first: at home there was little legislative achievement, abroad relations with Russia deteriorated, the success of Communist revolution in China was confirmed, and after 1950 America was heavily involved in the Korean War, which produced no quick victories and several nasty shocks. These alarms were exploited by Senator Joseph McCarthy, who used his position as chairman of a Congressional investigating committee to expose alleged subversion in high administration circles, among intellectuals, and even in the Churches. For three years 'McCarthyism' achieved a world-wide notoriety as the synonym for modern witch-hunting.

Tension was high during the election of 1952. The Democrats

---

[1] The twenty-second Amendment to the Constitution (which became law in 1951) states that 'No person shall be elected to the Office of the President more than twice'. If this Amendment remains as part of the Constitution Roosevelt will remain for ever the only man to serve three terms, and to be four times elected, as President of the United States.

nominated Adlai Stevenson, whose urbanity and quick intelligence made him the idol of American intellectuals; the Republicans chose Dwight D. Eisenhower, formerly Supreme Commander of the Allied Forces in Europe. Eisenhower was elected by a large majority, and was re-elected for a second term in 1956, though his personal success was always much greater than that of his party and for six of his eight years the Democrats had majorities in both Houses of Congress. Distinguished soldiers have seldom made good politicians, and Eisenhower's statesmanship has been the target of a good deal of criticism; but in retrospect it may appear that the United States were fortunate in having, as their leader during these years of anxiety, a man whose greatest talent lay in reconciling opposing views and whose strongest instinct was for compromise; nor is it possible to doubt that Eisenhower was and remained the most popular President of modern times. If his personal ascendancy never equalled that of Roosevelt he roused far fewer animosities, and for millions of Americans he seemed to embody the essential decency of their nation.

In 1960 John F. Kennedy, Democrat, Catholic and grandson of an Irish immigrant, became the youngest man ever elected to the Presidency. Vigorous, intelligent and sophisticated, Kennedy symbolized the coming-of-age of a new political generation, of men and women to whom the Depression was a childhood memory and the War a youthful experience; and if he was not called upon, like Roosevelt, to produce novel remedies for unprecedented problems he seemed to epitomize a new approach to politics. In point of fact the legislative experience of the President with his first Congress was disappointing, but the Kennedy magic was still fresh when an assassin brought his life to a sudden and tragic end. The shock of his death was deeply felt throughout the world, and the normal expressions of official regret were reinforced by the genuine sorrow of millions of humble people in distant places who felt that a bright and hopeful light had been extinguished. Nothing could have been more expressive of America's changed place in the world.

*   *   *   *

Modern American history is much concerned with material achievement and problems of economic organization, but if this were all that it consisted of the Americans would be as unattractive as some foreign critics imagine them to be. With all their pride in material achievement the Americans are a people of ideas; it is a nation which has been made by ideas and is conscious of its debt. The ideology of the Revolution, the phrases of the Declaration of Independence, the panegyrics on the Union, the belief in opportunity and freedom are the basic stuff of American education, and their frequent repetition does not diminish their attraction. In spite of all the anxieties of the past and present no nation is more convinced that it has in its hands the solution to the fundamental problems of human society. That arguments can be bitter is no disproof; for a freedom to differ and to express differences is a part of the solution. That the American way of life is free is no catchphrase but a truth which is embodied in the manners of the people, in their plethora of voluntary associations, and their dislike of subordination. That men are created equal is an awkward idea but most Americans manage to attach some meaning to it — political equality, racial equality, equality under the law, or equality of opportunity — and each of the phrases means something real, though each may have to be qualified. That men have inalienable rights is a difficult concept to explain philosophically but it is comparatively easy to treat it in the American way as an assertion that men ought to be treated as though they had rights. The absurdities of the American political system are not hard to find, but the American might reply that rational government is inevitably despotic. If American history seems to be strewn with grievous errors, the American may counter with the proposition that the most precious freedom is the right to be wrong. This body of ideas plays a unique part in American civilization; it is in fact the stuff of which it is made. No other nation depends less upon allegiance to race, to tradition or to necessity and more upon doctrine. It is an accepted doctrine which gives the American nation its cohesion, and if it ceased to be accepted some other unifying force would have to take its place. Americans do not like the alternatives and it is this which makes them sometimes intolerant of criticism which seems to sap at the foundations of their system. This survey of American history ends with two paradoxes. The first that a passionate attachment to freedom leads to an intolerance which is the denial of freedom. The other that these people, outwardly so confident and so practical, can only be understood in spiritual terms. Their material success is the by-product of belief; their national power depends upon their willingness to die for their faith.

APPENDIX I

Declaration of Independence

Extract from the Preamble [following original punctuation and capitalization].

We hold these truths to be self-evident, that all men are created equal, that they are endowed by their Creator with certain unalienable Rights, that among these are Life, Liberty and the pursuit of Happiness. That to secure these rights, Governments are instituted among Men, deriving their just powers from the consent of the governed, That whenever any Form of Government becomes destructive of these ends, it is the Right of the People to alter or abolish it, and to institute new Government, laying its foundation on such principles and organizing its powers in such form, as shall seem to them most likely to effect their Safety and Happiness. Prudence, indeed, will dictate that Governments long established should not be changed for light and transient causes; and accordingly all experience hath shown, that mankind are more disposed to suffer, while evils are sufferable, than to right themselves by abolishing the forms to which they are accustomed. But when a long train of abuses and usurpations, pursuing invariably the same Object evinces a design to reduce them under absolute Despotism, it is their right, it is their duty, to throw off such Government, and to provide new Guards for their future security.

APPENDIX II

Constitution of the United States of America

Preamble

WE THE PEOPLE of the United States, in order to form a more perfect Union, establish justice, insure domestic tranquillity, provide for the common defense, promote the general welfare, and secure the blessings of liberty to ourselves and our posterity, do ordain and establish this Constitution for the United States of America.

ARTICLE I

SECTION 1. All legislative powers herein granted shall be vested in a Congress of the United States, which shall consist of a Senate and House of Representatives.

SECTION 2. The House of Representatives shall be composed of members chosen every second year by the people of the several States, and the electors in each State shall have the qualifications requisite for electors of the most numerous branch of the State Legislature.

No person shall be a representative who shall not have attained to the age of twenty-five years, and been seven years a citizen of the United States, and who shall not, when elected, be an inhabitant of that State in which he shall be chosen.

Representatives and direct taxes shall be apportioned among the several States which may be included within this Union, according to their respective numbers, which shall be determined by adding to the whole number of free persons, including those bound to service for a term of years, and excluding Indians not taxed, three-fifths of all other persons. The actual enumeration shall be made within three years after the first meeting of the Congress of the United States, and within every subsequent term of ten years, in such manner as they shall by law direct. The number of representatives shall not exceed one for every thirty thousand, but each State shall have at least one representative;

and until such enumeration shall be made, the State of New Hampshire shall be entitled to choose three, Massachusetts eight, Rhode Island and Providence Plantations one, Connecticut five, New York six, New Jersey four, Pennsylvania eight, Delaware one, Maryland six, Virginia ten, North Carolina five, South Carolina five, and Georgia three.

When vacancies happen in the representation from any State, the executive authority thereof shall issue writs of election to fill such vacancies.

The House of Representatives shall choose their Speaker and other officers; and shall have the sole power of impeachment.

SECTION 3. The Senate of the United States shall be composed of two senators from each State, chosen by the legislature thereof, for six years and each senator shall have one vote.

Immediately after they shall be assembled in consequence of the first election, they shall be divided as equally as may be into three classes. The seats of the senators of the first class shall be vacated at the expiration of the second year, of the second class at the expiration of the fourth year, and of the third class at the expiration of the sixth year, so that one-third may be chosen every second year; and if vacancies happen by resignation, or otherwise, during the recess of the legislature of any State, the executive thereof may make temporary appointments until the next meeting of the legislature, which shall then fill such vacancies.

No person shall be a senator who shall not have attained to the age of thirty years, and been nine years a citizen of the United States, and who shall not, when elected, be an inhabitant of that State for which he shall be chosen.

The Vice President of the United States shall be President of the Senate, but shall have no vote, unless they be equally divided.

The Senate shall choose their other officers, and also a President pro tempore, in the absence of the Vice President, or when he shall exercise the office of President of the United States.

The Senate shall have the sole power to try all impeachments. When sitting for that purpose, they shall be on oath or affirmation. When the President of the United States is tried, the Chief Justice shall preside: And no person shall be convicted without the concurrence of two-thirds of the members present.

Judgment in cases of impeachment shall not extend further than to

s

removal from office, and disqualification to hold and enjoy any office of honor, trust or profit under the United States: but the party convicted shall nevertheless be liable and subject to indictment, trial, judgment and punishment, according to law.

SECTION 4. The times, places and manner of holding elections for senators and representatives, shall be prescribed in each State by the legislature thereof; but the Congress may at any time by law make or alter such regulations, except as to the places of choosing senators.

The Congress shall assemble at least once in every year, and such meeting shall be on the first Monday in December, unless they shall by law appoint a different day.

SECTION 5. Each house shall be the judge of the elections, returns and qualifications of its own members, and a majority of each shall constitute a quorum to do business; but a smaller number may adjourn from day to day, and may be authorized to compel the attendance of absent members, in such manner, and under such penalties as each house may provide.

Each house may determine the rules of its proceedings, punish its members for disorderly behaviour, and, with the concurrence of two-thirds, expel a member.

Each house shall keep a journal of its proceedings, and from time to time publish the same, excepting such parts as may in their judgment require secrecy; and the yeas and nays of the members of either house on any question shall, at the desire of one-fifth of those present, be entered on the journal.

Neither house, during the session of Congress, shall, without the consent of the other, adjourn for more than three days, nor to any other place than that in which the two houses shall be sitting.

SECTION 6. The senators and representatives shall receive a compensation for their services, to be ascertained by law, and paid out of the Treasury of the United States. They shall in all cases, except treason, felony and breach of the peace, be privileged from arrest during their attendance at the session of their respective houses, and in going to and returning from the same; and for any speech or debate in either house, they shall not be questioned in any other place.

No senator or representative shall, during the time for which he was elected, be appointed to any civil office under the authority of the United States, which shall have been created, or the emoluments whereof shall have been increased during such time; and no person holding any office under the United States, shall be a member of either house during his continuance in office.

SECTION 7. All bills for raising revenue shall originate in the House of Representatives; but the Senate may propose or concur with amendments as on other bills.

Every bill which shall have passed the House of Representatives and the Senate, shall, before it becomes a law, be presented to the President of the United States; if he approves he shall sign it, but if not he shall return it, with his objections to that house in which it shall have originated, who shall enter the objections at large on their journal, and proceed to reconsider it. If after such reconsideration two-thirds of that House shall agree to pass the bill, it shall be sent, together with the objections, to the other House, by which it shall likewise be reconsidered, and if approved by two-thirds of that House, it shall become a law. But in all such cases the votes of both Houses shall be determined by yeas and nays, and the names of the persons voting for and against the bill shall be entered on the journal of each House respectively. If any bill shall not be returned by the President within ten days (Sundays excepted) after it shall have been presented to him, the same shall be a law, in like manner as if he had signed it, unless the Congress by their adjournment prevent its return, in which case it shall not be a law.

Every order, resolution, or vote to which the concurrence of the Senate and House of Representatives may be necessary (except on a question of adjournment) shall be presented to the President of the United States; and before the same shall take effect, shall be approved by him, or being disapproved by him, shall be repassed by two-thirds of the Senate and House of Representatives, according to the rules and limitations prescribed in the case of a bill.

SECTION 8. The Congress shall have the power to lay and collect taxes, duties, imposts and excises, to pay the debts and provide for the common defense and general welfare of the United States; but all duties, imposts and excises shall be uniform throughout the United States;

To borrow money on the credit of the United States;

To regulate commerce with foreign nations, and among the several States, and with the Indian tribes;

To establish an uniform rule of naturalization, and uniform laws on the subject of bankruptcies throughout the United States;

To coin money, regulate the value thereof, and of foreign coin, and fix the standard of weights and measures;

To provide for the punishment of counterfeiting the securities and current coin of the United States;

To establish post offices and post roads;

To promote the progress of science and useful arts, by securing for limited times to authors and inventors the exclusive right to their respective writings and discoveries;

To constitute tribunals inferior to the Supreme Court;

To define and punish piracies and felonies committed on the high seas, and offenses against the law of nations;

To declare war, grant letters of marque and reprisal, and make rules concerning captures on land and water;

To raise and support armies, but no appropriation of money to that use shall be for a longer term than two years;

To provide and maintain a Navy;

To make rules for the government and regulation of the land and naval forces;

To provide for calling forth the militia to execute the laws of the Union, suppress insurrections and repel invasions;

To provide for organizing, arming, and disciplining, the militia, and for governing such part of them as may be employed in the service of the United States, reserving to the States respectively the appointment of the officers, and the authority of training the militia according to the discipline prescribed by Congress;

To exercise exclusive legislation in all cases whatsoever, over such district (not exceeding ten miles square) as may, by cession of particular States, and the acceptance of Congress, become the seat of the Government of the United States, and to exercise like authority over all places purchased by the consent of the legislature of the State in which the same shall be, for the erection of forts, magazines, arsenals, dock-yards, and other needful buildings;—And

To make all laws which shall be necessary and proper for carrying into execution the foregoing powers, and all other powers vested by the Constitution in the Government of the United States, or in any department or officer thereof.

SECTION 9. The migration or importation of such persons as any of the States now existing shall think proper to admit, shall not be prohibited by the Congress prior to the year one thousand eight hundred and eight, but a tax or duty may be imposed on such importation, not exceeding ten dollars for each person.

The privilege of the writ of habeas corpus shall not be suspended, unless when in cases of rebellion or invasion the public safety may require it.

No bill of attainder or ex post facto law shall be passed.

No capitation, or other direct, tax shall be laid, unless in proportion to the census or enumeration herein before directed to be taken.

No tax or duty shall be laid on articles exported from any State.

No preference shall be given by any regulation of commerce or revenue to the ports of one State over those of another: nor shall vessels bound to, or from, one State, be obliged to enter, clear, or pay duties in another.

No money shall be drawn from the Treasury, but in consequence of appropriations made by law; and a regular statement and account of the receipts and expenditures of all public money shall be published from time to time.

No title of nobility shall be granted by the United States: And no person holding any office of profit or trust under them shall, without the consent of the Congress, accept of any present, emoluments, office, or title, of any kind whatever, from any King, Prince, or foreign State.

SECTION 10. No State shall enter into any treaty, alliance, or confederation; grant letters of marque and reprisal; coin money; emit bills of credit; make any thing but gold and silver coin a tender in payment of debts; pass any bill of attainder, ex post facto law, or law impairing the obligation of contracts, or grant any title of nobility.

No State shall, without the consent of the Congress, lay any imposts or duties on imports or exports, except what may be absolutely necessary for executing its inspection laws: and the net produce of all duties and imposts, laid by any State on imports or exports, shall be for the use of the Treasury of the United States; and all such laws shall be subject to the revision and control of the Congress.

No State shall, without the consent of Congress, lay any duty of tonnage, keep troops, or ships of war in time of peace, enter into any agreement or compact with another State, or with a foreign power, or engage in war, unless actually invaded or in such imminent danger as will not admit of delay.

ARTICLE II

SECTION 1. The executive power shall be vested in a President of the United States of America. He shall hold his office during the term of four years, and, together with the Vice President, chosen for the same term, be elected, as follows:

Each State shall appoint, in such manner as the legislature thereof may direct, a number of electors, equal to the whole number of senators and representatives to which the State may be entitled in the Congress: but no senator or representative, or person holding an office of trust or profit under the United States, shall be appointed an elector.

The electors shall meet in their respective States, and vote by ballot for two persons, of whom one at least shall not be an inhabitant of the same State with themselves. And they shall make a list of all the persons voted for, and of the number of votes for each; which list they shall sign and certify, and transmit sealed to the seat of the Government of the United States, directed to the President of the Senate. The President of the Senate shall, in the presence of the Senate and House of Representatives, open all the certificates, and the votes shall then be counted. The person having the greatest number of votes shall be the President, if such number be a majority of the whole number of electors appointed; and if there be more than one who have such majority, and have an equal number of votes, then the House of Representatives shall immediately choose by ballot one of them for President; and if no person have a majority, then from the five highest on the list the said House shall in like manner choose the President. But in choosing the President, the votes shall be taken by States, the representation from each State having one vote; a quorum for this purpose shall consist of a member or members from two thirds of the States, and a majority of all the States shall be necessary to a choice. In every case, after the choice of the President, the person having the greatest number of votes of the electors shall be the Vice President. But if there should remain two or more who have equal votes, the Senate shall choose from them by ballot the Vice President.

The Congress may determine the time of choosing the electors, and the day on which they shall give their votes; which day shall be the same throughout the United States.

No person except a natural born citizen, or a citizen of the United States, at the time of the adoption of this Constitution, shall be eligible to the office of President; neither shall any person be eligible to that office who shall not have attained to the age of thirty-five years, and been fourteen years a resident within the United States.

In case of the removal of the President from office, or of his death, resignation, or inability to discharge the powers and duties of the said office, the same shall devolve on the Vice President, and the Congress may by law provide for the case of removal, death, resignation, or inability, both of the President and Vice President, declaring what officer shall then act as President, and such officer shall act accordingly, until the disability be removed, or a President shall be elected.

The President shall, at stated times, receive for his services, a compensation, which shall neither be increased nor diminished during the period for which he shall have been elected, and he shall not receive within that period any other emolument from the United States, or any of them.

Before he enter on the execution of his office, he shall take the following oath of affirmation:—'I do solemnly swear (or affirm) that I will faithfully execute the office of President of the United States, and will to the best of my ability, preserve, protect and defend the Constitution of the United States.'

SECTION 2. The President shall be Commander in Chief of the Army and Navy of the United States, and of the militia of the several States, when called into the actual service of the United States; he may require the opinion, in writing, of the principal officer in each of the Executive Departments, upon any subject relating to the duties of their respective offices, and he shall have power to grant reprieves and pardons for offenses against the United States, except in cases of impeachment.

He shall have power, by and with the advice and consent of the Senate, to make treaties, provided two thirds of the Senators present concur; and he shall nominate, and by and with the advice and consent of the Senate, shall appoint ambassadors, other public ministers and consuls, judges of the Supreme Court, and all other officers of the United States, whose appointments are not herein otherwise provided for, and which shall be established by law: but the Congress may by law vest the appointment of such inferior officers, as they think proper, in the President alone, in the courts of law, or in the heads of departments.

The President shall have power to fill up all vacancies that may happen during the recess of the Senate, by granting commissions which shall expire at the end of their next session.

SECTION 3. He shall from time to time give to the Congress information of the state of the Union, and recommend to their consideration such measures as he shall judge necessary and expedient; he may, on extraordinary occasions, convene both houses, or either of them, and in case of disagreement between them, with respect to the time of adjournment, he may adjourn them to such time as he shall think proper; he shall receive ambassadors and other public ministers; he shall take care that the laws be faithfully executed, and shall commission all the officers of the United States.

SECTION 4. The President, Vice President and all civil officers of the United States, shall be removed from office on impeachment for, and conviction of, treason, bribery, or other high crimes and misdemeanors.

ARTICLE III

SECTION 1. The judicial power of the United States shall be vested in one Supreme Court, and in such inferior courts as the Congress may from time to time ordain and establish. The judges, both of the supreme and inferior courts, shall hold their offices during good behaviour, and shall, at stated times, receive for their services, a compensation, which shall not be diminished during their continuance in office.

SECTION 2. The judicial power shall extend to all cases, in law and equity, arising under this Constitution, the laws of the United States, and treaties made, or which shall be made, under their authority; to all cases affecting ambassadors, other public ministers and consuls; to all cases of admiralty and maritime jurisdiction; to controversies to which the United States shall be a party; to controversies between two or more States; between a State and citizens of another State; between citizens of different States; between citizens of the same State claiming lands under grants of different States, and between a State, or the citizens thereof, and foreign States, citizens, or subjects.

In all cases affecting ambassadors, other public ministers and consuls, and those in which a State shall be party, the Supreme Court shall have original jurisdiction. In all the other cases before mentioned, the Supreme Court shall have appellate jurisdiction, both as to law and to fact, which such exceptions, and under such regulations as the Congress shall make.

The trial of all crimes, except in cases of impeachment, shall be by jury; and such trial shall be held in the State where the said crimes shall have been committed; but when not committed within any State, the trial shall be at such place or places as the Congress may by law have directed.

SECTION 3. Treason against the United States, shall consist only in levying war against them, or in adhering to their enemies, giving them aid and comfort. No person shall be convicted of treason unless on the testimony of two witnesses to the same overt act, or on confession in open court.

The Congress shall have power to declare the punishment of treason, but no attainder of treason shall work corruption of blood, or forfeiture except during the life of the person attainted.

ARTICLE IV

SECTION 1. Full faith and credit shall be given in each State to the public acts, records, and judicial proceedings of every other State. And the Congress may by general laws prescribe the manner in which such acts, records and proceedings shall be proved, and the effect thereof.

SECTION 2. The citizens of each State shall be entitled to all privileges and immunities of citizens in the several States.

A person charged in any State with treason, felony, or other crime, who shall flee from justice, and be found in another State, shall on demand of the executive authority of the State from which he fled, be delivered up, to be removed to the State having jurisdiction of the crime.

No person held to service or labor in one State, under the laws thereof, escaping into another, shall, in consequence of any law or regulation therein, be discharged from such service or labor, but shall be delivered up on claim of the party to whom such service or labor may be due.

SECTION 3. New States may be admitted by the Congress into this Union; but no new State shall be formed or erected within the jurisdiction of any other State; nor any State be formed by the junction of two or more States, or parts of States, without the consent of the legislatures of the States concerned as well as of the Congress.

The Congress shall have the power to dispose of and make all needful rules and regulations respecting the Territory or other property belonging to the United States; and nothing in this Constitution shall be so construed as to prejudice any claims of the United States, or of any particular State.

SECTION 4. The United States shall guarantee to every State in this Union a republican form of Government, and shall protect each of them against invasion; and on application of the legislature, or of the executive (when the legislature cannot be convened) against domestic violence.

ARTICLE V

The Congress, whenever two thirds of both Houses shall deem it necessary, shall propose amendments to this Constitution, or, on the application of the legislatures of two thirds of the several States, shall call a convention for proposing amendments, which, in either case, shall be valid to all intents and purposes, as part of this Constitution, when ratified by the legislatures of three fourths of the several States, or by convention in three fourths thereof, as the one or the other mode of ratification may be proposed by the Congress; provided that no amendment which may be made prior to the year one thousand eight hundred and eight shall in any manner affect the first and fourth clauses in the Ninth Section of the First Article; and that no State, without its consent, shall be deprived of its equal suffrage in the Senate.

ARTICLE VI

All debts contracted and engagements entered into, before the adoption of this Constitution, shall be as valid against the United States under this Constitution, as under the Confederation.

This Constitution, and the laws of the United States which shall be made in pursuance thereof; and all treaties made, or which shall be made, under the authority of the United States, shall be the supreme law of the land; and the judges in every State shall be bound thereby, anything in the Constitution or laws of any State to the contrary notwithstanding.

The senators and representatives before mentioned, and the members of the several State legislatures, and all executive and judicial officers, both of the United States and of the several States, shall be bound by oath or affirmation, to support this Constitution; but no religious test shall ever be required as a qualification to any office or public trust under the United States.

ARTICLE VII

The ratification of the conventions of nine States shall be sufficient for the establishment of this Constitution between the States so ratifying the same.

Done in convention by the unanimous consent of the States present the seventeenth day of September in the year of our Lord one thousand seven hundred and eighty seven and of the Independence of the United States of America the twelfth. In witness whereof we have hereunto subscribed our names.

GEO. WASHINGTON,
Presid't. and deputy from Virginia.

Attest:
WILLIAM JACKSON, *Secretary.*

New Hampshire

JOHN LANGDON   NICHOLAS GILMAN

Massachusetts

NATHANIEL GORHAM   RUFUS KING

Connecticut

WM. SAML. JOHNSON   ROGER SHERMAN

New York

ALEXANDER HAMILTON

New Jersey

WIL. LIVINGSTON   WM. PATERSON
DAVID BREARLEY   JONA. DAYTON

Pennsylvania

B. FRANKLIN   THOS. FITZSIMONS
THOMAS MIFFLIN   JARED INGERSOLL
ROBT. MORRIS   JAMES WILSON
GEO. CLYMER   GOUV. MORRIS

Delaware

GEO. READ   RICHARD BASSETT
GUNNING BEDFORD JUN.   JACO. BROOM
JOHN DICKINSON

Maryland

JAMES McHENRY   DANL. CARROLL
DAN. OF ST. THOS. JENIFER

Virginia

JOHN BLAIR—   JAMES MADISON JR.

North Carolina

Wm. Blount   Hu. Williamson
Richd. Dobbs Spaight

South Carolina

J. Rutledge   Charles Pinckney
Charles Cotesworth Pinckney   Pierce Butler

Georgia

William Few   Abr. Baldwin

Amendments

ARTICLE I

Congress shall make no law respecting an establishment of religion, or prohibiting the free exercise thereof; or abridging the freedom of speech, or of the press; or the right of the people peaceably to assemble, and to petition the Government for a redress of grievances.

ARTICLE II

A well regulated militia, being necessary to the security of a free State, the right of the people to keep and bear arms, shall not be infringed.

ARTICLE III

No soldier shall, in time of peace be quartered in any house, without the consent of the owner, nor in time of war, but in a manner to be prescribed by law.

ARTICLE IV

The right of the people to be secure in their persons, houses, papers, and effects, against unreasonable searches and seizures, shall not be violated, and no warrants shall issue, but upon probable cause, supported by oath or affirmation, and particularly describing the place to be searched, and the persons or things to be seized.

ARTICLE V

No person shall be held to answer for a capital, or otherwise infamous crime, unless on a presentment or indictment of a grand jury, except in cases arising in the land or naval forces, or in the militia, when in actual service in time of war or public danger; nor shall any person be subject for the same offense to be twice put in jeopardy of life or limb; nor shall be compelled in any criminal case to be a witness against himself, nor be deprived of life, liberty, or property, without due process of law; nor shall private property be taken for public use, without just compensation.

ARTICLE VI

In all criminal prosecutions, the accused shall enjoy the right to a speedy and public trial, by an impartial jury of the State and district wherein the crime shall have been committed, which district shall have been previously ascertained by law, and to be informed of the nature and cause of the accusation; to be confronted with the witnesses against him; to have compulsory process for obtaining witnesses in his favor, and to have the assistance of counsel for his defense.

ARTICLE VII

In suits at common law, where the value in controversy shall exceed twenty dollars, the right of trial by jury shall be preserved, and no fact tried by a jury, shall be otherwise reexamined in any court of the United States, than according to the rules of the common law.

ARTICLE VIII

Excessive bail shall not be required, nor excessive fines imposed, nor cruel and unusual punishments inflicted.

ARTICLE IX

The enumeration in the Constitution, of certain rights, shall not be construed to deny or disparage others retained by the people.

ARTICLE X

The powers not delegated to the United States by the Constitution, nor prohibited by it to the States, are reserved to the States respectively, or to the people.

Article XI

The judicial power of the United States shall not be construed to extend to any suit in law or equity, commenced or prosecuted against one of the United States by citizens of another State, or by citizens or subjects of any foreign State.

Article XII

The electors shall meet in their respective States, and vote by ballot for President and Vice President, one of whom, at least, shall not be an inhabitant of the same State with themselves; they shall name in their ballots the person voted for as President, and in distinct ballots the person voted for as Vice President, and they shall make distinct lists of all persons voted for as President, and of all persons voted for as Vice President, and of the number of votes for each, which lists they shall sign and certify, and transmit sealed to the seat of the government of the United States, directed to the President of the Senate. The President of the Senate shall, in the presence of the Senate and House of Representatives, open all the certificates and the votes shall then be counted. The person having the greatest number of votes for President, shall be the President, if such number be a majority of the whole number of electors appointed; and if no person have such majority, then from the persons having the highest numbers not exceeding three on the list of those voted for as President, the House of Representatives shall choose immediately, by ballot, the President. But in choosing the President, the votes shall be taken by States, the representation from each State having one vote; a quorum for this purpose shall consist of a member or members from two-thirds of the States, and a majority of all the States shall be necessary to a choice. And if the House of Representatives shall not choose a President whenever the right of choice shall devolve upon them, before the fourth day of March next following, then the Vice President shall act as President, as in the case of the death or other constitutional disability of the President. The person having the greatest number of votes as Vice President, shall be the Vice President, if such number be a majority of the whole number of electors appointed, and if no person have a majority, then from the two highest numbers on the list, the Senate shall choose the Vice President; a quorum for the purpose shall consist of two-thirds of the whole number of Senators, and a majority of the whole number shall be necessary to a choice. But no person constitutionally ineligible to the office of President shall be eligible to that of Vice President of the United States.

ARTICLE XIII

SECTION 1. Neither slavery nor involuntary servitude, except as a punishment for crime whereof the party shall have been duly convicted, shall exist within the United States, or any place subject to their jurisdiction.

SECTION 2. Congress shall have power to enforce this article by appropriate legislation.

ARTICLE XIV

SECTION 1. All persons born or naturalized in the United States, and subject to the jurisdiction thereof, are citizens of the United States and of the State wherein they reside. No State shall make or enforce any law which shall abridge the privileges or immunities of citizens of the United States; nor shall any State deprive any person of life, liberty, or property, without due process of law; nor deny to any person within its jurisdiction the equal protection of the laws.

SECTION 2. Representatives shall be apportioned among the several States according to their respective numbers, counting the whole number of persons in each State, excluding Indians not taxed. But when the right to vote at any election for the choice of electors for President and Vice President of the United States, Representatives in Congress, the executive and judicial officers of a State, or the members of the legislature thereof, is denied to any of the male inhabitants of such State, being twenty-one years of age, and citizens of the United States, or in any way abridged, except for participation in rebellion, or other crime, the basis of representation therein shall be reduced in the proportion which the number of such male citizens shall bear to the whole number of male citizens twenty-one years of age in such State.

SECTION 3. No person shall be a Senator or Representative in Congress, or elector of President and Vice President, or hold any office, civil or military, under the United States, or under any State, who, having previously taken an oath, as a member of Congress, or as an officer of the United States, or as a member of any State legislature, or as an executive or judicial officer of any State, to support the Constitution of the United States, shall have engaged in insurrection or rebellion against the same, or given aid or comfort to the enemies thereof. But Congress may by a vote of two-thirds of each house, remove such disability.

SECTION 4. The validity of the public debt of the United States, authorized by law, including debts incurred for payment of pensions and bounties for services in suppressing insurrection or rebellion, shall not be questioned. But neither the United States nor any State shall assume or pay any debt or obligation incurred in aid of insurrection or rebellion against the United States, or any claim for the loss or emancipation of any slave; but all such debts, obligations and claims shall be held illegal and void.

SECTION 5. The Congress shall have power to enforce, by appropriate legislation, the provisions of this article.

ARTICLE XV

SECTION 1. The right of citizens of the United States to vote shall not be denied or abridged by the United States or by any State on account of race, color, or previous condition of servitude.

SECTION 2. The Congress shall have power to enforce this article by appropriate legislation.

ARTICLE XVI

The Congress shall have power to lay and collect taxes on incomes, from whatever source derived, without apportionment among the several States, and without regard to any census or enumeration.

ARTICLE XVII

SECTION 1. The Senate of the United States shall be composed of two senators from each State, elected by the people thereof, for six years; and each senator shall have one vote. The electors in each State shall have the qualifications requisite for electors of the most numerous branch of the State legislatures.

SECTION 2. When vacancies happen in the representation of any State in the Senate, the executive authority of such State shall issue writs of election to fill such vacancies: *Provided*, That the legislature of any State may empower the executive thereof to make temporary appointments until the people fill the vacancies by election as the legislature may direct.

SECTION 3. This amendment shall not be so construed as to affect the election or term of any senator chosen before it becomes valid as part of the Constitution.

Article XVIII

Section 1. After one year from the ratification of this article the manufacture, sale, or transportation of intoxicating liquors within, the importation thereof into, or the exportation thereof from the United States and all territory subject to the jurisdiction thereof for beverage purposes is hereby prohibited.

Section 2. The Congress and the several States shall have concurrent power to enforce this article by appropriate legislation.

Section 3. This article shall be inoperative unless it shall have been ratified as an amendment to the Constitution by the legislatures of the several States, as provided in the Constitution, within seven years from the date of the submission hereof to the States by the Congress.

Article XIX

Section 1. The right of citizens of the United States to vote shall not be denied or abridged by the United States or by any State on account of sex.

Section 2. Congress shall have power to enforce this article by appropriate legislation.

Article XX

Section 1. The terms of the President and Vice President shall end at noon on the 20th day of January, and the terms of Senators and Representatives at noon on the 3rd day of January, of the years in which such terms would have ended if this article had not been ratified; and the terms of their successors shall then begin.

Section 2. The Congress shall assemble at least once in every year, and such meeting shall begin at noon on the 3rd day of January, unless they shall by law appoint a different day.

Section 3. If, at the time fixed for the beginning of the term of the President, the President elect shall have died, the Vice President elect shall become President. If a President shall not have been chosen before the time fixed for the beginning of his term, or if the President elect shall have failed to qualify, then the Vice President elect shall act as President until a President shall have qualified; and the Congress may by law provide for the case wherein neither a President elect nor a Vice

T

President elect shall have qualified, declaring who shall then act as President, or the manner in which one who is to act shall be selected, and such person shall act accordingly until a President or Vice President shall have qualified.

SECTION 4. The Congress may by law provide for the case of the death of any of the persons from whom the House of Representatives may choose a President whenever the right of choice shall have devolved upon them, and for the case of the death of any of the persons from whom the Senate may choose a Vice President whenever the right of choice shall have devolved upon them.

SECTION 5. Sections 1 and 2 shall take effect on the 15th day of October following the ratification of this article.

SECTION 6. This article shall be inoperative unless it shall have been ratified as an amendment to the Constitution by the legislatures of three-fourths of the several States within seven years from the date of its submission.

ARTICLE XXI

SECTION 1. The eighteenth article of amendment to the Constitution of the United States is hereby repealed.

SECTION 2. The transportation or importation into any State, Territory, or possession of the United States for delivery or use therein of intoxicating liquors, in violation of the laws thereof, is hereby prohibited.

SECTION 3. This article shall be inoperative unless it shall have been ratified as an amendment to the Constitution by conventions in the several States, as provided in the Constitution, within seven years from the date of the submission hereof to the States by the Congress.

ARTICLE XXII

No person shall be elected to the Office of the President more than twice, and no person who has held the office of President, or acted as President, for more than two years of a term to which some other person was elected President shall be elected to the office of President more than once. But this Article shall not apply to any person holding the office of the President when this Article was proposed by the Congress, and shall not prevent any person who may be holding the office of President, or acting as President, during the term within which this Article becomes operative from holding the office of President or acting as President during the remainder of such term.

A GUIDE TO FURTHER READING

WRITING on American history is very extensive and the following pages do no more than provide a highly selective list of books which will enable the student to progress from a generalized survey to a more detailed study. Little attention is paid to monographic work and preference is given to books which are accessible, readable and make definite contributions to historiography.[1] Most books on American history by American authors are particularly strong in bibliographical apparatus so that the advanced student will find it comparatively easy to extend his reading from the base provided in the following list; there is also the invaluable *Harvard Guide to American History*, which provides select bibliographies under subject headings, but there is, at present, no supplement to fill the gap between 1954 (its date of publication) and the present day. There are five leading journals in which articles on American history, and reviews of books on American history, appear regularly; they are the *American Historical Review, The Journal of American History* (formerly the *Mississippi Valley Historical Review*), the *Journal of Southern History, The William and Mary Quarterly*, and *The New England Quarterly*. There are also a large number of journals devoted to regional and state history.

REFERENCE WORKS

The Encyclopedia of American History (ed. R. B. Morris) is one of the best compilations of its kind and can be used to verify detail with some confidence; *The Dictionary of American History* (ed. J. T. Adams) in five volumes has many good essays on special subjects and there is an abridged edition entitled *The Concise Dictionary of American History*; the *Dictionary of American Biography* is of similar quality to the British *Dictionary of National Biography*.

A handy and accurate atlas of American history is that by C. L. Lord and E. H. Lord; a large standard atlas, particularly useful for

---

[1] Several works are cited more than once. The full title is given with each reference except where they follow closely upon each other.

political history, is O. G. Paullin, *Atlas of the Historical Geography of the United States*, and there is an Atlas volume in the *Dictionary of American History* cited above. *Historical Statistics of the United States* — an official publication — is an essential aid to any study involving economic problems.

DOCUMENTS

The best collection of official documents is H. S. Commager, *Documents of American History*; many leading documents are also found in R. S. Birley, *Speeches and Documents of American History* (World's Classics, 4 vols.), and there are several shorter collections. T. G. Manning and D. M. Potter (with W. E. Davies), *Select Problems in Historical Interpretation*: Vol. I, *Nationalism and Sectionalism 1775–1877*, Vol. II, *Government and the Economy 1870 to Present*, present well-chosen source-material arranged to illustrate various crucial problems. Donald R. McCoy and Raymond G. O'Connor, *Readings in Twentieth-Century American History*, is useful. One of the great achievements of modern American scholarship is the publication *in extenso* of the writings and papers of leading statesmen: so far complete or in progress are the writings of Franklin, Jefferson, Washington, Hamilton, the Adams family, Clay, Calhoun, Lincoln, and Theodore Roosevelt; there are also collections of the public papers of Woodrow Wilson, and Franklin D. Roosevelt. At a different level there are a large number of collections which select and compare the views of secondary authorities; the series published under the auspices of Amherst College (many titles and each volume devoted to a single major topic) are usually rewarding, and there is a particularly interesting collection in Sidney Fine and Gerald S. Brown, *The American Past.* Abraham S. Eisenstadt, *American History: Recent Interpretations* (2 vols.) reprints a large number of important articles from historical journals and extracts from recent books.

TEXTBOOKS

There are a very large number of these. S. E. Morison and H. S. Commager, *The Growth of the American Republic* has considerable literary merits; the authors are Northerners with Jeffersonian sympathies. J. D. Hicks, *The Federal Union* and *The American Nation from 1865 to the Present* is a straightforward and balanced history by a Mid-Westerner. C. A. and M. R. Beard, *The Rise of American Civiliza-*

tion is an interpretative survey rather than a textbook; it stresses economic factors and interpretations and has been a work of very considerable influence. There are two recent short surveys: R. B. Nye and J. Morpurgo, *Penguin History of the United States* and W. Miller, *A History of the United States*; the former is vigorous and good on the colonial and early national periods, but the latter is much better on the period since 1865.

R. A. Billington, *Westward Expansion: a history of the American Frontier* is an admirable textbook for the history of the West. F. B. Simkins, *A History of the South* is balanced in its treatment. J. H. Franklin, *From Slavery to Freedom* is a good history of the American Negro.

Economic history texts are fairly numerous. H. U. Faulkner, *American Economic History* avoids technicalities and is profusely illustrated; E. C. Kirkland, *A History of American Economic Growth* is more mature in its treatment; F. A. Shannon, *America's Economic Growth* is shorter and more provocative but less well balanced. Carl Wittke, *We Who Made America* is a general account of immigration and its consequences; Maldwyn Jones, *American Immigration* is the best short account of this subject.

The most generally useful text on Constitutional History is A. H. Kelly and W. A. Harbison, *The American Constitution*. The older *Constitutional History* by A. C. McLaughlin is still useful for its fuller treatment of the early national period. C. B. Swisher, *American Constitutional Development* is more technical in its approach and is valuable for a close study of constitutional development since 1865. The student of American history will find his path easier if he acquires some understanding of the modern American political system: E. S. Griffith, *The American Political System* and A. M. Potter, *American Government* are good outline studies; W. E. Binkley and M. Moos, *A Dictionary of American Politics* is very full and informative; D. W. Brogan, *An Introduction to American Politics* is especially good in describing the human motives behind the perplexing façade. W. E. Binkley, *American Political Parties; their natural History* is the best historical account of the subject but needs revision at several points.

The standard text on American intellectual history is Merle Curti, *The Growth of American Thought*, which is full and well-balanced but inclined to suffer from over-compression. R. H. Gabriel, *The Course of American Democratic Thought 1840–1930* is more limited in scope and time, but full and perceptive over the ground which it covers. V. L. Parrington, *Main Currents in American Thought* is an older but very readable work which also illustrates the continuing influence of Jeffersonian ideas upon modern American thought. A. M. Schlesinger, Jr., and Morton White (eds.), *Paths of American Thought* includes a number of essays, many of high quality, by various authors. Russell Kirk, *The Conservative Mind* is not confined to America and not generally acceptable to Americans, but it is interesting and provocative. W. J. Cash, *The Mind of the South* is a brilliant analysis which treats the subject historically. The history of American religion receives far less share in general histories than its importance warrants; W. W. Sweet, *The Story of Religion in America* is a good short survey, W. L. Sperry, *Religion in America* and L. Richard Niebuhr, *The Social Sources of Denominationalism* are valuable commentaries. There are brilliant comments upon American religion, and on many other topics, in Richard Hofstadter, *Anti-Intellectualism in American Life*.

There are two good standard histories of American Diplomacy: S. F. Bemis, *A Diplomatic History of the United States*, and T. A. Bailey, *A Diplomatic History of the American People*; Bemis is a robust nationalist, Bailey is more in sympathy with recent trends. W. Millis, *Armies and Men* is a stimulating essay on military history.

GENERAL HISTORIES

Modern American historians have not followed their predecessors in writing large multi-volume histories, but some of these older works are still valuable. E. Channing, *A History of the United States*, 6 vols., often provides the best summary account of complex problems. J. F. Rhodes, *A History of the United States from the Compromise of 1850*, 7 vols., is well balanced. E. P. Oberholtzer, *A History of the United States since the Civil War*, 5 vols., is comprehensive and restrained in judgment. In a rather different class is J. B. McMaster, *A History of the People of the United States from the Revolution to the Civil War*, 8 vols., which is a compilation rather than a history; it derives its usefulness from the extent to which the author used newspapers and other contemporary sources, and it can therefore give the reader a 'feel' for the period, but poor critical apparatus makes of little use for the scholar. *The New American Nation Series* (ed. H. S. Commager and R. B. Morris) and *The Chicago History of American Civilization* (ed. D.

Boorstin), each consisting of a large number of volumes by various authors, will eventually cover the whole range of American history; several of the titles in these series are separately noticed below.

SHORT SURVEYS AND INTERPRETATIVE ESSAYS

Under such a heading F. J. Turner, *The Frontier in American History* must have pride of place; Turner's 'frontier thesis' has been much criticized but is still resilient. Henry Nash Smith, *Virgin Land* describes brilliantly the place of the West in American imagination. In *The Great Experiment* an English scholar, F. Thistlethwaite, stresses the importance of migration in American social evolution. D. M. Potter, *People of Plenty* investigates the effects of material abundance on American evolution. R. Hofstadter, *The American Political Tradition* takes a fresh and often revealing look at the great figures of American political history, and D. J. Boorstin, *The Genius of American Politics* stresses (against determinists of all kinds) the pragmatic experience of the American people. Clinton Rossiter, *Conservatism in America* is a good survey of thinkers and trends which have not always received due recognition. Reinhold Niebuhr, *The Irony of American History* is a short essay by a distinguished theologian. Geoffrey Gorer, *The American People* brings psychology to the aid of history in a stimulating way. Of recent years a great many Americans have attempted to diagnose the peculiarities of their own civilization. Among such works, those which have more than an ephemeral value are: *U.S.A. The Permanent Revolution* by the Editors of *Fortune*, C. Wright Mills, *White Collar*, S. Lubell, *The Future of American Politics*, David Riesman, *The Lonely Crowd* and *Individualism Reconsidered*, W. H. Whyte, *The Organisation Man*, and *The Exploding City* by the Editors of *Fortune*. Many aspects of American life are examined and assessed in Max Lerner's massive *America as a Civilisation*. Amongst the periodicals in which important articles on American problems are likely to appear are *Harper's*, *The Nation*, *The New Republic*, *The Atlantic Monthly*, *The American Scholar*, *The Reporter*, and the News Review of the Sunday *New York Times*.

THE ERA OF THE REVOLUTION

Colonial society in the mid-eighteenth century has attracted a great deal of attention. C. M. Andrews, *The Colonial Background to the*

American Revolution is a good starting-point for the student. Carl Bridenbaugh, *Cities in the Wilderness* deals with aspects which have otherwise been somewhat neglected; the same author's *Myths and Realities in the Old South* is short and interesting. D. Boorstin, *The Americans: the Colonial Experience* contains new and interesting reflections. C. S. Sydnor, *Gentlemen Freeholders, Political Practices in Washington's Virginia* is an important book. L. H. Gipson, *The British Empire before the American Revolution* is a vast and leisurely work (nine volumes to date) but can be used for reference on special topics. L. B. Wright, *The Culture of Colonial America* provides a good overall survey. Carl Bridenbaugh, *Mitre and Sceptre* deals authoritatively with religious problems and their political repercussions. There are some good chapters in the *Cambridge History of the British Empire*, Vol. I.

A general survey of the origins and growth of the revolutionary movement is C. H. Van Tyne, *Causes of the American Revolution*. E. Channing, *History of the United States*, Vol. III still remains a most useful and well-written work. L. H. Gipson, *The Coming of the Revolution* provides an excellent survey of the decade preceding the Revolution in a mood which is somewhat more favourable to the British than a British historian would dare to be. J. C. Miller, *The Origins of the American Revolution* uses contemporary newspapers and similar sources but is somewhat neglectful of modern authorities. B. Knollenberg, *Origin of the American Revolution, 1759–1765* attempts to show, with a wealth of detail, that the 'origin' is to be found during these years. E. S. Morgan, *The Stamp Act Controversy* is thorough and interesting; O. M. Dickerson, *The Navigation Acts and the Revolution* also illuminates wider aspects of the revolution. A. M. Schlesinger, *Colonial Merchants and the American Revolution* and *Prelude to Revolution: the Newspaper War against Great Britain* are important works. T. P. Abernethy, *Western Lands and the American Revolution* is full of interest though stressing too heavily the importance of its subject. R. B. Morris (ed.), *The Era of the American Revolution* contains some valuable essays. R. R. Palmer, *The Age of the Democratic Revolution* has interesting comments upon the Revolution and traces its influence abroad. Robert E. Brown, *Middle Class Democracy and Revolution in Massachusetts* is an important monograph which attacks commonly held assumptions. William H. Nelson, *The American Tory* is a fresh and penetrating study of loyalism. This is, above all, the period in which the student should read source material, not only for its historical significance but also for its intellectual and literary content. Some of the material has been well selected in Max Beloff (ed.), *The Debate on the American Revolution.* S. E. Morison, *The American Revolution* is a collection of documents which includes contemporary pamphlets not readily available elsewhere; Merrill Jensen (ed.), *English Historical Documents, Vol. IX,* contains much interesting material; *Selected Writings of John and John Quincy Adams,* ed. A. Koch and W. Peden, and *Life and Writings of Thomas Jefferson,* by the same editor, contain well-chosen items. There is a splendid collection of contemporary description and comment in H. S. Commager, *The Spirit of Seventy-Six.*

The course of the Revolution itself is covered in a straightforward way by J. R. Alden, *The American Revolution,* and a sectional study is the same author's *The South during the Revolution.* E. Robson, *The American Revolution* is an incomplete essay published after the author's death, but particularly useful on military history. Esmond Wright, *Fabric of Freedom* is lucidly written and balanced in judgment. Carl Becker, *The Declaration of Independence* deals with the literary history and intellectual antecedents of the great document. R. G. Adams, *The Political Theories of the American Revolution* is a useful work. There are two good studies of Washington by Esmond Wright and Marcus Cunliffe. The history of the States during the Revolution can be studied in detail in Allan Nevins, *The American States during and after the Revolution,* but E. P. Douglass, *Rebels and Democrats* give a more stimulating account of the important political struggles which took place. Merrill Jensen, *The Articles of Confederation* is a first-rate book though the author may draw too sharp an antithesis between 'conservatives' and 'radicals'. J. F. Jameson, *The American Revolution considered as a Social Movement* was a pioneer work in shifting the emphasis away from the purely political aspects; R. A. East, *The Formation of Business Enterprise during the American Revolution* is a valuable monograph on the growth of commercial and financial interests. S. F. Bemis, *Diplomacy of the American Revolution* is a standard work on the subject.

NATIONALISM, LOCAL AUTONOMY AND DEMOCRACY

The Revolutionary origins of the great political struggles can be studied in the works cited above by Alden, Jensen and Douglass. Merrill Jensen, *The New Nation* is a well-documented work which attacks the conventional view of the Confederation period (as, for instance, in John Fiske, *The Critical Period*) and helps to explain the intensity of opposition to the Constitution. Charles Beard, *The Economic Interpretation of the Constitution* is a classic and influential work; modern criticism is inclined to the view that Beard over-rated the influence of a small minority group (the public creditors) and under-rated the force of eighteenth-century political perfectionism. Beard's work has been ably, if somewhat narrowly, criticized in Robert E. Brown, *Charles Beard and the Constitution*, and Forrest McDonald, *We the People* opens up a new field of detailed research. Pending a complete revision Max Farrand, *The Making of the Constitution* provides a straightforward and balanced account and J. R. Pole in *British Essays in American History* (ed. Allen and Hill) incorporates the findings of recent work on the subject. '*The Federalist*', written by Hamilton, Madison and Jay is essential reading for its commentary upon the Constitution, for its contribution to political argument, and for its subsequent influence upon constitutional interpretation.

Marcus Cunliffe, *The Nation takes Shape* is an excellent brief survey of the subsequent period from 1789 to 1837. The first decade under the Constitution arouses intense partisanship among American writers; Hamilton and Jefferson still stand at the head of two rival streams of American development, and the chasm between the two has yet to be bridged by impartial study. It is but recently that a start has been made in the task of getting behind the polemics of the period to the real structure of politics. Many years ago Charles Beard's *Economic Origins of Jeffersonian Democracy* pointed one line of investigation. More recently Manning J. Dauer, *The Adams Federalists* reveals the Federalist party as a more complex and socially more diversified organization than might be inferred from Beard or from C. G. Bowers, *Hamilton and Jefferson*. J. C. Miller, *The Federalist Era* is recent and useful. There are short readable biographies of Hamilton and of Jefferson by Nathan Schachner. A new biography of Hamilton by Broadus Mitchell promises to be a standard work, and the present writer has a brief account of Hamilton in *British Essays in American History* (ed. Allen and Hill). Stephen G. Kurtz, *The Presidency of John Adams* is sympathetic and scholarly. Russell Kirk, *The Conservative Mind* does justice to the political thought of John Adams, and Merrill D. Peterson, *The Jefferson Image in the American Mind* is a brilliant study of the use and misuse of Jefferson's ideas throughout American history. Max Beloff, *Thomas Jefferson and American Democracy* is very short but perceptive.

N. E. Cunningham, *The Jeffersonian Republicans: the formation of Party Organization* is a useful monograph on a neglected subject. Henry Adams (ed. Herbert Agar), *The Formative Years* remains the best general account of Jefferson's Presidency.

Any study of Hamilton will include some account of the principles of economic nationalism, but thereafter it will be difficult to find much which is useful. Raymond Walters, Jr., *Albert Gallatin: Jeffersonian Financier and Diplomat*, is thorough, but there is no study of the 'American System' as a political and social movement. After 1815 a part of the economic background is described effectively in G. R. Taylor, *The Transportation Revolution* and other aspects in P. W. Yates, *The Farmers' Age*; George Dangerfield, *The Era of Good Feelings* is a good political history which takes account of economic developments. Bernard Mayo, *Henry Clay* and the first volume of C. M. Wiltse, *John C. Calhoun* are helpful. Walter Buckingham Smith, *The Second Bank of the United States* is a useful monograph. O. and M. F. Handlin, *Commonwealth* uses a study of Massachusetts to demonstrate that *laissez-faire* was not the accepted social philosophy.

For legal nationalism a standard work is Charles Warren, *The Supreme Court in United States History*. W. W. Crosskey, *Politics and the Constitution* is a massive and learned work which challenges the accepted interpretations of the Constitution and of its early history; his arguments have impressed lawyers more than historians but should not be ignored.

The rise of the States' rights tradition can be studied in the works already cited on Jefferson, in Wiltse's *Calhoun*, in the short and readable biography of Calhoun by M. Coit, and in C. S. Sydnor, *The Rise of Southern Sectionalism*.

The democratic impulse is well illustrated in J. W. Ward, *Andrew Jackson: symbol of an age*, in the early chapters of C. G. Sellers, *James Polk: Jacksonian*, and in the same author's article on 'Politics and Banking in Eastern Tennessee' in the *Mississippi Valley Historical Review* for 1954. C. R. Fish, *The Rise of the Common Man* deals with the social history of the early nineteenth century. S. Rezneck, *The Depression of 1819–22* (*American Historical Review*, 1933) describes the effect of the depression upon the democratic upsurge. Marvin Meyers, *The Jacksonian Persuasion* is an interesting study. The later development of Jacksonian ideas can be studied in Arthur Schlesinger, Jr.'s brilliant and controversial *Age of Jackson* and in the very useful collection edited with a good introduction by J. L. Blau, *Social Theories of Jacksonian Democracy*. Bray Hammond, *Banks and Politics in America from the Revolution to the Civil War* is excellent and sharply critical of many accepted views about the Jacksonians.

As with the previous period contemporary sources are of great importance though the polemical literature is of less value and less readily accessible. The opinions of Hamilton and Jefferson on the Constitutionality of the National Bank, Hamilton's Reports on Public Credit and on Manufactures, the Virginia and Kentucky Revolutions of 1798, and the leading cases of John Marshall (especially Marbury *v.* Madison, Gibbons *v.* Ogden, McCulloch *v.* Maryland, and the Dartmouth College case) should all be read carefully. The relevant portions of the Diary of John Quincy Adams are of great interest, and the *Correspondence of Jefferson with John Adams* (ed. P. Wilstach) provides a delightful and often illuminating series of letters between the two ex-Presidents.

THE UNITED STATES IN A WORLD OF GROWTH AND CHANGE

The establishment of the United States as an independent world power can be followed in two standard works by S. F. Bemis, *Jay's Treaty* and *John Quincy Adams and the foundations of American Foreign Policy*, in J. B. Brebner, *The Atlantic Triangle*, a perceptive work which treats the North Atlantic as a single problem, in Alexander DeConde, *Entangling Alliance*, and in the early chapters of H. C. Allen, *Great Britain and the United States*.

Two sides in the controversy over the causes of the war of 1812 are represented by J. W. Pratt, *The Expansionists of 1812* (who stresses Western influences to the exclusion of almost everything else) and A. L. Burt, *The United States, Great Britain and British North America* (who reaffirms the traditional view that maritime disputes were the dominant issues). The pattern of trade and economic warfare in which the Americans had to find a place is described by E. Hecksher in *The Continental System* which can be supplemented by N. H. Buck, *The Organisation of Anglo-American Trade*. The developing commercial and financial links between the United States and Great Britain is described authoritatively in R. W. Hidy, *The House of Baring*, and F. Thistlethwaite, *The Anglo-American Connection in the Early Nineteenth Century* is a broad and interesting survey. M. Hansen, *The Atlantic Migration* is an excellent study of its subject to 1860.

Territorial expansion is best approached through R. A. Billington, *Westward Expansion* and *The North Western Frontier*, A. K. Weinberg, *Manifest Destiny*, and N. A. Graebner, *Empire on the Pacific*. Two books by Bernard DeVoto — *Across the Wide Missouri* and *1846: the Year of Decision* — are vividly written and full of information; Marquis James, *The Raven: a biography of Sam Houston* is an adequate life of the greatest Texan. Expansionism as a political movement can be studied in the later chapters of C. G. Sellers, *James K. Polk* and in *Polk's Diary* edited by Allan Nevins.

The intellectual and political ferment of the age is described by Arthur Schlesinger, Jr., *The Age of Jackson* (it has been said that he overestimates the role of Eastern labour in the Jackson movement and deals too unsympathetically with the Whig opposition). R. N. Current, *Daniel Webster and American Conservatism* does something to redress the balance but does not make the ideas of his subject very attractive. G. G. Van Deusen, *The Jacksonian Era, 1828–1848*, is a general survey. Lee Benson, *The Concept of Jacksonian Democracy* has more to say about the Whigs than the Democrats; it is challenging and opens a new field for enquiry about the party system between 1835 and 1850. In the more purely intellectual field Perry Miller, *The Transcendentalists* is a most useful collection of extracts from their writings; after 1840 R. H. Gabriel, *The Course of American Democratic Thought* is a good commentary. The impact of economic change is admirably sketched in the early chapters of T. C. Cochran and W. Miller, *The Age of Enterprise*. C. S. Sydnor, *The Rise of Southern Sectionalism*, and Clement Eaton, *The Growth of Southern Civilization* deal fairly with Southern history during this period. K. M. Stampp, *The Peculiar Institution* is sharply at variance with the older and apologetic view of slavery presented by U. B. Phillips in *American Negro Slavery* and *Life and Labor in the Old South*. A new and stimulating treatment is S. M. Elkins, *Slavery*. The anti-slavery movement can be studied in G. H. Barnes, *The Anti-Slavery Impulse*, Dwight Dumont, *The Anti-Slavery Origins of the Civil War*, and Louis Filler, *The Crusade against Slavery*.

The period from 1835 to 1850 has been less intensively studied than any other in American history. But it is possible to open a study of the period with an old classic — de Tocqueville's *Democracy in America* (supplemented by G. W. Pierson, *Tocqueville and Beaumont in America*) — and to close with a modern classic, the early chapters of

Allan Nevins, *The Ordeal of the Union* which survey American civilization about the year 1850.

THE GREAT CONFLICT AND ITS AFTERMATH

The best single volume survey of the whole subject is David Donald's revision of J. G. Randall, *Civil War and Reconstruction*; it contains a superlative bibliography which is an essential starting-point for specialized study. Thomas J. Pressley, *Americans Interpret their Civil War*, is an excellent study of historiography. The most important work upon the preliminaries of the Civil War is to be found in Allan Nevins, *The Ordeal of the Union* (2 vols.) and *The Emergence of Lincoln* (2 vols.). The first two volumes of J. F. Rhodes, *The History of the United States since the Compromise of 1850* are still useful. A. O. Craven, *The Coming of the Civil War* is a short book which leans toward the South in its sympathies; it is often stimulating and sometimes provoking. R. F. Nichols, *The Disruption of the Democracy* deals with party details but is more than a political chronicle. Among biographies J. G. Randall, *Lincoln* (4 vols. — the last compiled by R. N. Current) is important and well-written though it seems (to the present writer) to under-rate consistently the importance of anti-slavery feeling. B. Thomas, *Abraham Lincoln* is a good single-volume biography. D. M. Potter, *Lincoln and his Party in the Secession Crisis* gives the most balanced treatment of the highly controversial events of 1861. G. F. Milton, *The Eve of Conflict: Stephen A. Douglas and the Needless War* deals with the same events from a different point of view. O. G. Villard, *John Brown* is hagiographic but not entirely uncritical; the last chapter on Brown's influence on the anti-slavery movement is important.

An enormous amount of writing has been devoted to the military history of the war, but much of it is in the form of monographs on particular leaders, campaigns or units, and there is no thoroughly reliable single-volume history of military events. Bruce Catton, *This Hallowed Ground* deals eloquently with the military history of the North and his vividly written history of the war in three or more volumes is now in progress. Clement Eaton, *A History of the Southern Confederacy* is the best short treatment of the subject. David Donald, *Lincoln Reconsidered* contains some brief but important essays.

The history of Reconstruction bristles with controversy. Some Southern historians, such as E. M. Coulter, *The Southern States during*

Reconstruction, provide an unrelieved condemnation of Northern policy and of the reconstruction governments in the South. Equally biased on the other side was *Black Reconstruction*, by W. E. B. Du Bois, the patriarch of Negro historians. A recent general account by another Negro historian is *Reconstruction*, by John Hope Franklin, which is remarkable for its freedom from polemics. *The Tragic Era*, by Claude G. Bowers, has recently been reprinted, but readers should be warned of its undisguised anti-Republican partisanship. Hostility to Radical Republicanism was given deeper undertones by economic interpretations, as sketched in outline by Charles and Mary Beard, *History of American Civilization*, and Louis M. Hacker, *Triumph of American Capitalism*, and studied in detail in *The Critical Year*, by H. K. Beale; this economic interpretation has been sharply, and probably successfully challenged, by R. P. Sharkey, *Money, Class and Party*. The current interest in Reconstruction is witnessed by the recent appearance of three books which re-examine the political problems of Radical policy in great detail and with conclusions which differ sharply from older views: they are E. L. McKitrick, *Andrew Johnson and Reconstruction*, La Wanda and John H. Cox, *Politics, Principle and Prejudice, 1865–1866*, and W. R. Brock, *An American Crisis: Congress and Reconstruction 1865–1867*. F. Brodie, *Thaddeus Stevens* is an interesting analysis of a complex character; the less-critical biography by R. Korngold is also useful in showing how many men found this apparently unattractive man so worthy of support. The early chapters of C. Vann Woodward, *Origins of the New South* contain in some revealing information about the Southern 'redeemers' and the same author's history of Reconstruction in the South is now eagerly awaited.

THE BUSINESS CIVILIZATION

T. C. Cochran and W. Miller, *The Age of Enterprise* is a good survey of the progress of the economy and of its social implications. There is a great deal of information in two volumes in the *History of American Life* series: Allan Nevins, *The Emergence of Modern America* and Arthur Schlesinger, *The Rise of the City*. Two bitter contemporary attacks upon big business are Henry Demarest Lloyd, *Wealth against Commonwealth* and Ida M. Tarbell, *History of the Standard Oil Company* (but Miss Tarbell was much more sympathetic to business in her later years, as for instance, in her *Nationalizing of Business*). It is often forgotten by modern readers that the most influential critic was Henry George, and students should look at *Progress and Poverty* and read the biography of George by Charles Barker. An important aspect of intellectual history is covered by Richard Hofstadter, *Social Darwinism in American Thought*, and conservative thought is handled more sympathetically by Robert McCloskey, *American Conservatism in the Age of Enterprise*. H. S. Commager, *The American Mind* is detailed and interesting on the period since 1880.

The political history of the period has been written mainly through the eyes of contemporary critics and 'mugwumps' (the outlook is described by R. Hofstadter in the *Age of Reform*). The generally critical and contemptuous attitude is maintained in the readable and detailed work of Matthew Josephson, *The Politicos*. A more temperate assessment of Republicanism can be gained by scanning the pages of T. C. Smith, *Life and Letters of J. A. Garfield*, H. J. Eckenrode, *Rutherford B. Hayes*, and G. F. Hoar, *Autobiography of Seventy Years*. On the Democratic side Allan Nevins, *Grover Cleveland* is a thorough and sympathetic account. E. F. Goldman, *Rendezvous with Destiny* traces the reform movements of the period in an eminently readable book. *The Education of Henry Adams* by Henry Adams is an important and extraordinary work of American literature, but he was far from typical of his class or generation.

There are two contemporary studies of late nineteenth-century politics which have abiding significance: Lord Bryce, *The American Commonwealth* and Woodrow Wilson, *Congressional Government*. Both require considerable modification in the light of modern events and, in particular, both underestimated the potentialities of the Presidential office. L. D. White, *The Republican Era* is an excellent history of administration during the period and throws much light upon the contemporary struggle for civil service reform.

W. P. Webb, *The Great Plains* describes graphically the untamed Wild West. The best single-volume account of agrarian discontent is J. D. Hicks, *The Populist Revolt*; this should be read in conjunction with the chapter on Populism in R. Hofstadter, *Age of Reform* which stresses the limitations of the movement. The economic background to agrarian radicalism is provided by F. A. Shannon, *The Farmers' Last Frontier*. A companion volume on the industrial history of the period, *Industry comes of Age*, by E. C. Kirkland may serve to correct the agrarian bias which has characterized much of the writing about the period. Allan Nevins, *A Study in Power* (a much revised version of the same author's *John D. Rockefeller*) is a patient work, based upon an extensive acquaintance with the Rockefeller manuscripts, which succeeds in presenting its subject as a human being and not as a monster or bogy.

THE UNITED STATES IN A WORLD OF CONFLICT AND REVOLT

A good general account of the period since 1890 is A. S. Link, *An American Epoch*. T. C. Cochran, *The American Business System* 1900–1955 is a valuable survey. The works already cited on diplomatic history (Bemis and Bailey) are full and authoritative on the external relations of the United States in the late nineteenth and early twentieth centuries. A. S. Link's biography of Wilson has important material on the United States and the European war. L. M. Gelber, *Foundations of Anglo-American Friendship* is important though somewhat one-sided. George Kennan, *American Diplomacy* is a brief and challenging work, intended mainly for consumption at the date of publication (1950) but containing important reflections upon the principles of American foreign policy. Thorough and detailed works on the diplomacy of the 1930's are W. L. Langer and S. E. Gleason, *The Challenge to Isolation* and *The Undeclared War*.

Progressivism attracts more and more attention at the present time. Two good volumes in the New American Nation series — G. E. Mowry, *The Era of Theodore Roosevelt* and A. S. Link, *Woodrow Wilson and the Progressive Era* — will provide a starting-point. Two earlier works by Mowry, *Theodore Roosevelt and the Progressive Movement* and *The California Progressives* are also important. C. G. Bowers, *Beveridge and the Progressive Era* deals in full with the life of a Western progressive Republican who played an important secondary part in national politics. Lincoln Steffens, *Autobiography* is of absorbing interest. The *Selected Letters of William Allen White* (ed. Walter Johnson) are interesting reading and provide a great deal of illustrative material. The multi-volume collection of *The Letters of Theodore Roosevelt* (ed. E. E. Morison) contains much that is fascinating and illuminating, and H. F. Pringle's biography of Roosevelt is readable though unfriendly. There is a major biography of Woodrow Wilson by A. S. Link, and an important shorter study, *Woodrow Wilson and the Politics of Morality*, by John Blum. Herbert Croly, *The Promise of*

u

American Life was an influential book of the period. Theodore Roosevelt's *New Nationalism* and Woodrow Wilson's *New Freedom* have recently been republished in paperback.

By contrast the history of organized labour has had far less attraction for American historians. For some information the reader will still have to go back to the thirty-year-old work, *History of Trade Unionism in America* by S. Perlman or to the much larger compilation, *Labor in America* by John R. Commons on which Perlman's work was based. Henry Pelling, *Labor in America* is a short and penetrating survey by an English scholar. S. Gompers, *Autobiography* is an important source book, and Ray Ginger, *The Bending Cross* (a biography of Eugene Debs) is very well written and provides some real insight into the problems of organizing labour. C. Wright Mills, *New Men of Power* is a modern assessment of union leadership with some significant reflections upon its history. The Socialist minority has attracted more modern interest than the main current of trade union history: H. H. Quint, *The Forging of American Socialism*, D. D. Egbert (ed.), *Socialism and American Life*, and D. A. Shannon, *The Socialist Party in America* are interesting and fair.

The history of the South between 1877 and 1913 is admirably covered in C. Vann Woodward, *The Origins of the New South*, and the same author's *Strange Career of Jim Crow* deals briefly with the imposition of the segregation patterns upon the South. A thorough study of the Negro problem is Gunnar Myrdal, *An American Dilemma*; several of its sections contain good historical introductions. Here, as in earlier sections, W. J. Cash, *Mind of the South* is stimulating. Woodward and Cash are both liberal Southerners; Myrdal is a Swedish sociologist with pronounced liberal sympathies; it would therefore be fair to recommend a work exemplifying the conservative and segregationist point of view but there seems to be no such work above the level of polemical literature, though there is much that could be said against the view that racial conflict can be legislated out of existence.

CONSERVATISM AND LIBERALISM

The more tolerant attitude toward business conservatism in recent liberal writing is typified in F. L. Allen, *The Big Change*, which is also a good survey by an intelligent journalist of twentieth-century trends in America, and in J. K. Galbraith, *American Capitalism*, which can be read easily and with profit by those who are not trained economists.

P. W. Slosson, *The Great Crusade and After* was, when written, almost contemporary history; at this level it was surprisingly successful and remains a good short account of the nineteen-twenties. F. L. Allen, *Only Yesterday* is extremely amusing but should not be accepted as a complete picture of the decade. George Soule, *Prosperity Decade* covers economic aspects. The first volume of Arthur Schlesinger, Jr., *The Age of Franklin D. Roosevelt* entitled *The Crisis of the Old Order* is brilliantly written but is too partisan in tone to be taken as a reliable guide; it is, however, a very good account of the feelings of disgruntled intellectuals and of political rebels during the decade following the war. J. D. Hicks, *The Republican Era* is a useful survey of the period, but presents no new interpretations. W. Leuchtenberg, *The Perils of Prosperity* is the most interesting recent study of the decade. Andrew Sinclair, *Prohibition* is brilliant and readable though some of its judgments have been questioned. J. K. Galbraith, *The Great Crash* deals confidently with the events of 1920–30 from an economist's point of view.

The literature upon the New Deal promises to be as voluminous as that upon the Civil War, and unfortunately much was written before the passions of the period had had time to cool. The majority of writers have been emotionally committed to the New Deal, though Broadus Mitchell, *Depression Decade* is sharply critical of New Deal economics. William Leuchtenberg, *Franklin D. Roosevelt and the New Deal* supersedes earlier single-volume accounts, and has the merit of being very well written, but Sir Denis Brogan, *The Era of F. D. Roosevelt* is still useful for its penetrating judgments. The second and subsequent volumes of Arthur Schlesinger, Jr., *The Age of Roosevelt* succeed admirably in bringing to life the personalities of the New Deal and their ideas. James Burns, *Roosevelt: the lion and the fox* is a good study of Roosevelt as a politician, and there is a multi-volume biography of Roosevelt by Frank Freidel in progress. Memoirs from participants in these events continue to appear: Herbert Hoover, *Memoirs*, Vol. III, preserves the full bitterness of the time, but has many interesting comments; equally biased on the other side are Sam Rosenman, *Working With Roosevelt*, Frances Perkins, *The Roosevelt I knew*, and Rexford G. Tugwell, *The Democratic Roosevelt*. *The White House Papers of Harry Hopkins* (ed. R. S. Sherwood) and *The Morgenthau Diaries* (ed.

John Blum) provide invaluable first-hand material. Roosevelt's own published letters leave unsolved the problem of what he really thought about most things. The history of the United States since 1945 has yet to pass through the refining mill of scholarship. Mention may be made of some contemporary records: President H. S. Truman, *Memoirs* (2 vols.), Sherman Adams, *First Hand Report: the Eisenhower Administration*, Theodore White, *The Making of the President* (an absorbing account of Kennedy's campaign for nomination and election), and Douglass Cater, *Power in Washington*. On foreign affairs a good start can be made with Kenneth W. Thompson, *Political Realism and the Crisis of World Politics*, Louis Halle, *American Foreign Policy*, Max Beloff, *The United States and the Unity of Europe*, and H. G. Nicholas, *Britain and the United States*.

INDEX

Abolitionists, 111, 121, 131–2

Adams, Henry, on power of corporations, 23; on politicians, 176n

Adams, John, 50, 51, 80; on the revolution 52–3; on Declaration of Independence, 61n; opposition to 'unbalanced government', 65n, 86–7

Adams, John Quincy, 76

Adams, Samuel, 50, 51

Agricultural Adjustment Act, 217

Alabama, 13

Alien and Sedition Acts, 1798, 81

American Federation of Labor, 218, 246–7

Ames, Nathaniel, 82n

Anti-Trust Act 1890, 24, 174n, 190–1, 193, 237–8

Antietam, battle of, 142, 143, 147

Appomattox Courthouse, surrender of Lee at, 152

Arthur, Chester A., 179

Articles of Confederation, 67

Atlanta, capture of, 1864, 143

Bank of the United States, 72, 79, 91

Benton, Thomas Hart, on popular sovereignty, 127n, 128n

Bernard, Governor, 45

Beveridge, Albert J., 193n, 194n

Birmingham, Alabama, 167

'Black Codes', 159, 159n

Blaine, James G., 190n

Boston, 54, 58; 'tea party' 54

Brandeis, Louis B., quoted, 240n

Breckinridge, James, on Supreme Court and Congress, 73n

Brown, John, 132

Bryan, William Jennings, 180, 187–8

Buchanan, James, 125, 129; actions in 1861, 138–9

Bull Run, first battle of, 143

Bunker Hill, 58

Burke, Edmund, 32, 48

Calhoun, John C., 83, 123; on economic nationalism, 75n; political theory of, 118–19; and abolitionists, 121n; and slavery, 122n

California becomes part of U.S., 103, 123

Canada, attack on 1775–6, 59; attack on 1812, 99; boundary disputes settled, 101–2

Carnegie, Andrew, and 'Gospel of Wealth', 233–4

Chatham, William Pitt, Earl of, 39, 48

China, U.S. and, 224–5, 229; and Korean war, 229

Churchill, Winston Spencer, 222

Civil Rights Acts, 1875, 168n; 1957 and 1964, 254

Civil War 1861–5, 142–53 passim; causes of, 114–15, 116–23; character of, 141; effects of, 153–7

Clay, Henry, 75, 85, 125; proposes compromises of 1850, 123

Cleveland, Grover, 187; and labour disputes, 244n

Cold Harbor, battle of, 144

Colonies, American, character of society in, 5, 39; political institutions, 40–1; leadership in, 50–2; independence of, 61–2; suffrage, 9, 40; Great Britain and, 33–6; paper money in, 36; and Molasses Act, 36; loyalty of, 1763, 37–8

Committees of Correspondence, 49

Common sense, 60–1, 86

Communism, 229, 230, 248, 255

Concord, 58

Confederate States of America, formation, 136; difficulties during war, 150–1; collapse of, 151–3

Congress, Continental, 57, 67

Congress, of the United States, powers of, 68; and Reconstruction, 158–60

Congress, Stamp Act, 1765, 46

Conservatism in U.S., 230–5

Constitution, British, 38, 42–3; John Dickinson on, 42n

Constitution, of the United States, 25–8, 68–71, Appendix II; economic interpre-

PRINTED IN GREAT BRITAIN BY ROBERT MACLEHOSE AND CO. LTD
THE UNIVERSITY PRESS, GLASGOW

DATE DUE

GAYLORD			PRINTED IN U.S.A.